Ebor:

A History of the Archbis[...]

The front cover depicts:
> St. Paulinus (627-633) from a photograph of an early 15th century window in the north clerestory of York Minster. Courtesy Royal Commission on the Historical Monuments of England. Also the Arms of the See of York Ancient and Modern.

The title page design depicts:
> Archbishop Richard le Scrope 1398-1407. An illuminated page from *The Bolton Book of Hours* (c. 1420-30): Courtesy York Minster Library. – 'Sancte ricarde Scrope ora pro nobis'

The back cover depicts:

Upper: A reconstruction drawing by John Hutchinson F.S.A.I., F.R.Hist.S., of the Minster of Thomas (I) of Bayeux (c. 1080) from *The Cathedral of Archbishop Thomas of Bayeux. Excavations at York Minster, Volume II, by Derek Phillips.* Courtesy Royal Commission on the Historical Monuments of England.

Lower: Plan of Archbishops' former Palace (c. 1180) adjoining York Minster, re-drawn from Benson's *Later Medieval York* (1919). Courtesy York Minster Library.

Hadst thou faith as a grain of mustard seed,
thou wouldst say unto this mountain
be thou cast into that see.

— George Mountain (*Monteigne*) to Charles I before
Mountain's translation to York in 1628.

EBOR:

A HISTORY OF THE ARCHBISHOPS OF YORK

FROM
PAULINUS TO MACLAGAN
627 — 1908

by

A. TINDAL HART

William Sessions Limited
The Ebor Press
York, England
1986

ISBN 1 85072 002 9

Printed in 10/11 point Bembo Type
by William Sessions Limited,
The Ebor Press, York, England.

The Most Reverend the Lord Archbishop of York, Primate of England and Metropolitan

Foreword

By the Archbishop of York, Dr. John Habgood

The division of the Church of England into two provinces in uncertain relationship to one another was one of those accidents of history which for a time caused endless trouble, but in the end has revealed unsuspected advantages. Some of the rivalries and struggles for power recounted in this book make unsavoury reading. Canterbury and York have sometimes behaved more like warring monarchs than brother Archbishops. But out of the differences have emerged distinct and complementary roles, and a sense of identity in the Northern Province, which have been enriching for the whole church.

The story here set out lacks some of the glamour of an equivalent history of the Archbishops of Canterbury. Archbishops of York have not so frequently stood at the centre of national affairs, though it is worth noting that one of them crowned William the Conqueror and another was executed by royal command. But they have never been far from the centre of national and social life, and their story provides a fascinating glimpse from the wings at the whole panorama of English history.

For those who love York and can still see history written in its stones, this book will bring alive many of those who hitherto have been no more than names. And for those who have a more particular interest in the history of the Church of England in these northern parts it will be an essential reference book. I hope many others who dip into its pages will be tempted by it to read on.

For Dr. Tindal Hart himself it has been a labour of love. As the one who now stands at the head of the procession looking back over the long line of my predecessors, I am grateful for a work which at last gives proper recognition to the other half of the Church of England.

Bishopthorpe, York
March 1986

Contents

Illustrations

Preface

As far as I am aware this is the first time that a book has been published dealing with all the archbishops of York from the seventh to the twentieth century in one volume. Inevitably in the space available it has not been possible to do more than to draw each portrait in the broadest of outlines; but, I trust, enough has been said to show the part they played in shaping not only the history of their own diocese and province, but also that of England at large. As prelate follows prelate from the Saxon period to comparatively modern times, the importance of the northern province, which has all too often been over-shadowed by that of Canterbury in the story of *Ecclesia Anglicana*, clearly emerges; and the stature of its archbishops is revealed as only a little less than that of their fellow metropolitans in the south. This book, however, does not profess to be an original work of scholarship. It is a popular history, written primarily for the general reader; and consequently there are few footnotes. But the main sources from which it is drawn can be found in the bibliography.

I should like to express my grateful thanks to the librarians of York Minster, St. Anthony's Hall in York, Westminster Abbey, the Bodleian, and the many public libraries of Surrey and Sussex for providing me with so much of the raw materials needed for this study.

A. Tindal Hart, M.A., B.D., D.D., (CANTAB).
The College of St. Barnabas,
Lingfield, Surrey.

CHAPTER I

The Pre-Conquest Archbishops of York

There were christians in York before the end of the first century A.D., and it is known that they suffered persecution, although no named martyrs are recorded. Their worship was necessarily held in secret behind locked doors, and they must have been relatively few in numbers. However, it was at York that Constantine the Great was proclaimed Emperor, and his edict of toleration in 312 brought relief to the christians there, who now emerged into the light of day. Two years later a York bishop attended the Council of Arles; and by the time Theodosius I banned paganism, the city possessed a flourishing church. But the Roman withdrawal and the coming of the Saxons largely obliterated this tender plant, despite numerous legends connecting the Arthurian revival with York, and the fact that the tiny kingdom of Elmet in southern Northumbria remained christian until its conquest by King Edwin, who united the whole of the north under his heathen sway. Such was the position when Edwin himself married Aethelberga of Kent, and Bishop Paulinus accompanied her as chaplain to that northern kingdom.

Once Aethelberht, the Kentish monarch, had been baptised by St. Augustine, the latter sent Lawrence the priest and Peter the monk to Rome requesting Pope Gregory the Great for reinforcements. Accordingly a fresh band of missionaries arrived in Kent, which included Mellitus, Justus, Rufianus and Paulinus, bringing with them the papal demand that two synods should be established in England, one at London and the other in York, each containing 12 suffragan bishops. Subsequently Mellitus became bishop of London, and Justus bishop of Rochester. Each in turn succeeded Augustine at Canterbury, which, with papal approval, replaced London as the seat of the metropolitan province. But it was not until the archiepiscopate of Justus that Paulinus, after being consecrated bishop, went north to York with Aethelberga, in the year 625, after King Edwin had promised to tolerate christianity throughout his kingdom. The following Easter, Edwin miraculously escaped assassination, and Aethelberga bore him a daughter, Eanflaed; whereupon the king

1

promised that should he be successful in war against his would-be-assassin, he would become a christian. In the meantime he allowed his newly born daughter, together with 11 other members of her family, to be baptised at Whitsuntide. True to his word, after defeating the West Saxons, Edwin called a meeting of his Witan to consider adopting christianity as the official religion of his country. The heathen high priest, Coifi, was won over, who then led an enthusiastic mob to the profaning, burning and total destruction of the old temples. Edwin for his part built a wooden church at York, where in 627 he was himself baptised, later enclosing it in stone. It was dedicated to St. Peter.

Paulinus, now archbishop of the northern province by papal appointment, worked ceaselessly day and night during the next five years to convert the people to christianity, moving freely about the kingdom preaching and baptising. As at this date there were still no church buildings outside York, so he made it his habit to baptise his catechumens in streams and rivers, particularly favouring the Swale and the Trent. For example, at the royal residence in Yeavering, Glendale, where he stayed 36 days, he baptised large numbers in the river. Outside Northumbria Paulinus preached to the Lindissi, and built a stone church in Lincoln, where in 627 he consecrated Honorius as the next archbishop of Canterbury. Then came disaster: Cadwallon, the British king of North Wales, in alliance with Penda of Mercia, defeated and slew Edwin at the great battle of Hatfield on 12 October 633. Northumbria was overrun, and Edwin's queen, together with Paulinus, fled south to Kent. Here the latter, after serving a pastoral ministry in Romney Marsh, residing at Lyminge Minster (whose fine church was built in his honour), was appointed to the bishopric of Rochester in 635, where his pallium★ was laid up as a holy relic. He died in 644. In Northumbria James the deacon carried on his work; and Edwin's unfinished stone church in York was completed by his successor, Oswald.

But yet again the north was overrun by Penda and the British; and only after the battle of Winwaed was the Northumbrian monarchy once again firmly established. By that time the restoration of christianity in this part of Britain lay in the hands of the Celtic rather than the Roman Church, being led by St. Aidan, a wandering bishop, whose base was at Lindisfarne; and later by the equally famous St. Cuthbert. The bishopric of York, but not the archbishopric, was restored after the Synod of Whitby in 663 for Chad and then the Roman champion, St. Wilfred. But, nearly another 100 years had to pass, during which time the see was occupied by Bosa, St. John of Beverley and Wilfred II, before **Egbert** obtained his pallium at Rome from Pope Gregory III in 735, and thus became the second archbishop of York and metropolitan of the northern province, where previously such metropolitan authority as existed had been exercised from Canterbury by Theodore of Tarsus and his successors.

★ A vestment conferred by the pope on an archbishop to symbolise the jurisdiction delegated to him.

Egbert, a cousin of Ceolwulf, king of Northumbria, was a monk, who had been ordained at Rome. Appointed by the king in 732 to the bishopric of York, for the express purpose of reforming the clergy and monasteries, by putting an end to the clerical corruption then widespread throughout the diocese, he became archbishop in 735, working in perfect harmony with the new king, Eadberht, and seeking to carry out Gregory the Great's original scheme of establishing suffragan bishoprics in the north. He is reputed to have been learned, liberal and gracious, enriching the churches, ordaining worthy priests, and encouraging the use of church music. He founded a cathedral school at York under a famous headmaster, Ethelbert, which became known throughout Europe. Its curriculum consisted of the seven liberal arts, leading on to theology, philosophy, law and medicine. It possessed a comprehensive library, which Ethelbert constantly augmented when on journeys abroad in search of new books. A number of his pupils became famous, notably Eanbald, a future archbishop, and the great scholar Alcuin, who was appointed master of Charlemagne's palace school. Alcuin wrote of Ethelbert: 'he drew his scholars to him, brought them up and loved them'.

In *The Life of Alcuin*, which was founded upon information from his disciple Sigulf and written before 829, the following portrait is drawn of Archbishop Egbert:

> Egbert each morning, as soon as his business was transacted, used to sit on his couch and instruct his young clerks to midday: he then prayed privately and celebrated mass. At dinner he ate sparingly, and listened to his scholars discussing literary questions. In the evening he always said the compline with them, and then gave each his blessing separately.

The archbishop had been a pupil of the Venerable Bede, who urged him by letter always to be sure to study St. Paul's Pastoral Epistles and the works of Gregory the Great, in order to make certain that he trained up 'a godly household' unlike 'that attributed to some worldly bishops'. The training of the clergy in Pastoralia was the most important duty of an archbishop. Egbert was a prolific writer. He corresponded with that great missionary saint, Boniface, to whom Ethelbert also sent books, including Bede's *Commentaries*. Egbert himself was the author of the following works: *The Pontificale* on ritual; *The Penitentiale*; and a book of *Exceptions*, although this last may be of a later date. In 758 King Eadberht retired into a monastery, where he became a monk; and shortly afterwards Egbert died, on 19 November 766. He had ruled his diocese and province for 34 years; and during that time, in 741, the Minster was burnt down, which was not to be rebuilt until the archiepiscopate of Eanbald I. This church had been of wood, and quickly consumed in an age when fires all too frequently ravished the city. Its successor was to be of stone and much more durable. The only other important event during Egbert's tenure of office was the part he played, in response to Boniface's exhortations, trying to persuade the king of Mercia, Aethelbald, to abandon his scandalous way of life and prevent his thegns from stealing church property. Such representations made by both archbishops and other prominent ecclesiastics led eventually in 746 to the great reforming Synod of Clofeshoh, when the whole question of a secularised minster was settled, and other reforming canons passed. But, since this synod was held in the southern province and presided over by Cuthbert of Canterbury, Egbert did not attend and York was not represented.

Egbert had been able to exercise full authority in ecclesiastical matters throughout Northumbria because his brother happened to be king; and coins were actually issued bearing both their names. His successors were not always so fortunate. The next archbishop, **Ethelbert**, Egbert's old friend and ally, the master of the cathedral school, began the work of rebuilding the York churches. In addition to commencing the reconstruction of the Minster itself, with the assistance of his disciples, Eanbald and Alcuin, he completed an entirely new church, Alma Sophia, which subsequently entirely disappeared. Ethelbert also presented King Edwin's original church with many costly gifts, including a fresh altar dedicated to St. Paul. His reign otherwise was comparatively short and uneventful; he retired from the see in 778, and died two years later. He was succeeded by his pupil, **Eanbald I**, who, with Alcuin's help, completed the rebuilding of the cathedral, which, according to the latter, was an edifice of great splendour. He described it in his writings 'as lofty, supported by columns, and having round arches and panelled ceilings'. There were, Alcuin said, some 30 altars surrounded by many beautiful side-chapels. Ethelbert had left his library to Alcuin, who referred to it as 'a treasury of books . . . which were an aid to study and wisdom'.

It was King Aelfwold who sent a message to Rome asking Pope Hadrian I to grant Eanbald the pallium; and when this was agreed Alcuin went and fetched it. Hadrian then dispatched two legates to England, George and Theophylact, on a visit first to Offa of Mercia and then north into Northumbria 'to King Aelfwold and Eanbald, archbishop of York'. The upshot of all this diplomatic activity was the Council of Finchole near Durham, held in 787, where some 20 canons were promulgated. 'These decrees', the legates reported, 'O blessed Pope Hadrian, we presented publicly before King Aelfwold and Archbishop Eanbald and all the bishops, abbots and princes of the people of that region'.

The Vikings, who were now commencing their attacks on northern England, destroyed the church at Lindisfarne in 792, a dire warning of what was soon to befall the whole of the north of Britain. These coming disasters, or so it was said, were preceded by heavenly portents in the shape of whirlwinds, lightenings and 'five dragons flying in the air'. Alcuin, for his part, described them as a chastisement richly deserved by the Northumbrians on account of the corruptions of the clergy, and the rapacity of the nobility in their struggle for power. Eanbald had wished

4

Alcuin to succeed him, but the latter demurred, urging instead that there should be a proper election by the clergy.

In June 796 the archbishop crowned Eardwulf king of Northumbria, and by the following August he himself was dead. Instead of Alcuin, one of the late archbishop's pupils at the York school, described by him as 'dearest and most faithful son', **Eanbald II**, was elected to the archbishopric only four days after the death of his predecessor and namesake. He immediately turned to Alcuin for advice, both in regard to liturgical and pastoral matters, and in reply was exhorted to set himself a standard of holy life that others could follow, and at the same time to bear down ruthlessly on the unworthy actions and habits of his clergy, such as when 'they gallop across country, hallowing in the pursuit of foxes'. Instead they should be instructed to ride, 'singing psalms in sweet tunefullness', always carrying with them a copy of Gregory's *Liber Pastoralis*. Eanbald was granted the pallium by Pope Leo III, and enthroned at York on 8 September 797. Two years later yet another synod was held at Finchole near Durham, where five articles of faith were promulgated.

In 801 Alcuin sent his beloved friend and pupil 100 pounds of tin for roofing the Minster belfry, together with four screens to help keep the birds out of its windows. But in that same year Eanbald quarrelled with the king, who accused him of sheltering his Mercian enemies. This was probably true, since some little time later in 807 the archbishop openly assisted Cenwulf of Mercia in securing the deposition of Eardwulf. The king fled abroad and appealed for help both to Charlemagne and Pope Leo III, who espoused his cause, rejecting the arguments of Eanbald and Cenwulf, as 'evidence of craftiness'. A papal legate was despatched to England, and he ultimately succeeded in effecting Eardwulf's restoration.

Eanbald died in 810, still apparently in disgrace. He was undoubtedly a learned and vigorous prelate, whom Alcuin supported throughout his archiepiscopate, affectionately addressing him as 'Symeon' in his letters. Even when trouble broke out between Eanbald and the king, Alcuin continued to support his friend, exhorting him, under no circumstances, to quit his post. Like his namesake and predecessor the archbishop issued his own coinage, which bears the stamp of various moneyers.

Of the three archbishops who followed Eanbald we know very little. It was a period of conquest, darkness, confusion and turmoil. In 855 the Viking army wintered in England for the first time; some 10 years later the Danes had occupied East Anglia; and shortly afterwards they crossed the Humber and captured York. The Saxons had been weakened by civil war, but they rallied sufficiently to regain the city, only to lose it again in 869. Thereafter throughout the remainder of the ninth and most of the tenth century it changed hands several times. The Danes were driven out by King Alfred's successors; then it became occupied for a while by Norse raiders from Ireland; and it was not really until the reign of Edgar that Northumbria as a whole remained firmly established in English hands. During this troubled period little is known of the Church in York and its archbishops are shadowy figures. The Danes apparently tolerated christianity, and in some cases actually embraced the faith. Their king, Guthfrith, was a convert, who lies buried in the Minster, which not only survived and continued as a centre of worship, but actually received gifts of land and bells from Guthfrith's successors. The first of the three archbishops after Eanbald II was **Wulfsige**, who is reputed to have been a strong champion of Catholic orthodoxy and an enemy of heresy; and his successor, **Wigmund**, despite increasing Viking raids, upheld the traditions of York as a notable centre of learning, judging from his correspondence with the learned Abbot Lupus of Ferrières monastery that had established close links with the Minster through Alcuin. But all that is known of the next archbishop, **Wulfhere**, is that he received the pallium in 854, and then fled the city before the Viking invaders. Apparently he was reinstated in 873, and died in 900.

There then followed a vacancy of some eight years; and during this time the Vikings destroyed York's reputation for scholarship. In the 880's King Alfred lamented the fact that there were 'no good scholars in all the kingdom of the West Saxons'. Of Northumbria he made no mention at all. The next four archbishops were all undoubtedly of Danish origin, and of two of them we know little or nothing. **Wulfstan I**, who followed these unknowns, **Ethelbald** and **Hrotheweard**, was certainly much involved in politics. As a Dane himself he sympathised with the renewed attempts of the Vikings of Northumbria and Dublin to make Yorkshire into an independent kingdom under Olaf Guthfrethson. So, when the invading Danish army under Olaf took York, he, in collaboration with Oda, archbishop of Canterbury, helped to arrange a peace between Olaf and the Saxon king, Edmund. This treaty left the Danes in control of all the territory between Watling Street and the Northumbrian border. Then, on the death of Olaf, with Wulfstan's approval, Olaf Schtricson became king of York in 940; but four years later Edmund re-conquered York. However, this reconquest does not appear to have affected Wulfstan's position, since he remained archbishop until his death on 26 December 956. He is also remembered for his collaboration with Oda of Canterbury in another capacity, since between them they issued the following canons that demanded:

(1) The immunity of the Church from wicked persons.
(2) That princes should obey the episcopate.
(3) That bishops should visit their sees once a year.
(4) That priests should lead exemplary lives, clerks live honestly, and unlawful marriages, especially with nuns, should be prohibited.
(5) All christians must pay their tithes and give alms.

6

Wulfstan's successor, **Oskytel**, a nephew of Oda, and likewise of Danish origin, became a noted church reformer. He had been translated from the bishopric of Dorchester to York by the Saxon king, Edgar, and personally went to Rome to receive the pallium, accompanied by his own nephew, a later archbishop and saint, Oswald. Oskytel certainly inherited a shattered province, for the Danish raids, followed by their occupation of Northumbria, either put an end to or violently disrupted the tenure of such northern suffragan sees as Hexham and Whithorn, whilst the great Minsters of Ripon, Beverley and Medehamstede were plundered of their lands. In 886 the north-east of England was also conceded to the Danes, when the remaining bishoprics of Chester-le-Street, York and Elmham, suffered in a like manner.

The new archbishop quickly became known as a man 'of learning and piety'; and in his attempts to reform the clergy was ably assisted by Oswald, who had come to live with him after being brought up by Oda. Between them they introduced into the province the new monasticism of Fleury. Judging from the number of times the archbishop's signature appears on secular and political charters, he must often have been absent from his diocese in the south of England, where he became the close friend of St. Dunstan. But he was certainly in the north during 968, when he consecrated Elfsig, bishop of Chester-le-Street. He died on the 1 November 971 and was buried in Bedford Abbey.

Then, after the brief and undistinguished archiepiscopate of **Edwald**, he was followed by **Oswald**, who as already bishop of Worcester, continued to hold both sees until his death in 992. Oswald had inherited Oda's love of Benedictine monasticism, which had been further instilled into him by his long residence at Fleury Abbey. This love, as we have seen, he passed on to his uncle; together they sought strenuously to introduce and develop this system throughout Northumbria. Oskytel in his turn introduced Oswald to Dunstan; and, when the latter went to Canterbury, he persuaded King Edgar to nominate Oswald to his old diocese of Worcester in 961. Ten years later the same monarch, again on Dunstan's advice, chose Oswald as Oskytel's successor at York, which at that time possessed one suffragan see, Chester-le-Street, afterwards Durham; and there is little record that Oswald himself did much to improve the situation. For, apart from visiting Rome in order to receive the pallium at the hands of Pope John XIII, and shortly afterwards being solemnly enthroned in York Minster, there is only one definite act of his recorded as archbishop, namely, that, on a journey to Yorkshire, he visited the church at Ripon, where he collected and carried off the bones of St. Wilfred to Worcester. But even this is doubtful, since Oda, or so it was believed, had already removed them to Canterbury. Indeed, Oswald's fame rests not on what he achieved as archbishop, but rather on his achievements at Worcester, where he introduced the Benedictine monastic system, and sent forth missionaries to preach the gospel throughout that diocese. He may, of course, have tried to do the same in the north, seeking to reconvert Northumbria after the Viking conquests, but if so no records now remain. It would have been difficult, because York's continued paganism made it an insecure base for an archbishop, so that he could really only work from his southern see. In collaboration with Dunstan Oswald played an important part in the secular life of the nation. For example, together they secured the ratification of Edward as king by the Witan, and anointed him. The archbishop died on 29 February 992, and was buried at Worcester, when miracles were wrought at his tomb. He is remembered as a kindly and tolerant man, who, despite his zeal for monasticism, always refused to introduce it forcibly.

Eldulf, the next archbishop, had been chancellor to King Edgar; but, having the misfortune to overlay his own child, he atoned for this sin by becoming a monk at Medehamsted, now Peterborough, which he helped to rebuild. Later he was appointed abbot of Burgh, and 'greatly enriched the minster withal'. When elevated to York on the death of Oswald, he also inherited his predecessor's diocese of Worcester, but did not receive the pallium until 995/6. He continued to pursue Oswald's policies both of introducing the Benedictine rule into his dioceses, and of making benefactions to the Abbey of Fleury. On 15 April 1002 he translated Oswald's body into a costly shrine at Worcester Cathedral with great honours, but died himself the same year and was buried in the same church.

The Vikings had been in control of York for more than a century, a fact that is reflected in the large numbers of Norse names that have survived; and their occupation of large districts in eastern and northern England had caused that part of the country to revert to paganism. Hence Oswald and his successors, mainly working from bases in the south and south west, had to treat their province as once again a missionary area. But by the beginning of the eleventh century Northumbria was finally reconquered by the Saxons, when Eric Blood-Axe was expelled, his place being taken by an Earl appointed by King Ethelred II. However, the danger of new invasions remained, along with the possibility that the Northumbrians themselves, being now primarily of Danish origin, might declare their independence from the south and set up yet another Viking kingdom. Christianity in the north was certainly at a low ebb, with the mass of the people pagan or no more than semi-christian; the monasteries destroyed, and the clergy often lax, ignorant and superstitious. However, at York, Beverley and Southwell there were still canons living a community life; and, basing themselves on such establishments as these the eleventh-century archbishops of York sought to rebuild the Church.

None the less this century opened disastrously, with the reconquest of the whole of Britain by the Dane, Swein Forkbeard, and his famous son, Cnut, between 1013 and 1015. During the latter's reign England formed part of a 'North Sea Empire'; but his sons proved incompetent monarchs, and their short and troubled rule was followed by the return of the west Saxon dynasty.

Wulfstan II was the new archbishop at the beginning of the Danish occupation, and was acceptable to his countrymen, since he himself came from the eastern Danelaw. He had previously been bishop of London, but, like his immediate predecessors, now held York together with the see of Worcester, basing himself on the latter diocese rather than in the north. He was to be remembered as a great legislator and pastoral leader, who worked hard to reform the rank and file of the clergy. He was also a most eloquent preacher. His famous sermon on the wolf recalled the disasters of Ethelred's reign. 'A great breach', he said, 'will require much repair, and a great fire no little water, if the fire is to be quenched at all; and great is the necessity for every man that he keeps henceforth God's laws eagerly, and pays God's dues rightly'. Moreover he played a prominent part in secular as well as religious affairs, both in the reigns of Ethelred and Cnut. The archbishop was probably responsible for the Law Codes V–IX of Ethelred, and I–II of Cnut, besides being the author of some private Codes. Later he has also been credited with Codes dealing specifically with crime and punishment, the defence of the nation, and the maintenance of christian worship.

Cnut evidently thought highly of him, and, on at least one occasion, showed his regard by compelling Edgar Atheling to make concessions over a land dispute with the monks of Sherborne at the archbishop's request. At York Wulfstan's main task was two-fold: to reform the clergy and reconvert the people. To this end he drew up the famous 'Northumbrian Priests' Law', which covered a wide range of clerical conduct. For example: a priest is not to say mass without wine; is to be penalised if he misdirects his people in regard either to feasts or fasts; and to be strongly condemned for such abuses as heavy drinking, quarrelling, bringing weapons into church, or marrying more than one wife at a time. At the same time priests were exhorted to become active missionaries, to keep close to their people, and to be diligent in guiding and teaching them. The final injunction is typically Wulfstanian: 'We must all have and honour one God, and zealously hold one Christian Faith, and entirely cast out every heathen practice'.

The archbishop was likewise very active in seeking to preserve and maintain church lands in Yorkshire, whilst trying to get repossession of those that had been lost. In his writings, particularly in the homilies and *The Polity*, he stressed not only the needs of church reform, but issued a call for repentance and christian charity. Almsgiving, he insisted, was sorely much to be required after such long and grievous devastations. 'I will', he wrote, 'that ye daily deal alms to almsmen and the poor'. People ought to contribute up to a third of their incomes, and priests should make it their job to see that these moneys were distributed wisely. The recipients for their part must pray for their benefactors. 'A bishop', he declared, 'should first attend to his prayers, then to his books, to reading and writing, learning and teaching. He should say his offices at the proper times, wash the feet of the poor and give alms.' Furthermore in order to make sure that none of his time was wasted, a bishop, like St. Paul, ought to possess some craft or business. Wulfstan himself taught his people in public, and may well have tried to carry out the other precepts in *The Polity*; but he was not apparently above criticism, being accused by his contemporaries of cupidity, bribery and ambition. He has been described as 'repobus' for holding York and Worcester in plurality, despoiling the southern diocese, and putting on a display of worldly wealth unbecoming in a priest and a bishop. 'We catch', wrote Dr. Bethurum, 'a glimpse of a style of living which matched the archbishop's importance as the leading statesman of his time, and what is more, the representative of heavenly majesty on earth.' It is undoubtedly true that Wulfstan leased certain Worcestershire diocesan lands to his relations; and he himself seems to have taken a great personal interest in the work done on his own, describing what went on there in a book, *The Rectitudines*.

This provides us with a picture, if not of a magnificent prelate, yet of a careful landlord. He details the rights and duties of the peasantry, and of how their labours ought to be directed by the reeve, who must at once preserve old customs, whilst making sure the whole estate ran smoothly. As a valued royal adviser Wulfstan was present at most of the king's councils, both in the reigns of Ethelred the Unready and Cnut; and, during the vacancy at Canterbury, he became the foremost ecclesiastic in the realm.

He died at York on 28 May 1025, and was buried in Ely monastery. He was a learned man, quite apart from his legal expertise, being well read in the Fathers, and familiar with such modern works as those of Bede, Aldhelm and Alcuin. He corresponded with the homilist, Elfric. But perhaps his greatest achievement was a final codification of Anglo-Saxon Law. None the less for all his many talents as scholar, jurist, ecclesiastical reformer, teacher and preacher, besides the many miracles reputed to have been performed at his tomb, he was never canonised. He fell short in certain respects of the qualities of men like Dunstan and Oswald.

The following archbishop, **Aelfric**, was of West Saxon origin. He had been a monk and then dean of Winchester, before being appointed to York. An ardent supporter of Cnut's son, Harthacnut, in the latter's opposition to his brother, Harold, he actually went so far as to advise the king to insult that brother's body by having it mutilated; an act which he personally helped to carry out on Harthacnut's orders. He also played a leading part in accusing Earl Godwine and Bishop Lyfing of Worcester of the murder of the Atheling, Alfred, the son of Emma and Ethelred the

Unready. For this he was rewarded with the now vacant diocese of Worcester, where he took part in ravaging the city for its expulsion of himself and the murder of the king's tax-collectors. He was certainly something of a Vicar of Bray, since he cleverly accommodated himself to three such different kings as Harold, Harthacnut and Edward the Confessor, continuing to play a leading part in politics throughout all three reigns.

In 1026 he went to Rome for his pallium, and, in his capacity as archbishop, vigorously pursued Wulfstan's work of reformation in the north, and in particular increased the endowments of those great centres of evangelicalism and teaching, the houses of the secular canons at York, Beverley and Southwell. But at the same time he laid down some strict rules for governing their conduct: the canons were to avoid the company of women, sleep together in a single dormitory, sing the offices together in church, and eat together in the refectory. For this purpose Aelfric began the rebuilding of such dormitories and refectories, a work which was to be completed by his successors. At Beverley he translated the relics of St. John of Beverley into a costly shrine, and purchased further estates for that Minster. He likewise concerned himself with enlarging and extending the lands belonging to the see of York.

Aelfric's unscrupulous political career earned him the name of Puttoc, the kite, which was probably originally given him at Worcester after he took over that diocese, once again uniting it with York in 1040. He died at Southwell in 1051, and was buried in Peterborough monastery. Here he was venerated as a benefactor, although never selected, like his successor **Cynesige**, as a possible candidate for canonisation.

Cynesige himself came from the eastern Danelaw, and was reputed to have been born after a Caesarian operation, then considered almost a miracle. Originally a monk, he left the monastery for service in the king's chapel, before being appointed as archbishop of York in 1051. Unlike his predecessor he never became a politician, although on one occasion he accompanied Earl Tostig and Bishop Elthelwine of Durham in escorting King Malcolm of Scotland to a meeting with Edward the Confessor in the north of England, when border raids between the two countries were discussed. He is also known to have witnessed a number of charters. But, after Stigand, archbishop of Canterbury, fell under a papal anathema in 1058, Cynesige did not take his place as a political leader. This may possibly have been due to the fact that he was persona non grata with the all-powerful Earl Godwine. None the less, owing to Stigand's disgrace, Cynesige was able to usurp most of the latter's spiritual jurisdiction. In 1059, for example, he presided over a Church Council in London, when he consecrated Herewald to the bishopric of Llandaff; and, between 1052 and 1066, he consecrated most of the newly appointed bishops in the southern province, except for those who preferred to go to Rome. In the north Cynesige is supposed to have consecrated two bishops of Glasgow, Magsue and John; but as apparently there were no bishops residing at Glasgow at that time, in all probability these two men, finding themselves unable to function in Scotland, remained to work in the diocese of York.

Like his two immediate predecessors he patronised the houses of secular canons, both in Yorkshire and Nottinghamshire, particularly that of Beverley, where he continued the work on the refectory and dormitory, and added a stone tower to the church. According to the Peterborough chronicler, Cynesige was an ascetic and a most saintly character. This eulogy, however, may well have been partly inspired by the fact that not only had the archbishop provided the monastery with many gifts, but also lies buried there. The monks no doubt hoped that he might be canonised and so create a profitable cult. Yet to the impartial historian he does not seem to have been a man of strong character; and if he was a saint, his influence on others, even on the members of his own household, appears to have been slight. In public affairs he failed to profit from Stigand's anomalous position, and never became a really leading figure in the Anglo-Saxon Church. He died in 1060, and was succeeded by a much more formidable character: **Archbishop Ealdred**.

Ealdred was a West Saxon, a monk of Worcester, who followed Bishop Lyfing, first as abbot of Tavistock, and again as bishop of Worcester in 1046. From an early stage in his career he became closely associated with Earl Godwine, Lyfing's patron; and in all probability he was already assistant bishop at Worcester before succeeding the latter. In 1047 Ealdred played a leading part in defeating Welsh raiders, who were ravishing his diocese, although he himself, unlike other prelates of the day, did not actually indulge in any fighting. Later he was able to negotiate a peace with the Welsh king. From 1055 onwards he ruled 'a sort of ecclesiastical palatine on the Marsh', including the dioceses of Worcester, Herefordshire and Wiltshire, which made him probably the most powerful prelate in England, with Stigand hamstrung, and Cynesige failing to provide either ecclesiastical or politically strong leadership.

According to Florence of Worcester, Ealdred was on excellent terms not only with Earl Godwine, but also with Edward the Confessor; and so was able to act as mediator between the king and Swein Godwine, after the latter had slain his cousin, Earl Beon, and arrange for their reconciliation. He was employed by Edward on various diplomatic missions abroad: to Rome in 1050 with Bishop Herman; and again four years later to the Emperor at Cologne to try to secure the return of the Confessor's heir and nephew, Edward the Exile, from Hungary. But that Edward died in 1057, soon after his repatriation and Ealdred was sent abroad again to search for yet another heir to the English throne. That time his journey took him through Hungary to Jerusalem, where he offered up a golden chalice at the Holy Sepulchre. 'This pilgrimage', a contemporary wrote, 'was performed with such worship as none other did before'. Being in high favour with

King Edward, he was able to render further service to the Godwine family, when the Earl and his sons were outlawed by the Witan. They fled to Bristol, which lay in the Worcestershire diocese; and the bishop purposely delayed the pursuit until they had safely taken ship and escaped abroad. His excuses for doing so were graciously accepted by the king.

On Christmas Day 1060 Ealdred was elected archbishop of York; whereupon he relinquished his palatinate of the March, but retained the see of Worcester itself. However, this was to get him into trouble; for when in 1061, accompanied by Earl Tostig, he went to Rome, partly on the king's business and partly to receive his pallium, he met with a hostile reception from Pope Nicholas II. At a synod, which was already in session when they arrived, the archbishop was accused of ignorance, simony* and greed, of having accepted translation to York without papal approval, and above all of holding on to the see of Worcester along with the archbishopric. Consequently he was not only refused the pallium, but deprived of his episcopal rank altogether. Sadly his party set off for home, but was attacked by bandits, who forced a return to Rome. Then matters improved. Tostig threatened the pope with the witholding of England's Peter's Pence, Ealdred for his part grovelled and, after some tough negotiations, was forgiven, reinstated in his archiepiscopal office and received the pallium, but only on condition that he relinquished the see of Worcester, which was given to St. Wulfstan. However, by arrangement with the latter, Ealdred retained 12 of its manors.

Between 1061 and 1066 little is recorded of the archbishop's activities; but then he reappears to crown King Harold, who doubtless remembered his past services to the House of Godwine. Indeed, so greatly did he trust his loyalty that, when he marched south to meet William the Conqueror, he left all the booty taken at Stamford Bridge in Ealdred's keeping. None the less, when previously the king had gone on a tour of Northumbria to pacify its inhabitants, who seemed reluctant to accept his rule, he had preferred St. Wulfstan's company to that of the archbishop. But possibly this was no more than a reasonable precaution in view of the close relations that had once existed between Ealdred and his now rebellious brother, Tostig. After the Battle of Hastings the archbishop at first espoused the cause of the Saxon heir, Edgar Atheling, but he quickly abandoned the hopeless resistance, submitted to the Conqueror at Berkhamsted, crowned that monarch in Westminster Abbey on Christmas Day 1066, and Queen Matilda two years later. Henceforth William regarded him as one of the most trustworthy of his supporters; and he was to play a leading part in maintaining law and order in the north.

Ealdred was no sycophant; and when the royal sheriff sought to encroach on the rights of the Church of Worcester he boldly withstood him, uttering the defiant words:

Highest thou Urse
Have thou God's curse.

* Buying and selling of ecclesiastical preferments.

Then, on hearing that the Conqueror himself had broken the coronation oath administered to him by the archbishop, i.e. to defend the Church, rule justly, and establish good laws, Ealdred not only appeared before William to protest, but turned his blessing into a curse. The story that the king threw himself at the archbishop's feet to beg forgiveness for the depredations of his sheriff at York, may well be apocryphal; but the very fact that such a story could be told at all indicates the respect in which Ealdred was held by the Crown.

He died on 11 September 1070, at the very moment that a Danish fleet was sailing into the Humber, and the whole of the north about to rise against the Normans. Indeed he is said to have prayed that he might not live to see the evil days that, as he forsaw, were about to dawn for his church and people alike. He was buried in the Minster, which shortly afterwards was burnt to the ground, and the whole of York put to the sack, during the Conqueror's ferocious harrying of the north in 1070.

In his York diocese Ealdred had been even more lavish than his predecessors in enriching the houses of the secular canons, providing them with new lands and creating fresh prebends. He not only completed the refectory and dormitory at Beverley, but also those at Southwell and York. Beverley church was redecorated throughout, received a new presbytery, and furnished with a pulpit of bronze, silver and gold. The archbishop carried through a number of synodical reforms that are recorded by the monk Folcard in his *Life of St. John of Beverley*, which enforced order and decency among the clergy, especially in the manner of their dress. They also demanded much higher educational standards for ordinands. For Ealdred had the greatest possible contempt for semi-literate clerics and 'whiskey' priests. He himself was a noted patron of letters, especially encouraging Folcard in his work on *The Anglo-Saxon Chronicle*, who spoke highly of his patron's literary gifts and treasured his friendship. For, at the queen's request, Ealdred had taken Folcard under his wing, and further persuaded him to write *The Life of St. John of Beverley*.

Like Archbishop Wulfstan, Ealdred provided yet another example of 'episcopal magnificence'; and probably of all the pre-conquest archbishops of York, he approached closest to the concept of a 'prince bishop', who was at once a professional politician, an able administrator, and an important ecclesiastical reformer, instilling the discipline he had found at Cologne into the English Church. Yet no attempt was ever made to canonise him; and in fact no-one has written his biography.

CHAPTER II

The Struggle between
Canterbury and York over the Primacy

In the year 601 Pope Gregory the Great sent the pallium to St. Augustine as the first English archbishop, together with certain directions: he was to consecrate 12 suffragan bishops, and the metropolitan see should be sited in London, 'so that for ever in time to come the bishop of the city of London shall be duly consecrated by his own synod, and shall receive the pall of honour from this holy apostolic see, which by the authority of God I serve'. At the same time the pope ordered St. Augustine:

> . . . to send to the city of York a bishop whom you yourself shall think fit to ordain, on this condition only, that, if that city with its neighbourhood receives the Word of God, he also shall ordain 12 bishops and enjoy the dignity of a metropolitan. For to him also, if we live, we intend with the Lord's favour, to give the pall; but we wish him nevertheless to be subject to your brotherliness's disposal. After your death, however, he shall so preside over the bishops whom he appoints as *in no way* subject to the jurisdiction of the bishop of London. But between the bishops of London and York there shall be hereafter this distinction in dignity that priority shall belong to the one who has been consecrated first. Let them with one mind, with common counsel and harmonious action, order all that is to be done for the fervent love of Christ. Let them think aright, and put their thoughts into deed without difference of opinion.

These directions are clear enough. As long as St. Augustine lived he was to have supreme authority over all the churches in Britain, including apparently the ancient British Church in Wales; but after his death the metropolitans of London and York were to rule with equal powers, except that priority should belong to the archbishop who was consecrated first.

Gregory did not then contemplate the permanent establishment of the southern archiepiscopal see at Canterbury; but subsequent events were to bring this about. Augustine died before York had been christianised, and

15

was succeeded first by Mellitus, bishop of London, and then by Justus, bishop of Rochester, both of whom migrated to Canterbury, which, with papal approval, became firmly established as the southern metropolitan see. It was Justus who consecrated **Paulinus** and sent him north to York in 625; and it was not until some years later that King Edwin and his Northumbrian kingdom embraced the true faith. However, Gregory's directions had not been forgotten; and in 634 Pope Honorius I sent palliums to both archbishops; Honorius of Canterbury and Paulinus of York. But in the latter case it arrived too late, since King Edwin had been slain in battle by the heathen Penda of Mercia, Northumbria over-run, and Paulinus forced to flee back to Kent in the company of Edwin's queen, where he was appointed bishop of Rochester.

For the next 30 years the see of York lay vacant; and even after restoration its bishops were not given the pallium until Archbishop **Egbert** received that honour in 735. Meanwhile Canterbury took over. Her autocratic archbishop, Theodore of Tarsus, may well have heard of Gregory the Great's directions, but he had no intention of being bound by them. So during his time and that of his immediate successors, Canterbury firmly established its authority over northern Britain; and this remained true even after Egbert had obtained the pallium. For the ideal of a northern province with 12 bishops subject to the metropolitan see of York had never been realised. The bishopric of Hexham disappeared, that of Lindisfarne was destroyed by the Danes, and the see of Lindsey was wrested from York and came under the jurisdiction of Canterbury.

On the other hand the southern province flourished. The short primacy of Lichfield, under the Mercian kings, had come to an end; and a full complement of 12 subject sees acknowledged Canterbury as their metropolitan, the bishops making their profession of obedience to the primate at their consecration. Indeed by the tenth century this number had risen to 15. York, ravaged and now largely dominated by the Vikings, was certainly in no position to compete with or question the dominating rôle of her sister metropolitan. **St. Oswald**, for example, as has been seen, whilst archbishop of York, spent most of his time in his southern diocese of Worcester, a bishopric professing obedience to Canterbury. None the less, after the Battle of Hastings, the position, for the moment at least, was reversed. Stigand, the then archbishop of Canterbury, lay under a deprivation, and it was **Ealdred**, the last Saxon archbishop of York, who crowned William the Conqueror; and, for the next three years, there was no other primate in England.

Ealdred died in 1070, and the new archbishop, the Norman **Thomas I**, found himself the metropolitan of a devastated province, a ruined cathedral, and only one suffragan see, that of Durham, subject to his authority, beyond a vague claim, strongly resisted, to a suzerainty over the Scottish bishoprics. Moreover another Norman, Lanfranc, had been appointed to Canterbury, who was determined to re-assert his authority over the north. This he considered essential for two reasons: to help maintain and stabilise the new political settlement after the Conquest, and to carry through successfully the necessary religious reforms required by the whole country. Thomas, anxious to be conciliatory, and unable in any case to muster sufficient suffragans of his own for the purpose, came to Lanfranc for consecration. But before the latter would perform the ceremony, a profession of obedience was demanded both written and verbal. This Thomas refused to give unless the validity of such a claim could be proved, and left Canterbury without being consecrated. He appealed to the king, who at first appeared sympathetic, until Lanfranc convinced him that the unity of the kingdom needed the overall authority of one primate. If the archbishop of York was given equal status, he might well join with the northern rebels and crown some Scandinavian monarch. The north also possessed practically no suffragans, was savage and impoverished, and thus in every way vastly inferior to the southern province. So, finding the king also against him, the wretched Thomas, in reply to Lanfranc's question: 'Will you be subject to the holy church of Canterbury and to me and my successors?' said in tears: 'I will be subject to you, as long as you live, but not to your successors, unless the pope so decrees'; but declined to sign any written declaration.

Both archbishops now appealed to the pope, Alexander II, who decreed that the whole matter should be settled by the bishops and abbots of England. Consequently a royal council met at Winchester in 1072, where Lanfranc produced evidence taken from letters by Popes Gregory, Boniface, Honorius, Sergius and Leo. These were undoubtedly forgeries, concocted by the monks of Christ Church, Canterbury; and even *they* were unable to prove that either a verbal or written promise of obedience had ever been made by York to Canterbury. Thomas, for his part, relied solely on the instructions of Gregory the Great to St. Augustine. None the less judgment was given in favour of Lanfranc, and Thomas formally made a written profession of obedience, but without taking an oath; and the final sentence ran: 'I promise to obey thee without conditions, but thy successors conditionally'.

This left the door open to further disputes. The council also drew up certain guide lines: the archbishop of York and his suffragans must attend any council called by the archbishop of Canterbury. The former archbishop must, after appointment, be consecrated by the latter in Canterbury Cathedral; but York could himself consecrate Canterbury in the same cathedral. These decisions were communicated to Alexander II, who never formally confirmed them. As long as Lanfranc lived Thomas loyally abode by his promise. Thus in 1075 at an ecclesiastical council in London attended by the bishops of both provinces, and presided over by the archbishop of Canterbury as Primate of All England, Thomas sat meekly on his right hand, with the bishop of London on his left. But, on

Lanfranc's death, the tables were turned, when York exercised the metropolitan jurisdiction over the whole of the country during the vacancy. Then, when Anselm, the new archbishop of Canterbury, asked that the claim of the southern province to hold the primateship should be confirmed, Thomas, who was about to consecrate him, replied:

> Since there are only two metropolitans in Britain, neither can be primate without authority over the other. If I have done obedience through fear or affection, or for the sake of a quiet life, personally and improperly, I am now freed from it. I will consecrate no-one to be primate.

This bold utterance was prompted by the knowledge that in his original submission to Lanfranc, he had implicitly excluded his successors. Whereupon Anselm dropped the demand and was simply consecrated as metropolitan of the southern province.

In making his stand Thomas knew that he had the papacy on his side, since some four years earlier Pope Urban II had supported Thomas' refusal to give lasting obedience to Canterbury. **Gerard**, his successor, likewise resisted Anselm's plea for a profession of obedience, although he only obtained permission to go to Rome for his pallium on the understanding that 'when he came back he would do all that could be justly demanded of him'. This vague promise he studiously ignored; and, at an important council meeting held at Westminster in 1102, he furiously kicked over the lesser seat, which had been prepared for him, pronouncing a curse 'in the vulgar tongue on the head of the author of such an indignity', and refusing to take his place except on a level with the archbishop of Canterbury. Whereupon Anselm appealed to Pope Paschal II, who both confirmed his personal precedence, and ordered Gerard to promise obedience. But this papal decree also contained the saving clause that such a primacy could be enjoyed only in so far as it had been exercised by Anselm's predecessors, which was the precise matter under debate. None the less, as Professor Southern points out, this was the only advance for 30 years and represented the high water-mark in Canterbury's case, since from henceforth the papacy was increasingly on the side of York.

Gerard soon had his revenge. For when Anselm quarrelled with Henry I over the investiture of bishops and was driven into exile, the king called upon the archbishop of York to restore discipline in the southern province. However on his return, Anselm, having patched up his differences with the king, made a further determined effort to extract an unambiguous profession of obedience before consecrating the next archbishop of York, **Thomas II**, a nephew of Thomas I. This Thomas refused to give, although it had been supported by a royal command; and his stand was strongly supported by the York cathedral chapter, who told him that if ever he made a profession of obedience to Canterbury they would publicly disown him. Anselm replied by not only declining to consecrate Thomas, but also declaring that from henceforth he himself would perform all episcopal functions in the northern province. Furthermore he asked Pope Paschal II not to grant Thomas the pallium, reminding His Holiness that unless he could extract a firm profession of obedience from York,

> . . . the Church of England would be torn asunder and brought to desolation in the word of the Lord that every kingdom divided against itself will be desolate . . . and the vigour of the apostolic discipline would be in no small measure weakened . . . As for myself I could on no account remain in England, for I neither ought nor can suffer the primacy of our Church to be destroyed in my life time.

But the papacy now favoured the York side in this dispute, and the pallium was sent. Anselm replied by both refusing to consecrate Thomas and threatening to excommunicate him should he seek for consecration elsewhere; whilst at the same time again demanding submission to his primacy.

The whole matter was now referred to the king; and, at a Whitsuntide court held in London during 1109, Henry I finally pronounced judgment: Thomas must either submit or resign his archbishopric. Anselm had died, so Thomas agreed to make a profession of obedience to Canterbury in writing, in return for which he was consecrated at St. Paul's by the bishop of London and six other bishops. The York chapter, who had staunchly supported their archbishop throughout the entire contest, reluctantly acquiesced in this surrender, commenting: 'If he [Thomas] had not been so fat and consequently unfitted to bear exile and worry, he would never have given way.'

But once again the surrender was not absolute. Thomas had pleaded that he had acted only in obedience to the king, and consequently the profession was neither legal nor created a precedent; moreover it contained saving clauses regarding his loyalty to the pope and the rights of the Church of York. Indeed, even Henry recognised that this profession was no more than a temporary arrangement, which could not prejudice the Church of York in the future. Thomas, of course, was aware that he had the support of the papacy; and this became even more apparent in the case of the next archbishop, **Thurstan**. For Thurstan, backed by Rome, was to fight a short, sharp battle with the king and Canterbury and win, although at the cost of some sacrifice. Indeed, it is noteworthy that from this time onwards no archbishop of York has made a profession of obedience to his fellow metropolitan. Thurstan had only a deacon's orders when nominated to York on 15 August 1114; and, when Archbishop Ralph of Canterbury summoned him to Christ Church for priesting and consecration, he refused to go, since he was also expected at the same time

19

to make a profession of obedience. Instead he persuaded Ralph Flambard, bishop of Durham, to priest him; and, supported by a petition from the York chapter, sent messages to Rome asking to be freed from any servitude to Canterbury.

Pope Paschal II, who had already granted palliums to Thurstan's two predecessors despite protests from Anselm that they would create a schism in England, now ordered the archbishop's immediate consecration. Henry I replied, as he had done in Thomas' case, by telling Thurstan either to make a profession of obedience or resign; and, when the archbishop chose the latter alternative, pressure was immediately brought to bear upon the king both from the papacy and the York chapter to restore him to office. This was eventually done; but meanwhile Ralph had sent a mission to Rome, who took with them a long letter that set forth in detail the arguments for Canterbury's primacy over all Britain, which they were instructed to present to the new pope, Calixtus II. This missive declared that Gregory the Great's directions to St. Augustine had proved unworkable.

Paulinus was appointed by Justus, and no sooner had he received the pallium than he became a fugitive. Thereafter the see lay vacant for 30 years, during which time the archbishops of Canterbury had exercised primacy in the north as well as in the south. This continued even after Archbishop Egbert had received the pallium, since the diocese, having no suffragans, was far too weak to become another metropolitan see. The northern bishoprics, such as Ripon and Hexham, had been instituted by Canterbury, and York possessed no valid claim to suzerainty over Scotland. But later archbishops of York stole what by right belonged to Canterbury. They said: 'Others have laboured, let us enter into their labours. Naboth is stoned; and there is no-one to hinder us. Let us take his vineyard.' The letter concluded by stating that Canterbury would not give up its heritage, and demanded as its right the homage and subjection of York, along with a profession of obedience. These arguments were rejected in toto by Calixtus, who proceeded to consecrate Thurstan himself at the Council of Rheims in 1119. Henry I promptly forbade him to return to England or indeed to enter any of the king's French dominions, seized his estates and deposed him from the archbishopric. But Thurstan was welcomed at Rome, where a bull was published freeing York from making a profession of obedience to Canterbury, and he received the pallium.

Negotiations with England followed, with the papal legate in that country acting as a mediator, when Calixtus even threatened to lay the whole of Britain under an interdict unless Thurstan was restored to office without having to make any profession of obedience to Canterbury. Reluctantly Henry agreed to his return, and reinvested him with the archbishopric; but continued to demand that at least he should give a personal verbal assurance to Archbishop Ralph of his submission, which Thurstan steadfastly refused to do. Then, when William of Corbeil succeeded Ralph, and York once again declined to acknowledge him as Primate of All England, he by-passed Thurstan, being consecrated by his own suffragan bishops. Both archbishops then resorted to Rome for a final papal decision on the whole matter. Here, in a famous scene at the papal curia in 1125, the Canterbury forged documents were laughed out of court, and Pope Honorius II made it abundantly clear that the metropolitan dignity of York was not to be compromised.

However, as a sop to Canterbury, William was made vicar-general and papal legate, which in theory at any rate gave him authority over Thurstan; but, in a personal letter to the latter, the pope absolved him from the profession of obedience and the jurisdiction of Canterbury. At the same time he licensed the archbishops of York, in case Canterbury should refuse to consecrate any of them, to be consecrated instead either by their suffragans or the pope himself. Armed with these assurances Thurstan appeared the next Christmas at Windsor dressed in his archiepiscopal robes and preceded by his cross, when he claimed an equal right with the archbishop of Canterbury to place the crown on the king's head. He was ejected from the chapel by royal command; but none the less he had made his point. A battle had been won, but the war went on. One of the principal symbols adopted by either archbishop to assert his rights was to have his cross borne erect before him in his rival's province, which could and did sometimes lead to violent clashes.

The next archbishop of York, the gentle and saintly **St. William Fitzherbert**, had enough troubles of his own without getting involved in further disputes with Canterbury; although it is noteworthy that he was consecrated not by his fellow metropolitan, but at the hands of Henry de Blois, bishop of Winchester, then the papal legate in England. However, his subsequent deposition at the Council of Rheims in 1147 by Pope Eugenius III, under pressure from St. Bernard and the Yorkshire monastic leaders, for alleged simony, led to the elevation of a much tougher character, **Henry Murdac**, abbot of Fountains, who was consecrated by the pope himself as William's successor. His bold defiance of Canterbury caused Archbishop Theobald to accuse him to Eugenius, 'as setting up his seat in the north as though his honour was equal to Canterbury's'. This protest was brushed aside, and the same privileges granted to Thurstan by Honorius II were confirmed by Pope Alexander III to **Roger of Pont L'Eveque**, who, although a former archdeacon of Canterbury, once he became archbishop of York showed himself to be one of the fiercest champions of the northern see, and a bitter enemy of Thomas Becket. When consecrated by Theobald of Canterbury in Westminster Abbey on 10 October 1154, he flatly declined to make any kind of profession of obedience; and some eight years later refused to consecrate Becket, since it was conditional on him making an act of submission to Canterbury.

Henry II adopted the policy of playing off one archbishop against the other in order to prevent the Church as a whole uniting against him; and to this end asked the pope to make Roger a legate, which would give him the whip hand over Becket. The pope agreed, and at the same time gave Roger authority to carry his cross erect before him anywhere in England, together with the right to crown kings. He told Roger: 'It has never occurred to us and never shall, God willing, to wish your church to be subject to any but the Roman Pontiff'. Becket, not unnaturally, reacted angrily, and forbade Roger to carry his cross in the southern province, an edict studiously ignored. There is the story that on one occasion Roger entered into the castle hall at Northampton with his cross erect, to find Thomas already seated with cross in hand. Thomas' biographer commented: 'Two crosses like hostile lances at rest'.

In the struggle that now developed between Becket and the king, the archbishop of York inevitably took the latter's side in upholding the Constitutions of Clarendon; but this meant that he lost papal support, and his authority to crown kings was withdrawn. None the less Roger defiantly placed the crown on the head of the young Henry in June 1170, and consequently was not only suspended from office, but threatened with excommunication by the papacy.

Unable to prevent Becket's return to England from his long exile, Roger has been credited with his murder: inciting the four knights to that deed, giving them money, and actually suggesting the very words they should use when confronting Thomas. But, after stoutly protesting his innocence, Roger obtained papal absolution.

His relations with Richard, the new archbishop of Canterbury, were no better; and once again his claim to carry his cross erect in the southern province was upheld by the pope. In 1175 there was even a physical tussle between the archbishops over priority. At a council held in St. Catherine's Chapel, Westminster, presided over by the papal legate to try yet again to settle this perennial question of cross-bearing, Archbishop Richard, in order to demonstrate his precedence, took his seat on the right-hand side of the legate, whereupon Roger endeavoured, in the words of Gervase of Canterbury, 'to squeeze his buttocks between the archbishop of Canterbury and the legate, ending up on the legate's lap.' Richard's servants seized and hurled Roger to the ground, tearing his vestments. In a rage he betook himself to the king, who simply roared with laughter and would do nothing to help him; however, later that year, Henry held another council, where he persuaded both archbishops to agree to suspend hostilities for five years. None the less Roger's position was reinforced at the Lateran Council of 1179, when a decree was made confirming the independence of York from Canterbury, and declaring that no profession of obedience was due to her.

Roger's successor, the blue-blooded **Geoffrey Plantagenet**, reputedly the illegitimate son of Henry II and 'Fair Rosamund', likewise came to blows with his rival at Canterbury, Hubert Walter, who claimed to be able to carry his cross erect throughout England, whilst denying the same right to York in the southern province. Consequently when the two archbishops met face to face at Nottingham in March 1194 to greet King Richard I, Geoffrey protested because Hubert had erected his processional cross; to which the latter replied: 'I carry my cross throughout all England, as I ought since I am Primate of all England'. Probably only the presence of the king then prevented the Yorkists from attacking him. Richard, who secretly sympathised with Geoffrey, none the less advised him to stay away from the coronation at Winchester, to which the archbishop agreed. But six days later on 23 April 1194 he joined the king at Waltham still defiantly carrying his cross erect. So the struggle between the two metropolitans continued.

Walter de Grey of York found a formidable adversary in the person of Stephen Langton of Canterbury. So the former, being essentially a peaceable man, sought as far as possible to avoid confrontation by keeping away from occasions likely to provoke it, such as the second crowning of Henry III. This, however was not always possible. At a council held in St. Paul's, the papal legate had himself to intervene to settle a fiercely contested dispute over precedence, by placing Canterbury on his right and York on his left. Walter, however, was followed by some more aggressive archbishops; and, when Archbishop Boniface of Canterbury forcibly prevented **Walter Giffard** from carrying his cross erect in the southern province and barred him from taking part in the coronation of Edward I, Giffard once again appealed to Rome.

His successor **Wickwane**, who went to Rome for his coronation and to receive the pallium, when returning defiantly hoisted his cross in mid-channel, and then marched through the Canterbury diocese and province with his cross borne erect before him from Dover to York. This action provoked a riot, and more than once the archbishop was attacked by a mob and his cross broken. The official reaction from Canterbury took the form of issuing inhibitions addressed to the rural deans, forbidding the people of each district that Wickwane passed through to supply him with food or any kind of hospitality.

Nothing daunted the next archbishop of York, **John le Romeyn**, continued his predecessor's policy of carrying his cross erect in the south, where he encountered an equally violent opposition. However, what was sauce for the goose could be the same for the gander. So when the archbishop of Canterbury attempted to assert his primatial rights in the north, he found himself facing a similar hostility. **Corbridge**, who followed Romeyn, did his best to prevent this by sending Bishop Langton of Lichfield to try and persuade his brother metropolitan, Archbishop Winchelsey, to stay out of his province.

By this time these archiepiscopal disputes had become a first class church scandal, which was not helped by the action of Corbridge's successor, **Greenfield**, who, on his return to England after his consecration by Pope Clement V, boldly proceeded to march through London with his cross erect under the protection of King Edward I. But then Edward back-tracked; and, fearful that Greenfield's appearance at Westminster in similar guise would provoke hostile demonstrations, appealed to the pope to restrain him. The whole position had reached an impasse. On the one hand Rome undoubtedly believed that by backing York's claims to parity with Canterbury, the papacy was helping to prevent the Church of England from becoming too independent, which might well happen should that Church become united under one metropolitan. It was the age old policy of divide and rule. On the other the English kings normally backed Canterbury with just that end in view: a strong independent Church controlled by a single primate. For the moment the monarch prevailed and Greenfield had reluctantly to submit and allow Archbishop Reynolds of Canterbury to carry his cross erect even in York itself, when parliament met there.

This truce, of course, did not last; and, under Archbishop **Melton** of York, the war increased, and chaos prevailed. The visits of one archbishop to the province of the other led to anathemas, riots, and people being threatened with excommunication should they provide hospitality or even pay reverence to the intruder. Melton was forbidden to take part in the coronation of Edward III; but got his revenge when he officiated at the marriage of Edward to Philippa of Hainault in York Minster. His successor, **William de la Zouche**, adopted a more pacific attitude, and sought to avoid further conflict by residing 'almost entirely in the north, where he busied himself with the affairs of the diocese'. Then, with the election of **John Thoresby** to the York archbishopric in 1352, who became known as 'the peace maker', this long and fierce controversy was at last settled.

Archbishops Thoresby and Islip agreed on the following terms: Each archbishop was at liberty to have his cross borne erect before him in the other's province. Canterbury would receive the title of Primate of All England, whilst that of York simply Primate of England. The Primate of England should acknowledge the seniority of the Primate of All England, by sending to Canterbury by his official a golden ornament worth £40, preferably the image of an archbishop, carrying a cross, within two months of his entering the southern province carrying his cross erect before him. It was also agreed that Canterbury had the right of sitting next to the king in parliament, and on the chief seat in Convocation; and at the same time it was understood that the archbishop of York could only crown the monarch under exceptional circumstances.

Finally, in order to avoid further confrontations, they agreed that when the two archbishops with their crosses met face to face in a broad way, they would pass each other by; but, if in a narrow passage or entry, then Canterbury's cross should pass first. This concordat was confirmed by the pope in 1354; and thus it appeared that the centuries' old struggle over the primacy had come to an end.

However, two vexed questions remained: those of legateships and cardinalates. As we have seen Pope Honorius II in 1126 conferred on William of Corbeil, the then archbishop of Canterbury, legatine authority in England, which in theory at any rate gave him undisputed supremacy as the pope's representative over all the English bishops, including the archbishop of York. But at the same time Honorius made it clear that the metropolitan dignity of York should not be compromised. Furthermore this legatine authority, apparently, was not given to William's immediate successors, since Henry of Blois, bishop of Winchester, was granted it next, who, on the strength of such an authority, consecrated William Fitzherbert as archbishop of York. Later still Roger of York received that office; and the archbishops of Canterbury did not become automatically *legatus natus* by virtue of their see until the thirteenth century. Not unnaturally York demanded the same legatine status as his fellow metropolitan; and, after overcoming considerable opposition, it was granted to the northern archbishop as a matter of course by the middle of the fourteenth century.

The position moreover became further complicated by the fact that from time to time the pope dispatched one or more of his own personal legates to England, who as *legati à latere* had precedence over both archbishops. On occasion too the pope exercised his power to appoint an ordinary English suffragan bishop as *legatus à latere*, as when Pope Martin V nominated Henry Beaufort, bishop of Winchester, to that office in 1419. A century later **Thomas Wolsey**, archbishop of York, was granted this honour, which gave him the whip hand over Warham of Canterbury.

In the reign of Henry IV the English archbishops were freed by the crown from the obligation to resign their sees once they had been made cardinals. **John Kempe**, archbishop of York, became a cardinal in 1439, and promptly claimed precedence over Archbishop Chichele of Canterbury in the king's council, which was granted him despite Chichele's protests. 'The matter', we are told, 'was referred to Pope Eugenius IV, who declared that even in his own province an archbishop should go after a cardinal, since the latter was the first degree in the Church next to the Papacy'.

These disputes came to a head in the reign of Henry VIII, when Thomas Wolsey combined in his person not only a cardinalate and the office of *legatus à latere*, but was also Lord Chancellor. It is scarcely surprising then that Warham, who was not a cardinal and only held the title of *legatus natus*, became subordinated to his fellow metropolitan. Wolsey could and did overrule the decisions of the ecclesiastical officers and their courts in the southern province, and presided himself over

Convocation. Indeed so potent was his authority that whenever he celebrated mass, which incidentally he very rarely did, all the worshippers present automatically received absolution from their sins. His fall from power, however, followed as it was by a final break with Rome, and eventually by the establishment of the Church of England as a truly national church under the supreme government of the crown, put an end to both legateships and cardinalates, and so brought peace at last to the archiepiscopal scene. This was also made possible by the fact that as early as 1462 the northern synod had agreed to the amalgamation of its own constitution with that of the southern province, which meant that both Canterbury and York were now subject to the same body of ecclesiastical law. Never again was an archbishop of York to challenge Canterbury's incontestible right, as the successor of St. Augustine, to be and act as the Primate of All England.

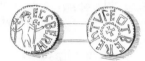

Archbishop Egbert (735-766)
Silver sceat, also citing
his brother Eadberht, king
of Northumbria

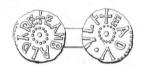

Archbishop Eanbald II (796-808)
Silver sceat

Gold solidus of Archbishop Wigmund (837-854)

Archbishop Wigmund (837-854)
Copper sceat

Archbishop Wulfhere (854-900)
Copper sceat

CHAPTER III

The Early Medieval Archbishops of York

Up to Norman times the diocese of York consisted of the three Ridings, Nottinghamshire, Cumberland, Westmorland and the northern part of Lincolnshire, with the see of Worcester attached to the archbishopric. But most of this was soon to disappear. North Lincolnshire was quickly lost, the archbishops ceased to be also bishops of Worcester from the time of Ealdred's relinquishment of that see, and Cumberland and Westmorland became part of the new bishopric of Carlisle in 1233. The rest remained until after the Reformation, but still proved so unwieldy that only one archbishop, Melton, is known to have crossed the watershed on a pastoral visitation. The wild and poverty-stricken archdeaconry of Richmond was ruled by its official with dictatorial powers, and only once received a visit from York. Outside its own boundaries, however, the archdiocese claimed a considerable territory in Durham, and another in Gloucestershire, including the monastery of St. Oswald and a couple of parishes. But within the see itself the archbishop found himself confronted by the fiercely independent chapters of York, Beverley, Ripon and Southwell, together with some other minor 'peculiars'. Two periods during the medieval archiepiscopate are covered in this chapter: the first from 1070 to 1215; and the second from 1215 to 1373.

York and Yorkshire had been devastated by William the Conqueror's harrying of the north; but under the new Norman archbishop, **Thomas I**, a born administrator, a wonderful transformation took place: the cathedral rose from its ashes; the prebendal chapter, with dean, precentor, treasurer and chancellor, came into being; and the archdeaconries of York, Richmond, Nottingham, East Riding and Cleveland were established. Thomas was followed by three other clerics from Normandy: **Gerard**, **Thomas II** and **Thurstan**, during whose reigns monastic communities were planted in strategic centres all over the diocese; the see of Carlisle was created; and the Gregorian reforms were put into practice. The famous cathedral school at York became almost a university. Then, for the next 60 years two worldly, quarrelsome and ambitious prelates, **Roger** and **Geoffrey**, occupied the see; and during their time the attempts of York to establish effective suzerainty over the Scottish bishoprics were finally frustrated by the steady resistance of the people of that country, their independence being confirmed by a papal decree of 1188. Only Whithorn remained within the York orbit until the fourteenth century. These turbulent years then gave place to an age of able, learned archbishops, drawn from the universities of Oxford and Paris and elected by the chapter, of which they were themselves originally members, beginning with **Walter de Grey** in 1215. Competent administrators, and well versed in civil and canon law, they put the finances of the Minster onto a sound footing, reorganised the parochial system, built churches, instituted vicarages, and began to keep careful registers. But, apart from Grey himself, **Melton**, **de la Zouche** and **Thoresby**, none of them were very distinguished; and probably Grey was the only really strong character. The average expectation of the life of an archbishop was between 11 and 12 years, although Grey ruled the diocese for 40, the longest in its history apart from **Vernon Harcourt** in the nineteenth century.

We now turn to the individual stories of these earlier medieval archbishops of York:

Thomas I, who succeeded Ealdred in 1070, came of a noble family from Bayeux, whose father and brother, Samson, were already priests. Thomas and Samson had been educated by Bishop Odo of Bayeux and became his clerks. The former acted as the bishop's treasurer, and followed him to England, where he was chosen as one of the royal chaplains; whilst the latter ultimately rose to be bishop of Worcester. Thomas, who had studied not only in France and Germany, but also under Saracen teachers in Spain, was a recognised scholar, and William I quickly came to appreciate his wisdom, diplomatic skills, sophisticated and polished manners. So much so indeed that on Ealdred's death the king appointed him to the vacant archbishopric as the right man for tackling the formidable task of restoring a ruined city and a devastated diocese and province.

As the whole subject of the struggle between Canterbury and York has been dealt with in the previous chapter it will only be touched on briefly here in so far as it affected each archbishop personally. Thomas' consecration was delayed owing to his refusal to make a profession of obedience to Lanfranc; but, having given way, and after consecration, he and Lanfranc went to Rome for their respective palliums. Here the pope, Alexander II, raised the question of Thomas' illegitimacy as the son of a priest, but at Lanfranc's intercession he relented and Thomas received the pall.

At York the new archbishop found himself with only one suffragan bishopric, Durham, together with a vague suzerainty over Scotland that could not be enforced, and a devastated province. Moreover he now lost the 12 Worcester estates, and henceforth the York connection with that diocese was finally broken. The city of York had been burnt and the Minster was a ruin; so he must needs set about rebuilding not only the cathedral, but the buildings belonging to the restored canons, whom he endowed out of his own properties. According to Hugh the Chanter the archbishop appointed new archdeacons, founded the chapter dignities of dean, treasurer and precentor, revived the chancellorship, restored the cathedral school and filled the Minster 'with clerks, books, ornaments . . . above all he desired to have good and reputable clerks'. In other words he created a first class chapter of secular prebendaries with the archdeacons as canons. However, another writer, William of Malmesbury, accused Thomas of impoverishing the archbishopric for the sake of providing funds for the chapter.

Thomas and Lanfranc were now firm friends; and, with the help of the latter, the archbishop was able to extend his authority over Scotland, consecrating the bishop of Orkney and obtaining a profession of obedience from the bishop of St. Andrews. Then, when William of Calais, bishop of Durham, was accused of treason, Thomas not only refused to support him, but sat as one of his judges. He attended Lanfranc's funeral; and, during the ensuing vacancy at Canterbury, became the leading ecclesiastic in the kingdom, consecrating new bishops, even for the southern province. Taking advantage of this position he boldly claimed the bishopric of Lincoln for the York province, which was rejected by William Rufus, who gave him instead the abbeys of Selby and Gloucester.

In 1093 he consecrated Anselm, but only as the southern metropolitan; and had hopes, in the absence of the latter abroad, of crowning Henry I. However, that monarch declined his offer, and the ceremony was performed by the bishop of London, on the lame excuse of the need for haste; although the real reason was undoubtedly that the king did not wish to offend Canterbury. Thomas grudgingly accepted the *fait accompli* and did homage, an acquiescence appreciated by Henry, who relied upon his loyalty to keep the north quiet and prosperous. This was not easy, since there were still frequent Viking raids either from Denmark or Norway. Indeed in 1075 York had again been plundered and the partially restored Minster seriously damaged.

Thomas died on 18 November 1100 at York, 'full of years, honours and divine grace'. Physically the archbishop was tall, handsome and robust; a first class scholar and a good musician. He wrote the epitaph for the Conqueror's tomb. At Durham he freed the convent and its churches from all dues payable to him by charter; and he founded the provostship at Beverley for his nephew and future successor, Thomas II. His generosity towards Durham was a reward for his cure at the tomb of St. Cuthbert, and also because its bishop had substituted monks for secular canons in the

29

cathedral. The provostship of Beverley, on the other hand, can only be attributed to an act of nepotism.

His immediate successor, however, was not Thomas II, but a distant kinsman of William I, named Gerard, and this connection served him well, as he quickly became a canon and precentor of Rouen and a clerk to William Rufus. The king sent him on a secret mission to Rome in 1095 to bargain with the pope over Rufus' dispute with Anselm, putting forward the suggestion that in return for England's recognition of Urban as the true pope instead of his rival, the papacy in return would grant William both a pallium and a legatine authority, which he could bestow on whom he pleased. This mission proved successful, and Gerard returned triumphantly in the company of a papal legate, Cardinal William of Albano, who brought the pallium in his luggage. Gerard's own reward was the bishopric of Hereford, when Anselm not only ordained him deacon and priest on the same day, but on the following consecrated him as bishop. As a favourite of the next king, Henry I, Gerard was not only present at his coronation, but one of the witnesses of the king's famous charter, and he himself crowned Queen Matilda, despite the archbishop of Canterbury's protests.

Three weeks later Thomas I was dead, and Henry promptly appointed **Gerard** in his place. There were the usual disputes over Canterbury's demand for a profession of obedience, but none the less the new archbishop obtained permission to go to Rome for his pallium; and in the subsequent struggle between Henry I and Anselm over the investiture of bishops, Gerard undertook the task of pleading the king's cause before the pope. The papacy, however, backed Anselm, ordered Henry to submit, and excommunicated Gerard and the other bishops who had supported him. But when Anselm refused to consecrate certain bishops because they had received investiture from the king, Gerard defiantly offered to take his place. The bishops themselves, however, objected to such a substitution, the whole assembly broke up in disorder, and Anselm went into exile.

Despite a papal rebuke Gerard now took over his authority and became metropolitan for the whole of Britain; but, after some conciliatory correspondence, Anselm was persuaded to return, became reconciled to Gerard and his supporting bishops, and the investiture dispute was settled. As a token of their renewed cordiality the two archbishops jointly performed the deferred consecrations at Canterbury on 11 August 1107.

Gerard himself died the following May at his Southwell palace, whilst on his way to London for a church council that was to consider the enforced celibacy of the clergy. He died in his sleep with a book on astrology under his pillow, a death therefore without the rites of the Church, and this was regarded as a judgment on him for his interest in magical and forbidden arts. His bier was pelted with stones as it entered York, and his remains were refused interment in the Minster. Instead they had to be content with a turf grave outside the cathedral. But Thomas II, his successor, had them translated to the church. His epitaph was written, like his predecessor's, by Hugh the Chanter.

Gerard had a great reputation for learning and eloquence. he wrote elegant little latin verses; and Raine says of him: 'Gerard was a reformer and a successful politician, and in both these characters he would be sure to create enemies'. Certainly he was not popular, being accused of covetousness, leading a licentious life, and practising magical arts. Furthermore he was at odds with his canons. In 1103 he wrote to Anselm: saying how lucky he was to have monks given to prayer and piety, while he had to deal with refractory canons, who were often only in minor orders, but refused to proceed to major ones lest they found themselves committed to celibacy. They took the revenues from their prebends, but lived away from the Minster, providing substitutes to serve its altars. They also got round the celibacy laws by saying: 'precisely as the Council has laid down we shall not keep women in our houses; but there is nothing in the decree of any general council forbidding us to entertain women alone and without witnesses in the houses of our neighbours.' This was the kind of attitude, reflecting dislike of monasticism, that Gerard most resented. But unfortunately the previous year the archbishop himself had blotted his copybook by being justly accused of simony, when he sold a prebend of York to the son of one of his archdeacons. Realising his error too late he tried in vain to buy it back.

He is credited with enriching the Minster by securing five churches for it from Henry I; but, like his predecessor, helped to impoverish the archbishopric itself by a prodigal distribution of its lands. At the Minsters of Beverley, Ripon and Southwell Gerard aroused a storm of protest against his attempt to introduce certain reforms. When, for example, a reputed miracle took place during his celebration of mass at Beverley, a servant of his being restored to speech and hearing, and the archbishop took advantage of the occasion to laud the power of St. John of Beverley, one of the local nobility stood up and said that they were well accustomed to St. John's miracles; but it would be well if Gerard himself took this event to heart and so stopped interfering in the affairs of Beverley. No one, however, could deny the archbishop's own religious zeal; and in 1106 he actually proposed joining one of the crusades.

The next archbishop, **Thomas II**, son of Thomas I's brother Samson, had been brought up by his uncle at York where he was popular. In 1092 he became provost of Beverley and one of the king's chaplains. He was actually on the point of being elected bishop of London, when the news arrived of Gerard's death, and he was immediately nominated by Henry I to York, where Hugh the Chanter played a dominant part in securing his election by the chapter. Thomas attended a London council called by Anselm; but shortly afterwards relations between the two archbishops

31

grew sour over the inevitable question of a profession of obedience to Canterbury. Consequently Anselm forbade any of the northern bishops to consecrate the new bishop of St. Andrews, which, he claimed would have infringed Canterbury's rights; and further demanded that in future he himself should perform all episcopal functions in the York province. He forbade Thomas to go to Rome for his pallium, urged the pope not to grant it, and threatened to excommunicate any prelate who should dare consecrate the new archbishop.

The York chapter, who supported Thomas wholeheartedly, wrote to Anselm expressing their supreme contempt for the Canterbury monks, whom, they declared, 'do not cease to aim at and shamelessly demand what is unjust'. The death of Anselm and Thomas' conditional submission at the behest of the king opened the way for his consecration at St. Paul's, in June 1109, and his investiture with the pallium by the papal legate at York shortly afterwards. He now felt able to consecrate Turgaot as bishop of St. Andrews, and himself received professions of obedience from the bishops of Glasgow, the Isle of Man, and the Orkneys.

Owing to an incurable disease, which he was told could only be remedied by violating his chastity, a solution he at once rejected, Thomas became enormously fat and died still a comparatively young man at Beverley on 24 February 1114. As Hugh the Chanter put it: 'he was full-bodied and fatter than he should have been'. This physical condition no doubt explains the fact that he was notoriously indolent and had to be pushed into any kind of action by the York chapter, of whom he was mortally afraid. On the other hand he was known to be cheerful, benign, very liberal in his religious views, a learned scholar and an eloquent preacher. Fond of music he composed a number of hymns. Generous to a fault, he freed the Southwell canons from their episcopal dues, and endowed the Augustinian canons in the diocese with lands, books and ornaments. But at Hexham he unwittingly stirred up a hornet's nest. For in attempting to reform that church he replaced certain clerks, who, although adequately compensated, resented their expulsion. One of them, Eilaf, hearing of Thomas' death broke into joyful laughter and commented most unkindly on his supposedly evil way of life; in particular his attempt to remove the body of St. Eata from Hexham and have it reburied in the Minster. In this, Eilaf said, he was rudely rebuffed by the saint himself, who appeared to Thomas in a dream and roughly demanded: 'Why have you decided to disturb my peace, and take me from the place where I am sleeping contentedly with my brethren, and bear me into foreign parts?' He then informed the terrified archbishop: 'This is not the Will of God but your own presumption for which you will now be punished.' The apparition then raised its pastoral staff, struck Thomas twice on the shoulder, and vanished. The screams of the archbishop brought his clerks running, whom he begged to pray for his forgiveness; and for three days he lay in a deadly sickness. On the fourth he recovered, and hastily left Hexham with its saint's bones intact. He lies buried in the Minster.

His successor, **Thurstan**, was born near Bayeux in Normandy, his father being a priest, and he was sent to Caen for his education. But on his father, Auger, receiving a prebend in St. Paul's Cathedral, London, he brought his two sons, Audouen and Thurstan, to England with him. The latter, following in Auger's footsteps, also secured a St. Paul's prebend, and made some valuable contacts, which included William Giffard, bishop of Winchester, and Archbishop Anselm, whose saintly character and reforming principles greatly attracted Thurstan. These brought him into the royal household, first as a clerk at Rufus' court and then secretary to Henry I, who came to esteem his abilities so highly that, on Thomas' death, he appointed his young secretary to the vacant archbishopric of York on the Feast of the Assumption, 15 August 1114, but without making any attempt to consult the York chapter, which, according to recent precedent, should have had at least some say in the choice of their archbishop, especially as Thurstan was then no more than a sub-deacon. However, they acquiesced, and were later to back him to the hilt in his campaign against the demands of Canterbury for submission and a profession of obedience; although at his enthronement in December 1114 he had still risen no higher in the Church than the full diaconate.

Skipping the controversial struggle over the primacy, which was dealt with in Chapter II, Thurstan finally arrived back in England from exile in January 1121, determined to devote himself in future to the affairs of his northern diocese and province. Hugh the Chanter wrote of his tumultuous reception at York as follows:

> The archbishop set off to meet his bride so long widdowed by his absence, that is to say the church of York. And as he drew near the city there came out to meet him such a great crowd of clerics, knights, nobles and monks, and men and women on horse and foot, that certain of those present called to mind what was written about St. John: 'When he was returning from exile St. John was met by the whole population, men and women alike, acclaiming him in the words Blessed is he that cometh in the name of the Lord'. Then on the Sunday when the service begins with the words of Esto mihi in deum protectorem he was received in the church in the manner worthy of an archbishop so long exiled from his church's freedom; he was taken into the bosom of his bride with exultation and rejoicing. In the presence of that great multitude was read out and explained the apostolic privilege confirming the liberty of the church, at which everyone rejoiced and gave thanks to God.

Thurstan now vigorously set about the task of reform; and he began by remitting the fee payable by parishes for the holy chrism, whilst at the same time forbidding the clergy to exact such fees for burials, baptisms or anointing the sick, unless they were freely offered. The archbishop was also resolved not only to encourage and strengthen existing ecclesiastical institutions in the archdiocese, but to found new monastic centres. For example he increased the number of York prebends, already enlarged by Thomas II, by adding those of Salton, Weighton and Bramham; but at the same time decreed that all vacant prebends, which formerly had been treated like any other kind of personal property to be disposed of as the late tenant indicated in his Will, should now remain firmly in the hands of the chapter and solely at their disposal. These decrees were likewise to apply to Ripon, Beverley, Southwell and St. Oswald's in Gloucestershire as well as York, but at the same time he increased the finances of the chapters without seeking to change their status quo by converting them from secular to monastic establishments. On the other hand Thurstan became a famous patron and founder of northern monasteries. At first he favoured the Austin canons, who were already settled at Hexham, Nostell and Bridlington, protecting and encouraging them; whilst also setting up further foundations at Guisborough, Embsay (later Bolton), Worksop and Kirkham. In such endeavours he found an ally in Alexander I of Scotland, who promoted Robert, prior of Nostell, to the see of St. Andrews, thus healing a previous breach with Thurstan over his support of John, bishop of Glasgow's, refusal to profess obedience to the archbishopric of York. John for his part was excommunicated.

The archbishop's links with the next Scottish king, David, were to be even closer; and together they successfully revived the ancient see of Whithorn in 1125. Another king, Olaf of Man, co-operated with Thurstan in establishing an abbey, Rushen, on that island, which was staffed by the Augustinians from the abbey of Furness. This led to the creation of an episcopal see, whose first bishop was consecrated by the archbishop.

But a much more important bishopric than that on Man now came into existence: Carlisle, which was founded under the auspices of Henry I and Thurstan. John of Glasgow had intruded into the Carlisle area, and as a counter measure the monasteries of Wetheral, St. Bees and Embsay were established by Thurstan, which as monastic strongholds in the north-west, the first two Benedictine and the last Augustinian, sought to buttress the already flourishing abbey of Furness, and firmly entrench the archbishop's rule against that of John of Glasgow. Then, with the co-operation of Henry I and King David, all this religious zeal was harnessed for a 'major stroke of policy in the north east,' namely the setting up of the see of Carlisle, whose first bishop, Athelwold, was Thurstan's friend and confidant, who was consecrated at York in August 1133. Indeed by 1133 Thurstan could feel well satisfied with the state of his archbishopric. When he had arrived at York 20 years previously the province was largely in a chaotic condition. Now the archbishop, with reliable suffragans both at Durham and Carlisle, a screen of churches in the hands of his associates running along the Scottish border, flourishing monasteries everywhere,

34

and the ancient Minsters in good shape, had become the outstanding personality in northern England.

Perhaps his most outstanding achievement was the founding of the great Cistercian abbey of Fountains. In 1131 a group of these Cistercians sponsored by St. Bernard, arrived in Yorkshire under a Yorkshireman, William, and established themselves at Rievaulx. Thurstan was most impressed by their saintliness and other-worldliness; so, when trouble broke out at St. Mary's Priory in York between those monks, headed by the prior, Richard, who wished to imitate the Cistercians, and the abbot, Geoffrey, who, with the majority in the monastery, clung to the old ways, the archbishop backed the reformers. Consequently on these men being expelled from St. Mary's, he took them under his wing and settled them on one of his estates near Ripon. From these small beginnings emerged the famous abbey of Fountains with Richard as its first abbot. Thurstan himself practised what he preached, living a disciplined, holy and ascetic life: he wore a hair shirt, flagellated himself, ate and drank very sparingly, was constant in prayer, and lavish with alms for the poor. As a result he became the trusted spiritual adviser of a large number of individuals, particularly of women, among whom were numbered Adela, Countess of Blois, William the Conqueror's daughter; that remarkable female recluse, Christina of Markgate, and Gundreda de Mowbray. Indeed Thurstan's chief claim to fame rests on his patronage of the monastic ideal, and, as the instigator of the monastic renaissance that took place in his province during the last years of his life. For his name is not only associated with the Cistercian foundations of Fountains, Newminster, Calder and Byland, but also with the revival of such older diocesan houses as Selby, Whitby, and Pontefract, as well as those of Holy Trinity and St. Peter's Hospital in York itself.

Thurstan, however, was much more than simply a religious leader, for he had an important part to play in the politics of the north. Hitherto his relations with the Scottish kings had been good and friendly; but, with the death of Henry I, there came a change. The archbishop, loyal to the House of Blois, supported Stephen's claim to the throne, whilst King David of Scotland backed his niece, the Empress Matilda. So David invaded England, seizing the towns, of Carlisle, Carham, Alnwick, Norham and Newcastle; but then came to terms with Stephen on the understanding that his son, Henry, would ultimately succeed as king of Northumbria.

Thurstan, handicapped now by old age and growing infirmities, at first took little part in this struggle; and, owing to his difficulty in taking long journeys, was even prevented from attending the important council at Oxford, where a sweeping charter of ecclesiastical liberties was issued by Stephen. Moreover, a disastrous fire on Friday, 8 June 1137, that destroyed much of York, burnt down the Minster, and even spread outside the walls, damaging both St. Mary's Priory and St. Peter's Hospital, naturally distracted both his attention and energies from the political conflict. But when the Scots again entered England, in order both to ravage Northumbria and seize it for Henry, at a time that Stephen was absent on the continent, the archbishop took action. As the king's representative in the north, and backed by a large army based on Newcastle, he successfully negotiated a temporary truce with King David at Roxburgh. None the less the Scots were determined to annex Northumbria, and, on Stephen's refusal to meet their demands, they prepared to renew the conflict. Thus in January 1138 further invasions began, and by July an army estimated at 20,000 strong was preparing to strike into the heart of Yorkshire. To combat this menace Thurstan mobilised the nobility and clergy of the north, who, under a banner depicting the five wounds of Christ, won a decisive victory over the Scots on 22 August near Northallerton that came to be known as 'The Battle of the Standard'.

The papacy now intervened; a small mission headed by Cardinal Alberic, bishop of Ostia, arrived in England, and a treaty of peace was eventually signed which surrendered Northumbria and the area of the north-west to Henry; but Athelwold was restored to the see of Carlisle, and David promised a full indemnity for all the damage his troops had inflicted. The archbishop, who now had to be carried everywhere in a litter, was unable to attend this peace conference at Carlisle, or indeed the council of the English Church held at Westminster Abbey in December 1138, where, under the legate's guidance, a series of reforming decrees were passed against clerical marriage, lay investiture, and the hereditary succession to spiritual offices. Yet even from a distance he was still able to make his influence felt, as when he got his friend, Theobald, abbot of Bec, appointed to the vacant archbishopric of Canterbury, and succeeded in quashing the election of Alselm, abbot of Bury St. Edmund's, to the see of London, informing the legate: 'he deserved to lose his abbey rather than being given a see'.

But by now Thurstan himself was preparing to resign his archbishopric and retire into a monastery. This he did, despite the eloquent pleas of St. Bernard that he should remain at his post, and became a cluniac monk at Pontefract on 25 January 1140, dying 12 days later:

> Surrounded by the dignitaries of the church of York and other men of religion, as the hour of his summons drew near, he himself celebrated the vigils for the departed, none other but himself reading the nine lessons. And when he came to the verse of the response, Diesilla, dies irae, he laid significant and awful emphasis on each word. At the end of the Lauds the monks being all assembled at prayer, he gave up the ghost. He was buried, with becoming honours before the high altar of the church of St. John the Evangelist.

Before Thurstan left York he had as a good businessman put all his affairs in order, making sure that every member of his familia had received his wages in full. He confessed his sins before the chapter, and, naked on the ground, was physically chastised, 'weeping from the depth of a contrite heart'. The monks of Pontefract were hoping that he might be canonised; but this expectation was never fulfilled.

The discipline and order that Thurstan had imposed upon his province broke down almost immediately after his death; a not unnatural occurrence in view of the struggle that now commenced between Stephen and David as to which of them should control the north of England and secure their own candidate for the archiepiscopal throne. David proposed his stepson, Waltheof, prior of Kirkham, who was promptly vetoed by Stephen, who in his turn put forward his nephew, Henry de Sully, abbot of Caen. Now the pope intervened, refusing to allow the latter to become archbishop, unless he first resigned his Normandy abbey. This Henry refused to do; and so Stephen, supported by Henry de Blois, suggested yet another member of the same family, albeit from an illegitimate branch, **William Fitzherbert**, treasurer of the York chapter and one of the king's chaplains, despite bitter opposition from the monks, who resented such secular interference in ecclesiastical affairs. None the less William was elected by the York chapter; whereupon some of the leading northern abbots, backed by a dissident section of the chapter headed by the archdeacon, Walter of London, appealed to Rome against what they considered irregularities in the archbishop's election, whom they described as no more than a royal pawn and the nominee of Henry de Blois, 'the whore of Winchester'.

Moreover this election had been opposed by the powerful St. Bernard, who alleged that Fitzherbert had been guilty of simony. He called upon the pope to repudiate him, 'lest the authority of St. Peter succumb to these new and great humiliations, lest religion should grow cold in the diocese of York, yes, lest it be wholly uprooted and scattered to the winds'. Stephen retorted by imprisoning the archdeacon of York, along with his fellow archdeacons, including Osbert of Bayeux, Thurstan's nephew, at Byrham Castle in Lincolnshire. Then he himself welcomed Fitzherbert to Lincoln and conferred upon him the temporalities of the see. Theobald, archbishop of Canterbury, refused to consecrate him, so William went to Rome, and here, despite the clamour raised against him by St. Bernard and the whole Cistercian Order, Pope Innocent II agreed to consecrate the archbishop provided he was able by oath to dispel the accusations of royal pressure and simony. The dean of York, who had accompanied William, gave firm assurances that the charges were untrue, and added: 'all clamour for his consecration'. None the less the pope hesitated and finally delegated the consecration to Henry de Blois, then acting as papal legate, which took place on 26 September 1143.

At first William was generally accepted in York, despite the continued hostility of the Cistercians; and he set about reforming the clergy, settled a dispute at Durham, and consecrated the dean of York as its bishop. Then came disaster. A Cistercian in the person of Eugenius III became pope; and in 1147, at the insistence of St. Bernard and the Yorkshire monastic leaders, ordered a fresh election. William was first suspended and then deposed, while the pope himself consecrated Henry Murdac, abbot of Fountains, William's fiercest enemy, as the new archbishop. In vain William had gone to Rome to plead his cause. He was described as 'the Idol that the Whore of Winchester had set up in St. Peter's Minster', and could get no redress, although he had had to sell some of the Minster's treasures in order to pay for his expenses. At the Council of Rheims, held the same year, his deposition was formally confirmed, and he retired in shame to Sicily, whilst Murdac reigned in his stead.

The usurper found no easy throne. William's friends burned and plundered Fountains Abbey, the York citizens compelled him to quit and take up his residence at Beverley, and even here the wrath of Stephen pursued him by fining the Minster for receiving him. Murdac replied by excommunicating his chief enemy at York, Hugh of Puiset, the treasurer, and placing an interdict on the city itself. But this last was disregarded since Hugh compelled the clergy to go on performing the services, and himself excommunicated the archbishop.

However, Murdac had his friends. He won the support of King David, of the bishops of Durham and Carlisle, and of the future Henry II. Moreover he appealed to the pope, who threatened Stephen with dire consequences unless he accepted Murdac; and eventually, with Stephen's son, Eustace, acting as mediator, peace was made between the king and the archbishop. So Murdac was enthroned at York on 26 January 1151; and in return not only absolved Hugh, but promised to use his influence with the pope to get Eustace recognised as Stephen's heir.

But, once in office, his high handed conduct again aroused hostility, by his ruthless reforms of the monasteries and by thrusting regulars into the place of the secular canons at the Minsters. Then he refused to recognise Hugh's election to the bishopric of Durham excommunicating the archdeacons and the prior of Brinkham who had protested. Again the York citizens rose, drove him out of the city, and petitioned the king and the archbishop of Canterbury to get these excommunications lifted. This was done after the culprits had submitted to a symbolic scourging.

Murdac now turned his attention to the forthcoming crusade, so eagerly preached by his friends, St. Bernard and Pope Eugenius III, and sought to whip up enthusiasm for it throughout the north of England. It ended in disaster, and all its three main champions died the same year, 1153, Murdac himself at Sherburn. A stern and righteous ascetic he wore the traditional hair shirt and endured flagellation, raising the Cistercian order to the height of its fame in England, but failing to extend its ideals into the northern Minsters. He, together with St. Bernard and Eugenius, were described by the monastic chronicler at Fountains, somewhat over-enthusiastically, as 'the guardians of the Lord's flock, columns of the Lord's house, and lights of the world'.

By May 1154 William Fitzherbert was once again in occupation of the archbishopric. A kindly but sluggish man he had found refuge during the usurpation with Henry de Blois at Winchester, where he devoted himself to prayer and study, eschewing every kind of luxury, and acquiring a reputation for sainthood. Now, after Murdac's death, he found support for his cause from the new pope, Anastasius IV, who, after reviewing his case, reinstated him as archbishop of York. Here he received a tumultuous welcome from the citizens and most of the chapter, although still bitterly opposed by the dean and Archdeacon Osbert. An auspicious event greeted his arrival and confirmed his claims to sainthood: the procession of clergy and laity coming to welcome him was suddenly precipitated into the river Ouse as its wooden bridge gave way under their weight. But thanks, or so it was believed, to the prayers of William no lives were lost; and later a chapel was erected on the new stone bridge to commemorate this miracle. For the rest of his life, which only lasted a few months, William ruled his archbishopric in peace. He won over the Cistercians by visiting their monasteries, promising restitution to burnt-out Fountains, and confirming Murdac's grant to the new foundation at Meaux.

So at first it seemed that the Blois family had reasserted its authority in the north; but not for long. The death of Stephen and his son, Eustace, and the elevation to the throne of Henry II entirely changed the situation. Henry refused to recognise the title of William of Aumale, the most powerful Blois supporter in the north, to the Earldom of York, and Henry de Blois himself wisely retired to the continent for four years. How Archbishop William would have fared under the new regime none can say, since he had died under very suspicious circumstances. The rumour ran that Archdeacon Osbert had put poison into the chalice at mass, illustrating once again the bitter divisions into which the York chapter had sunk since Thurstan's time. Osbert, of course, denied the charge; but, even after compurgation, this denial failed to carry conviction and he was unfrocked. However, as a layman he continued to flourish, becoming steward to Hugh de Tilly, marrying and begetting a large family. Opinions as to his guilt varied, and nothing was ever proved; but so judicious a character as John of Salisbury firmly believed that he was a murderer.

William had designated **Roger**, archdeacon of Canterbury as his successor, to which office he was duly appointed by Henry II and elected by the chapter. William himself, whether poisoned or dying of a fever, became canonised in 1227 by Pope Honorius III, after miracles had been wrought at the tomb of this supposed martyr. Then, on 9 January 1283, his remains were enclosed in a shrine behind the high altar at the Minster in the presence of Edward I and at the instigation of the powerful Bishop Bek of Durham. His festival was fixed for 8 June; but he never rose above the stature of a purely local saint, whose shrine never attracted the type of popular pilgrimage accorded to that of Thomas Becket.

Roger of Pont L'Eveque, then archdeacon of Canterbury, immediately succeeded William and reigned as archbishop from 1154 to 1181. At the court of Archbishop Theobald he and Thomas Becket had become deadly foes, an enmity that was to continue until the latter's death. Roger, as one of King Stephen's chaplains, attended the council in Rheims under Pope Eugenius III, where he did his best to persuade the papacy to acknowledge Eustace as Stephen's heir, whilst also secretly inciting Rome against Archbishop Theobald in support of the king.

The next step in his career was the appointment to the provostship of Beverley, to be followed by his elevation to the archbishopric of York. Consecrated by Theobald on 11 October 1154 in Westminster Abbey, he was present at Henry's coronation; and then quickly came to blows with the new archbishop of Canterbury, Thomas Becket. The struggle between them over the primacy has been dealt with in chapter II, but this inevitably led to Roger supporting the king over the 'criminous clerks' controversy, and assenting to the Constitutions of Clarendon. He even went so far as to demand Thomas' imprisonment for opposing them. Becket for his part referred to his enemy as *'malorum incentor et caput'*.

On 27 February 1155 Roger became a papal legate, and went on an embassy to Rome for the purpose of trying to persuade Pope Alexander III to disown Becket. In this, as always, he failed dismally, since both the pope and Louis VII of France were prepared to back Becket to the hilt. Roger, indeed, was ordered in no uncertain terms to do Thomas justice; but, studiously ignoring such a papal appeal, he continued to support the king, and told the English clergy to repudiate Becket. In reply the pope withdrew his permission to crown kings in general, and young Henry in particular.

Defiantly the archbishop crowned Henry II's eldest son on 14 June 1170, thereby earning for himself a suspension from office, with every prospect of an excommunication to follow. He was forced to submit, and found himself unable to prevent Thomas' return to England. However, he secretly warned the king that there would be no peace in the Church until Becket was dead, and succeeded in preventing young Henry from receiving him when he landed. Roger, indeed, has even been accused of urging on the four knights to commit the murder, giving them money, and actually suggesting the very words they should use when confronting Thomas. For thus supposedly acting as an accessory to murder, he was excommunicated by the pope, but later absolved after taking a solemn oath protesting his innocence. In a long letter to Hugh de Puiset he expressed his joy at this absolution; and at the same time sent another to Rome thanking the pope profusely for his kindness.

However, his relations with the next archbishop of Canterbury, Richard, were no better than they had been with Thomas. The controversy over the primacy continued; and, at the Council of Northampton in January 1175/6, Roger not only claimed that all the Scots' churches were subject to him as metropolitan, which was denied by Richard, but also the right of supervision over the sees of Lichfield, Hereford, and Lincoln. Furthermore he maintained that St. Oswald's, Gloucester, belonged to him. In 1180 Pope Alexander III recognised York's claim to the sees of Whithorn and Glasgow, and made Roger the papal legate for Scotland. Whereupon the archbishop excommunicated the Scots' king, William the Lion, for contumacy. Always a loyal adherent of Henry II, he gave him valuable support in his struggle with the barons and his own sons. In return he received the castle of Scarborough, and, during the last 10 years of his life, was constant in his attendance at the royal councils. Indeed, along with his friends, Gilbert Foliot, bishop of London, and Hugh de Puiset, bishop of Durham, Roger represented that section of the English Church which steadfastly upheld Henry's cause.

In his rôle as archbishop Roger proved himself both harsh and arrogant, becoming at once a bitter foe of monasticism and an oppressor of monks. For instance he carried out a long and venomous vendetta with the canons of Newburgh. On the other hand he was a sumptuous builder, enriching the Minster, erecting an episcopal palace at York, of which the ruins still remain, and, despite his dislike of the religious, founding new monasteries with splendid buildings. According to John of Salisbury he amassed a very large fortune, but used much of it to endow churches in the diocese. So much so indeed that he has been described as 'the most munificent ruler that ever presided over the see of York'. Not unnaturally his enemies, and they were many, charged him with odious vices; and certainly he was lacking in spiritual fervour. 'He was', wrote William Hutton, 'one of Henry II's statesmen–prelates, and as bishop he shaped his course to satisfy a political ambition.' None the less when in 1181 he knew himself to be dying, he called his clergy together and ordered the distribution of his property for the benefit of the poor. He died in York, and at first was buried in the Minster choir; but later his body was moved to a new and splendid tomb by Archbishop Thoresby. It is to be noted in his favour that, unlike St. William or Henry Murdac, he commanded throughout his archiepiscopate the united and fervent loyalty of the York chapter.

He was followed by that formidable blue-blooded bastard, **Geoffrey Plantagenet**, the supposedly illegitimate son of Henry II and 'Fair Rosamund', of whom D. I. Douie wrote: 'he played a modest but decisive part in the political history of England'. Born about 1153, he was forced at an early age into the clerical profession, for which he had neither taste, inclination nor aptitude, being like his step-brothers addicted to the arts of sport and military adventure. As a mere boy he became a prebendary of

41

St. Paul's, next the archdeacon of Lincoln, and then in 1175 its bishop, when he played a prominent part in the suppression of the insurrection that broke out in the north and midlands during that year. But during his seven years episcopate he did not entirely neglect his see: redeeming the sacred vessels pledged by his predecessors to the Jews; and appointing men of learning and ability to the canonries in his gift. His loyalty to his father and later to Richard I was absolute, causing the former to say of him: 'Baseborn indeed have my other children shown themselves; this is my true son'. His chastity was never impuned; but his imperious and over-bearing temper brought him into conflict with everyone he had to work with.

His repugnance to the clerical profession revealed itself in the fact that for many years he refused to be ordained, holding on to his see as a layman by reason of a dispensation from the pope. But obviously this state of affairs could not continue indefinitely, and in 1181 the pope told him he must either be ordained or resign the bishopric. He chose the latter, informing His Holiness that he much preferred military action to a clerical career, and became instead Chancellor of England, whilst receiving permission to retain a number of clerical offices, including the arch-deaconries of Lincoln and Rouen, and the treasurership of York Minster, besides several benefices. His father heaped upon him castles and other secular honours; but was determined that, despite Geoffrey's reluctance to become ordained, his son should succeed the deceased Roger as archbishop of York.

At this time Geoffrey was commanding Henry's troops in the French wars; and attended his father's deathbed in Chinon, when, in the words of the chronicler: 'his patient devotion won back the dying king from his ravings against his undutiful children, to die with a blessing on his one loyal son.' But Richard I was swift to fulfil Henry's wish and nominate his half-brother to the archbishopric of York. But this action of the new king's split the York chapter right down the middle. Apparently both Hubert Walter, the dean, and Hugh de Puiset, bishop of Durham, had hoped to obtain the archbishopric, the former for himself, and the latter for a nephew. An appeal therefore went to Rome against Geoffrey's appointment, citing his illegitimacy, secular tastes and refusal to be ordained. The king at first supported his brother, who was present at his coronation; and later at the Council of Pipewell on 3 September confirmed his election by a majority in the chapter. But, in order to placate the opposition, Richard then appointed Hubert Walter to the see of Salisbury, and Bouchard de Puiset to the York treasurership, now vacated by Geoffrey; while at the same time nominating Henry Marshal as dean. Geoffrey, however, had had his own candidates for the last two posts, and bitterly resented the king's appointments, even going so far as to refuse to install the new dean. Richard promptly changed sides, confiscated Geoffrey's estates, and prevented him from going to Rome for his pallium. A compromise was then arrived at, whereby in return for the archbishop's agreeing to confirm the new dean and treasurer in their offices and providing Richard with £2,000 out of his own pocket, he himself was priested by the bishop of Whithorn, and the papal legate, John of Anagni, sanctioned his election.

This truce did not last long; for on arriving at York late in order to attend vespers on the Vigil of the Epiphany, Geoffrey found the office already in full swing presided over by the dean. He immediately demanded that it should begin again; and since the choir obeyed him, despite the dean's plea to continue, the treasurer caused all the lights to be extinguished. The archbishop replied by laying the cathedral under an interdict, which far from producing an apology from dean and treasurer, only goaded them into heaping abuse on his head. The citizens of York, who were on Geoffrey's side, were only prevented from attacking them by the archbishop's intervention, and they were allowed to retire into hiding. None the less Geoffrey excommunicated them both, which enraged the king, who sent an embassy to Rome asking Pope Clement III to quash his election; whilst the bishop of Durham, as justiciar of the north, prevented the archbishop from raising the £2,000 he had promised Richard. The pope for his part tried to pour oil on troubled waters by confirming Geoffrey's election and giving him the pallium, and then absolving the dean and treasurer from their excommunications, besides granting the bishop of Durham an exemption from taking the oath to Geoffrey and thus rendering him independent of his metropolitan.

The next pope, Celestine III, took a very different line, withdrawing this privilege from Durham and exempting York from obedience to anyone except a visiting legate. This last shaft was aimed at the justiciar, Longchamp, who was attempting to force the York clergy to accept himself as legate, and proposed to deal severely with Geoffrey's allies in the chapter, especially Homo, the precentor. The archbishop now bought himself back into favour with Richard by paying him 800 marks and promising the rest of the £2,000 in instalments. Consequently, with the help of an old ally, Eleanor, the queen mother, he obtained permission from the king to be consecrated at Tours, some two years after his election.

Fearful of his many enemies Geoffrey returned to England in disguise on 14 December 1191, but only to be discovered by his inveterate foe, Longchamp, and forced to take refuge at the priory of St. Martin's in Dover, from which sanctuary he was dragged by Longchamp's men and imprisoned in the castle. Prince John and his mother now brought pressure to bear upon the justiciar, the archbishop was released and this high-handed outrage precipitated Longchamp's own downfall. Enthroned in York Minster on All Saints' Day 1191, amid scenes of great rejoicing, when he was hailed as a hero and a victim of sacrilege, Geoffrey took advantage of this popular acclaim to seek revenge upon his enemies. Consequently, when Hugh de Puiset, bishop of Durham, refused to appear as summoned to take an oath of obedience and pay his dues to the archbishop, the latter excommunicated him. But as he continued to celebrate mass, the archbishop ordered his altars to be overthrown and his sacred vessels shattered. Furthermore he excommunicated the dean, treasurer and their other allies in the York chapter and had their livings sequestrated. In order to obtain absolution, he said, they must come barefoot to York and do penance. With this ultimatum they all complied with the exception of the dean and the bishop of Durham, who both appealed to Rome. The Government again intervened; and with the help of Queen Eleanor, peace was again restored.

This happened to be all the more necessary in view of Prince John's rebellion during Richard's imprisonment in Germany; which caused all his friends, including Geoffrey, to rally to his cause. But it was not long before the archbishop was once more at odds with his chapter over the appointment of a new dean. Henry Marshal had become bishop of Exeter, and in his place Geoffrey proposed his bastard brother, Peter; and then, when such a choice proved impracticable, his clerk, Simon of Apulia, the York chancellor. Richard's nominee was Philip of Poitou; and eventually the archbishop dropped Simon in his favour. But the chapter continued to back Simon and appealed to Rome, to Richard's wrath, who summoned Geoffrey to meet him in Germany for a consultation. Unfortunately, however, the archbishop had barely started on his journey, when he was recalled to York to settle a clerical strike that had broken out against his order that the chapter should contribute a quarter of its annual income towards the king's ransom. This took the form of the canons refusing to serve the Minster, stripping the altar bare, locking up the archbishop's stall, and sealing the door through which he entered the cathedral from his palace. Geoffrey replied by getting his own personal clerks to perform the services. Meanwhile Pope Celestine III took the side of the chapter, provided Simon with the deanery, absolved them from the archbishop's excommunication, and restored their livings, which he had sequestered.

Their morale boosted by such support, the canons now went further and asked the papacy to depose Geoffrey from the archbishopric on the following grounds: that he had refused to obey papal orders, neglected his spiritual duties in favour of secular pursuits such as hunting and hawking, and most unbecomingly gloried in military adventures. During his period of office, they declared, he had held no ordinations, called no synods, dedicated no churches, and blessed no abbots. On the other hand he was over-lavish in bestowing excommunications both on the secular and religious clergy; and, most outrageous of all, had brought armed men into the Minster and seized the canons property for his own treasury. Celestine listened carefully to all these charges, and then informed Geoffrey that he had three months in which to issue an appeal against a sentence of deposition.

Richard had by now returned to England, and the archbishop turned to him for help, paying him 3,000 marks and promising an annual contribution of 400 more in return for the Shrievalty of York. At the Council of Northampton in 1194 he sat proudly on the king's left hand; but was none the less assailed from all sides, his servants arrested, his clerks ejected from the Minster and his estates seized. But with the king on his side Geoffrey was able to obtain royal letters ordering the restoration of his estates and forbidding anyone to interfere with him in the exercise of his ecclesiastical duties.

Simon, the new dean, arrived in York to a magnificent reception; and, when the archbishop's clerks tried forcibly to prevent him from entering the Minster, they were driven out by the citizens. The victorious canons then forbade Geoffrey's suffragan to consecrate the chrism; and when he did so instead at Southwell, they refused to accept it, the archdeacon of Cleveland going so far as to pour it into a cesspool.

So the struggle between the archbishop and his chapter continued, the former supported by Richard, and the latter by the pope, by Hubert Walter now archbishop of Canterbury, and by the citizens of York. At Christmas 1195 Celestine suspended Geoffrey from office, but St. Hugh of Lincoln declined to publish such a suspension until there had been a fresh investigation into the charges against him; and the papal commissioners in England did so instead, instructing the dean of York to exercise the archiepiscopal jurisdiction. Geoffrey was with Richard in Normandy at the time, and no doubt expected royal support; but very foolishly he then forfeited the royal regard by publicly rebuking the king for his sins. Richard, whose rages were notorious, promptly turned on the archbishop, deprived him of his estates, removed him from the Shrievalty of York, and nominated two of his own clerks to the then vacant offices of the archdeaconry and treasurership of York, which by law and custom were in the gift of the archbishop.

Geoffrey took himself off to Rome, where he managed to get his suspension revoked; but quickly found further trouble. For one of his clerks confessed that, at his master's bidding, he had sent forged documents to England; and another alleged that at Geoffrey's behest he had dispatched poison to Simon and other hostile members of the York chapter, contained in a ring and girdle. These Simon actually produced, and had them burnt publicly on the orders of the archbishop of Canterbury. However, the next pope, Innocent III, came down heavily on Geoffrey's side, threatening Richard with excommunication unless he restored the archbishop's estates, allowed him to return to York, and ceased to interfere in his ecclesiastical appointments.

But all attempts to heal the breach between Geoffrey and his chapter failed; and the king remained hostile. So when the archbishop gave the archdeaconry of Richmond to M. Honorius, the dean promptly installed the royal candidate, M. Roger, and then excommunicated one of the canons for daring to protest against such an action. Moreover upon this

45

canon, Hugh Murdac, entering the Minster during Vespers, the dean stopped the service and had all the lights extinguished, presumably in order to avoid contact with an excommunicated person. Richard too remained obdurate, despite a papal threat to lay an interdict on York, and then if need be on the whole kingdom; but Richard's death, King John's warm championship of the archbishop, and the mediation of the papal legate, Peter of Capua, eventually led to a reconciliation between Geoffrey, the dean and the canons of York.

At Westminster in 1200 the archbishop formally exchanged the kiss of peace with Simon and his other enemies in the chapter; but, as Howden wrote: 'the peace was not of long duration'. First Geoffrey fell out with the new king, then again with the dean and chapter over vacancies in the precentorship, the archdeaconry of Cleveland and the provostship of Beverley; whilst that of the archdeaconry of Richmond still remained unsettled, with the two candidates, Honorius and Roger, both trying to gain royal support by large bribes. Geoffrey, for his part was equally lavish with his excommunications and suspensions, besides placing interdicts on the churches of his enemies. Pope Innocent III's patience became exhausted, and he began seriously to wonder whether, after all, in view of these interminable disputes between the archbishop and his chapter, the former was really the right man for his office. A papal commission was therefore appointed to look into the whole matter; but soon got bogged down in a welter of arguments and counter-arguments.

Geoffrey escaped deposition; and instead embarked on a new dispute in 1204 over the mastership of St. Leonard's Hospital. In his usual high-handed manner the archbishop ejected the chapter's candidate, Ralph of Nottingham, although the chapter was undoubtedly the legal patron, and instead installed the man elected by the brethren of the hospital itself. But in the subsequent litigation he was defeated and compelled to pay the costs of the case. None the less the very next year he again found himself in hot water, when the bishop of Durham, Philip of Poitou, and the heads of 14 religious houses in the north appealed to Rome and the king against the excommunications and suspensions pronounced against them by the archbishop.

Finally Geoffrey and King John came to blows in 1207 over a proposed tax on clerical incomes. Geoffrey was driven into exile; but found an unexpected ally in the pope, who despite his previous doubts about the archbishop's fitness for office, now rallied to his side, threatening John with an interdict, which became a reality not so much on this issue as over the election of Langton to the archbishopric of Canterbury. Geoffrey himself never returned to England, dying in Normandy during 1212 and being buried near Rouen, where no doubt, 'after life's fitful fever he sleeps well'.

By the time of Geoffrey's death the York chapter was in a most unhappy state with pope, archbishop, the king and members of the chapter itself all competing for the control of its patronage; and this sorry story was to continue throughout the rest of the Middle Ages, creating an unedifying atmosphere of intrigue and bitterness, with so many of its richest stalls held by absentees, many of them foreigners. For three years after Geoffrey's death the archbishopric remained vacant, and then the canons elected **Simon Langton**, a younger brother of Stephen, archbishop of Canterbury, one of the prebendaries, on account of 'his learning and widsom', but in opposition to the king's nominee, Walter de Grey, whom they denounced as illiterate. Simon had been a zealous champion of his brother against King John, and a supporter of the barons in their struggle against both king and pope. His election took place in June 1215, and a couple of months later was quashed by Innocent III at John's instigation.

Simon's subsequent stormy career, encouraging the barons and citizens of London to disregard the papal excommunication of Louis of France and his partisans, who were seeking to oust John; and later, as archdeacon of Canterbury, denouncing the Christ Church monks, usurping the prior's functions during the vacancy in the Canterbury archbishopric, and inciting the secular clergy against the religious, do not really concern us here. But it is noteworthy that Gervase of Canterbury referred to him as 'accursed'; and Matthew of Paris wrote: 'It is no wonder if he was a persecutor and disturber of his own church of Canterbury, seeing he was a stirrer up of strife throughout the whole realm of England and France.'

His successor at York was a very different character, a member of an important family that had already held high positions in Church and State, his uncle, John de Grey, being an outstanding bishop of Norwich. A favourite of King John's, **Walter de Grey** had been his chancellor, becoming bishop of Lichfield in 1210, and bishop of Worcester two years later, when he resigned the chancellorship. At Runnymede on 15 June 1215 he appeared as one of the king's stoutest supporters, and was nominated to York by John the following November in the teeth of the chapter's opposition, but with papal approval. Innocent III, after quashing Simon's election, provided Grey in his place, commending him for 'his chastity of life', and giving him the pallium. For the last privilege, however, the new archbishop promised to pay £10,000, which he could well afford as he had inherited great wealth.

Henceforth Grey proved himself a tower of strength on John's side against the barons and the French, excommunicating all the king's enemies; and this loyalty was extended to his son, Henry III. He absolved Alexander II of Scotland, and in return was allowed to take over Carlisle for Henry; helped to crush a rebellion in the north under William Aumale, and on 25 June 1220 married Alexander to Henry's sister, Joanna of York. He also served on a number of embassies abroad. In ecclesiastical matters he continued to refuse York's obedience to Canterbury, but strongly maintained his own claim to such an obedience from the Scottish churches, which, however, was finally decided against him by Pope Innocent IV in 1251. Some 10 years earlier the Roman curia itself had been in trouble, when after the death of Pope Gregory IX, the Emperor, who was then triumphant in Italy, attempted to interfere with the papal election. Grey headed a deputation of bishops and other church dignitaries to remonstrate and persuade him to withdraw.

In his own province of York he consecrated Nicholas of Farnham to the bishopric of Durham, and received from him a profession of obedience; but it was largely in the political field that the archbishop made most mark. During Henry's absence abroad from 1242 to 1243 he was named as 'the king's chief justiciar', with the bishop of Carlisle and William Cantilupe as his advisers. In this rôle he proved most efficient in supplying his master with money, stores and troops for the French war; but came to blows with the Cistercians, who refused to let him have their wool. Whereupon he banned their abbots from attending the General Chapter of their Order. Then, with growing troubles at home, and French attacks on the Cinque Ports, he urged Henry to return home, providing the ships needed for the crossing and meeting the monarch himself at Portsmouth in September 1243.

The following year he became Warden of the Tower of London, from which the Welsh prince, Griffith, seeking to escape, fell and broke his neck; for that unfortunate accident Grey was exonerated from all blame. In 1245 he attended the Council of Lyons, and subsequently was employed on various royal missions abroad as a man whose diplomatic skills and complete loyalty had won the king's absolute trust. In England he became noted for his magnificence; and this was never more lavishly displayed than at the marriage of Henry's daughter to Alexander III of Scotland in 1252. But soon afterwards he withdrew from political life on the excuse of old age and ill-health, but more probably because of the king's mismanagement of the country that he was unable to prevent. Consequently he declined to take charge of England once again whilst Henry and his queen were in Gascony. However, he did make a supreme effort to attend the parliament which met on 6 April 1255, but only to die a month later in the bishop of London's palace at Fulham. His body was embalmed and buried in York Minster, where his monument and effigy still exist.

In his diocesan affairs Grey showed himself to have been both active and wise. In the disputed election between Simon Langton and Grey, Pope Innocent III had clinched the argument in favour of the latter by telling the York canons: 'By St. Peter, virginity is a great virtue, and we will give him to you'; thus implying that Grey's chastity was of far greater importance than Simon's learning. Yet Grey was certainly no illiterate, being an Oxford graduate. During his archiepiscopate he re-organised the parochial system, extended the Minster by building the south transept, where he founded a chantry where he was himself ultimately buried, encouraged monasticism, and translated St. Wilfred's remains to a new shrine at Ripon. On the whole, unlike his predecessor, he retained the goodwill and willing co-operation of the York chapter, even those members of it who had originally opposed his election. On the other hand he did not scruple to introduce his own kinsmen into it, one of whom, William de Langton became dean, and another, Walter Giffard, was eventually to succeed him in the archbishopric. Under the *statuta de residentia* the four dignitaries were required to keep continuous residence, and every canon was expected to spend at least half the year near the Minster, attending matins, vespers and mass. They were to be well paid; but the absentees would lose part of their income.

Grey was able substantially to increase the cathedral's wealth by appropriating to it the four Yorkshire parishes of Mappleton, Wawne, Thurnstale and Witherwick. He also founded some new prebends; and it is of interest to note here in passing that the creation of the prebend of Bilton in 1294 finally brought the number up to 36. At the same time Grey separated the treasurership from the archdeaconry of the East Riding, whilst endowing it with the prebends of Sherburn and Wilton. Despite the *statuta de residentia* Grey kept the four cathedral dignitaries with him wherever he went in the diocese, when he was also accompanied by a select group of clerical professional administrators. He made use of his own wealth to buy the village of Bishopthorpe for the archbishopric, besides the house in London that became known as York Place, and which was to remain in the hands of the archbishops until the fall of Cardinal Wolsey.

He showed himself to be a generous patron of the monasteries; but in some other respects was reputedly harsh and avaricious. One particular story to his discredit appears in the chronicles, but may well have been apocryphal. In a time of famine the archbishop agreed to supply his villeins with a quantity of decaying wheat, provided they promised to refund the full amount with the new grain they reaped after the next harvest. But the barn containing the stuff was found to be full of toads and snakes. None the less an attempt was made to weigh it out to the poor, which was only frustrated by its appalling stench. Then a heavenly voice was heard to exclaim: 'put no hand to the grain, for the archbishop and all that he has are the Devil's due'. The whole lot was then burnt. This story may well have some connection with the fact that because, as a patriotic Englishman, Grey had stoutly opposed the excessive interference of the Roman curia in English affairs and its oppressive taxation, he had been excommunicated by the papacy, and died before he could be absolved. Consequently he

49

could not be buried in consecrated ground; and his body was encased in a monument raised above the level of the floor in the south transept of the Minster. So it was believed; but when in modern times this monument was examined it proved to be solid.

Chancellor Raine said of Grey: 'When he came north he found his province a barren wilderness, and after ruling over it for nearly 40 years he left it a fruitful field'. Raine then went on to list his achievements: he reorganised the parochial system, subdivided parishes, redistributed endowments, and raised funds for the building of chapels, bridges and roads. Parishes were united in certain districts where it led to a more efficient ministry, incumbents were chosen with care, and he steadfastly refused to institute unworthy clerics or permit an hereditary succession to livings. He took a great interest in the monasteries, insisting on a tighter discipline; and helped to provide financial aid for their rebuilding. He was probably responsible for the construction of the west front at Ripon Minster, and likewise embellished those at Southwell and Beverley. Apart from the south transept with its chantry, he made many valuable gifts to York Minster, including a gold chalice and paten, which were encrusted with jewels, and a number of costly vestments. A good business man, he did much to restore the prosperity of the archiepiscopal estates. Raine concluded his account of this archbishop with the words; I am not giving him too high praise when I call him the greatest prelate of the century in which he lived'.

Of the next 13 archbishops of York from Grey to Thoresby, little of a personal nature is known, and that little concealed in the formal phraseology of the correspondence conducted in their names. **Walter Giffard**, who reigned from 1266 to 1279, is chiefly remembered for his stately presence, his sociability and his extreme corpulence; **William Wickwane**, 1279-1283, was noted for his intransigence and austerity, 'esteemed as a petty saint in that age'; and **John le Romeyn** is recalled for a curious combination of excessive avarice, magnificence, and a much publicised liberality, the last of which, or so it was said by one of his admirers, was 'unsurpassed by any of his predecessors or successors'.

Eleven of them were professional clerical administrators, mostly from humble origins; but learned men, doctors from either Oxford or Paris in theology and civil law. Only Walter Giffard and **William de la Zouche** were from the nobility; and **William Melton** alone, the son of a franklin, was a non-graduate. They were, too, largely drawn from the York chapter itself: **Sewal de Bovill** and **Geoffrey Ludham** had been deans, William Wickwane and **Thomas Corbridge** chancellors, whilst John le Romeyn was the illegitimate son of one of its treasurers. Then from 1304 to 1374 the archbishopric lay in the hands of four ex-royal clerks, **William de Greenfield**, **William Melton**, William de la Zouche and **John Thoresby**. The last had served as the king's chancellor and keeper of the privy seal. All of these archbishops were to devote themselves to the business of their diocese and province once they had been elected to that office, and, apart from Giffard, did not hold any high political place in the Government afterwards. Corbridge never left the north; and William de la Zouche and John Thoresby withdrew into diocesan affairs once they had been enthroned.

Despite frequent attempts by the pope and king to exercise their prerogative of provision and appointment, these archbishops, with the exception of Giffard and Thoresby, were freely and remarkably unanimously elected by the chapter, often in the face of both papal and royal opposition; and it is of interest to note that almost invariably pope and king accepted their choice in the end. William de la Zouche, for example, was chosen in preference to Edward III's candidate, William de Kildesby. In order to avoid having to go to Canterbury for consecration, these archbishops went to Rome where they also received the pallium. The one exception was **Henry de Newark**, who was consecrated by his suffragan, Anthony Bek, bishop of Durham at York in 1298, These journeys caused long delays before they could be enthroned, which was compensated for by the spectacular magnificence of the occasion. It also meant that these archbishops came to be much under papal influence; and, as a quid pro quo, the pope was able to provide for most of the major York dignitaries. However, Archbishops Sewal de Bovill and William de la Zouche put up a strong resistance to such demands and were excommunicated for their pains.

None the less by 1296 at least a third of the canons were Italians and also absentees. A letter of Romeyn's is extant lamenting the plundering of the Minster by Rome; and Giffard once told Cardinal Ottobuono to keep his clerks out of the chapter, protests that apparently had little effect. But since these foreigners, together with the royal nominees, took little interest in the affairs of the cathedral, although at one time they represented a majority in the chapter, its day to day working was in the hands of a small group of canons carefully selected by the archbishops themselves, although, of course, such prelates had no statutory right to attend chapter meetings, which were presided over by the dean; and therefore no power to help in either drafting chapter statutes or over the Minster's worship and way of life, since the archbishop had no hand in the appointment of the dean. The Minster, in fact, was an 'ecclesiastical Republic' that remained static, whilst the archbishops were constantly on the move, perambulating from one of their dozen or so manors to another. They had, indeed, less authority over their own cathedral than in any of their parish churches. But they did have the right of visitation in order to maintain discipline, which was seldom enforced owing to the hostility of the chapter. Wickwane fought shy of doing so altogether; Romeyn obtained a concession from the chapter that he could visit once in five years, provided he was accompanied by two of the canons, asked no questions in writing, and refrained from interrogating individuals against their will; and Melton was allowed a four year visitation, to introduce four clerical assessors into the chapter house, and produce written statements based on the private examinations of individuals. But it proved impossible to discipline the canons, and the subsequent visitations of Zouche in 1343 and Thoresby in 1362 proved complete failures. Consequently the archbishops turned instead to trying to strengthen their authority over the rest of the cathedral clergy, in which they met with more success.

This period witnessed three royal marriages at the Minster in 1221, 1251 and 1328*. The last between Edward III and Philippa of Hainault was an especially splendid affair. The cathedral, too, became the centre for the northern convocations and synods, and much political activity revolved round it. In the 1330s for example, the Chancery met in its chapter-house. These factors all tended to enhance the archbishop of York's standing both in ecclesiastical and state matters; whilst this was increased by the popularity during these years of the cult of St. William. His shrine behind the high altar, with his head in a bejewelled reliquary, became the cathedral's 'greatest treasure'; and thousands of pilgrims were attracted to his tomb every year, when they were blessed by the occurrence of many miracles, all of which were carefully recorded in a volume kept in the vestry, that survived until 1736.

Against this background, covering the next period from 1256 to 1375, we will now deal with the stories of the individual archbishops concerned. **Sewal de Bovill** had been a pupil of St. Edmund Rich at Oxford, whose canonisation he himself urged upon Pope Innocent IV. In 1240 he was appointed both dean of York and prebendary of Fonton; and then some 15 years later was elected by the chapter as their archbishop. At first the king refused to give his consent because of Sewal's illegitimacy, but relented when the pope granted him a dispensation; and he was consecrated by de Cantilupe, bishop of Worcester. But shortly afterwards he quarrelled with the pope over the latter's nomination of an Italian, Jorden, to the deanery of York, thereby bringing down upon his head first a suspension and then an excommunication. However, this resistance to papal interference gained him much popular support in anti-papal Yorkshire, which was enhanced by his own christian character and way of life. Matthew Paris described him as 'a humble and holy man, well skilled in the law and other sciences'. He died on 10 May 1257, still an excommunicate, but defiant to the last, summoning the pope to judgment on his deathbed. He played no part in politics beyond once serving on a commission seeking to reconcile Alexander of Scotland with his nobles. He lies buried in the south transept of the Minster. Apparently a very learned man, he was well versed in science and law as well as theology; various literary works have been attributed to him.

---

* On 25 June 1221, Archbishop Walter de Grey married Alexander I of Scotland to Henry III's sister, Joanna in York Minster. Again in 1251 he married Henry's daughter, Margaret, to Alexander III of Scotland. The last marriage cost the archbishop some 4,000 marks.

Of the next archbishop, **Geoffrey Ludham**, even less is known; so much so indeed that he is not even included in the *Dictionary of National Biography*. Elected to the archbishopric on 23 July 1258, he was consecrated the following September, receiving the temporalities at the beginning of December. Selected by the York chapter, he enjoyed their full support throughout his term of office, and is remembered as a conscientious administrator of his see and province, but played no part in public affairs either before or after his appointment. It was during his time that, with the backing of the resident canons, conscious that they alone fulfilled their duties, an approach was made to Pope Alexander IV asking him to censure their non-resident colleagues, who neither played a part in the running of the cathedral nor contributed money to meet its burdens. There were then only eight or nine resident canons, a body with a growing sense of *esprit de corps*, and it was from among their number that Ludham and future archbishops like William Wickwane were chosen. On 4 February 1969 Ludham's tomb of Purbeck marble, a slab with a cross and supported by arcading, was opened, and found to contain intact a pallium, an episcopal ring containing an uncut sapphire, a silver chalice, paten and staff.

Following Ludham's death in January 1265 there was a protracted struggle over the next appointment between the chapter, the pope and the king. The chapter elected William Langton on 12 March 1265; but this election was quashed in November by Pope Clement V, who in his stead provided that famous medieval saint, Bonaventura, then minister-general of the Franciscans and nicknamed 'the Seraphic Doctor'. However, in the end the king prevailed, Bonaventura resigned the archbishopric, and the royal nominee, **Walter Giffard**, was accepted by the papacy and chapter alike. Giffard did not come from York, but had been successively, canon, archdeacon and bishop of Bath and Wells, where he had shown himself a strong supporter of Henry III, excommunicating Simon de Montfort and his party. After the battle of Evesham he became chancellor and helped draw up the award of Kenilworth that restored the baronial estates. A handsome man with a gay and genial disposition, Giffard was fond of every kind of luxury, and grew corpulant through over-indulgence; but, beneath an outward bonne-hommie, the new archbishop possessed a fiery temper likely to explode at any moment, when he could be both cruel and ruthless. After his enthronement at York on 1 November 1266, he resigned the chancellorship and for the time being retired from politics, devoting himself to the affairs of his diocese and province, where he became known as a 'strict and fearless reformer of abuses'. However, his high-handed methods brought him into conflict with the see of Durham, where he was shut out of the cathedral whilst attempting to visit it during a vacancy. In reply he excommunicated the prior and monks.

Prince Edward, the future Edward I, greatly admired his abilities and sought to bring him back into public affairs. He was appointed tutor to the prince's children, and on 13 October 1269 officiated at the translation of Edward the Confessor's remains to Westminster Abbey. Then Edward secured the archbishop's help in bringing Earl Warenne to justice for the murder of Alan de la Zouche at Westminster. On the death of Henry III, Giffard was made first lord of the council, and once again had charge of the great seal. The new king being absent abroad, the archbishop acted as one of the regents governing the kingdom until Edward's return in August 1274. The continuing quarrel with Canterbury prevented him from attending the coronation; but once more he was a guardian of the country during the king's absence abroad in 1275.

He died at York four years later and was buried in the choir, his remains being later removed by Archbishop Thoresby to a tomb in the presbytery. Admirable as had been his loyalty to the crown in public life, and his fearless reforming of clerical abuses, his private extravagances led him, despite his immense wealth, into the hands of Italian and French money-lenders, whom he was only able to repay in full by later instituting the strictest economies. Then, once out of debt, he swore 'to keep out of the whirlpool of usury', an oath he kept for the remainder of his days. He was also charged with nepotism, a fault not uncommon among archbishops, getting his brother, Geoffrey, a minor, appointed to the archdeaconry of York. Geoffrey was said to be 'unlearned', and complaints reached Rome about him. Other kinsmen likewise benefited from his patronage, and one of them, William Greenfield, was maintained by him at Oxford.

William Wickwane, canon and chancellor of York, was elected to the archbishopric with the king's consent on 22 June 1279. At first this election was quashed by Pope Nicholas III, but he than gave way under pressure and not only provided him with the see, but consecrated the archbishop himself on 17 September, giving him the pallium. His temporalities were restored the following October, and he was enthroned in 1280. The dispute with Canterbury over the primacy continued, and another arose with Durham. For when the archbishop conducted a visitation of his province, particularly of the northern monasteries, he was refused admission to Durham Priory, and replied by excommunicating the monks from the roadside. There followed the usual appeals and counter-appeals to Rome; and then, when some three years later Wickwane entered Durham to renew his excommunication against the prior, he was driven out by the citizens. As the chronicler recorded: 'he was forced to flee, one of his palfrey's ears was cut off, and he is said to have been in danger of his life'.

On 8 January 1284 he had the body of St. William translated to its new shrine, when the king, Edward I, attended the ceremony; and shortly afterwards consecrated Anthony Bek to the bishopric of Durham, an act he regretted to the day of his death, since Bek promptly took the side of the Durham monks and became his deadly enemy. Consequently the feud with Durham became greatly intensified, and the archbishop obtained the king's leave to go to Rome and lay his complaint against the priory before the pope. But he never reached his destination, falling ill and dying at Pontigny, where before his demise he took the habit of a Cistercian monk. He lies buried in its abbey church.

This last action of his has raised the question whether at the same time he resigned his archbishopric, but of that there is no concrete evidence. A man of an austere and ascetic life, his habits were of the simplest, and he was greatly revered for his holiness. Miracles were said to have occurred at his tomb. His register from 1273 to 1285 has been published by the Surtees Society, showing that he was both industrious and conscientious in administrating the affairs of his diocese and province, visiting the parishes and monasteries, and making sure that his own archiepiscopal estates were well worked and stocked. He was also a learned man, who had left behind him a commonplace book, *Memoriale*.

Wickwane died on 26/27 August 1285, and **John le Romeyn** was elected by the chapter in his place the following October, being consecrated on 10 February 1286, and the temporalities restored in April. An illegitimate son of the subdean and treasurer of York, he had originally obtained a papal dispensation in order to be ordained, but this did not include an advancement to a bishopric. Consequently, immediately after his election, he went to Rome, where Pope Innocent IV both renewed his dispensation, to include his promotion to the archbishopric, and consecrated him himself under a papal mandate. Enthroned on 9 June 1286, he henceforth devoted himself almost exclusively to his see and province, taking only a very small part in public affairs. An Oxford graduate, Romeyn had come to York from Lincoln, where he had been chancellor and precentor prior to his election to the archbishopric. Hence he was not unfamiliar with the north, and, like his predecessor, soon found himself in trouble with the turbulent Anthony Bek and the Durham chapter. Edward I sought in vain to mediate between them, but with a bias in favour of Durham. So, when Bek imprisoned two of Romeyn's officials and was excommunicated by the archbishop for his action, the latter found himself imprisoned by the king in the Tower of London, from which he could only secure his release by paying Edward 4,000 marks. But in other respects he was less controversial and more successful: rendering yeoman service in military service against the Scots; in continuing the rebuilding of the Minster, where he completed the nave by means of persuading the pope to grant him the papal first fruits for that purpose; and in founding Bilton, the last of the prebends. He is also remembered as a generous benefactor of Southwell Minster. He died in 1292 and lies buried in the cathedral. His enemies denounced him as quarrelsome and indiscreet; but his many friends recalled his lavish hospitality, his zeal for the Church, and his ardent promotion of education.

Henry Newark, the next archbishop, had been a clerk of Edward I's, and, as one of the king's favourites, was employed by him at the Roman court from 1276 until 1277. Then, after Archbishop Giffard's death, as archdeacon of Richmond and a canon of York, he became guardian of the temporalities during the vacancy. In these capacities he did yeoman service for the crown in collecting a subsidy for the Welsh war and arranging for knights' service north of the Trent. The new archbishop, Romeyn, made him his vicar-general and gave him a prebend of Southwell, which favours he repaid by lending the latter money. Two years later he became dean of York, when he helped to play an active part in the king's negotiations with the Scots, and continued to serve Edward in a variety of ways, as for example in settling disputes with the Court of Holland and treating with the Counts of Guilders. His reward was not long in coming, being elected to the archbishopric by the York chapter on 7 May 1296, as the king's nominee. Edward's recommendation also secured his acceptance by Pope Boniface VII. But, owing to the Scottish war, Newark was unable to go to Rome either for his consecration or pallium, so the latter was sent to him, and Anthony Bek performed the consecration. He is remembered in the north as a conciliator, who patched up the old quarrel between York and Durham, making Bek his friend, and also as a liberal benefactor of his diocese; but his main activities were still political. At a synod of his clergy he persuaded them to grant a subsidy of one fifth for the war-effort, was regular in his attendance at the parliamentary sessions, and became a member of the Prince of Wales' Council. He died on 15 August 1299, and lies buried in the Minster.

Thomas Corbridge, described by Stubbs as 'an incomparable professor of all the liberal arts', was elected by the York chapter as Newark's successor on 12 November 1299, an election approved by the king; but, when he went to Rome to be consecrated and receive his pallium, Pope Boniface insisted on re-appointing him on his own authority, thus re-asserting the papal right to provide to this office. At the same time he gave Corbridge permission to hand over his previous ecclesiastical appointments to his grand-nephew. These offices, which included the sacristy of St. Sepulchre's Chapel and a York prebend, had already aroused considerable controversy. Corbridge, who had then been chancellor and a prebendary, resigned those posts in order to obtain the sacristy; but shortly afterwards demanded them back from the sitting incumbent, Thomas Wakefield. Wakefield, backed by Archbishop Romeyn, refused to give way, whilst the dean and most of the chapter supported Corbridge. An appeal to Rome led to Corbridge's excommunication, and he was only absolved on agreeing to relinquish the chancellorship. However, he retained the sacristy and the prebend, which he now bequeathed to his grand nephew.

Corbridge, unlike Newark, was no politician, although he attended parliament and helped in the war against the Scots; his main interests were ecclesiastical, and in their defence he was prepared to fight like a tiger even against royalty itself. The fact that the northern war brought Edward frequently to York aggravated the situation, when two strong men met face to face, neither of whom was prepared to give way to the other. Consequently there were a number of clashes. When Corbridge quarrelled with the provost of Beverley over his visitation of that church, the king took the provost's side. Edward then tried to thrust one of his clerks, John Bush, into a York preferment in opposition to the candidate of both archbishop and pope, Gilbert Segrave. Upon the archbishop protesting over Bek's siege of the prior and convent of Durham (cutting off their supplies of food and water), the king, who supported Bek, became so exasperated with Corbridge's interference that he confiscated the archbishop's temporalities, which remained in royal hands until the archbishop's death. So little influence indeed did Corbridge exert in public affairs that his name rarely appears either on state papers or in the chronicles, and his register contains very few political documents. But in his own province he often acted in a masterful and aggressive fashion: compelling the bishop of Whithorn to restore the goods he had taken from Robert Bruce's son, Alexander; forbidding the nobility to hold tournaments and duels in Lent; and boldly asserting his right to coin his own money. A notorious nepotist like his predecessors, he provided rich preferments for his kith and kin; and, as a fierce champion of the pope against the king, he remained in royal disgrace until his death on 22 September 1304. He lies buried in Southwell Minster.

Less than three months after Corbridge's death another royal clerk, **William Greenfield**, was elected to succeed him, on 4 December 1304. A kinsman of the late Archbishop Walter Giffard, who had paid for his Oxford education, William became an Oxford doctor of civil and canon law, and rose swiftly in the church, acquiring numerous livings and prebends before being appointed chancellor of Durham Cathedral and dean of Chichester. As clerk and counsellor to Edward I he was employed by that king to negotiate with Rome over the crusading tenth, and took part in helping to bring about the treaty between Charles of Sicily and Alfonso of Aragon, besides conducting the inquest into the Scottish succession at Norham. As a reward for such services Edward made him his chancellor in 1302; an office he resigned two years later when with the royal blessing, he was elected to the archbishopric of York. But, owing to troubles in the papal curia, this election was not confirmed by the pope until 1306, when in January that year he was consecrated by Pope Clement V and received the pallium; the following March the temporalities were restored. For these last, however, Greenfield had to pay considerable sums both to the crown and to certain noblemen in bribes before they were yielded up. This outlay, together with the heavy expenses he had incurred whilst awaiting consecration at Rome, got him into the hands of Italian money-lenders, from whom he was only able to extricate himself by taxing his clergy and borrowing from all the church dignitaries of the north.

During the Scottish wars Edward had made York his headquarters, which considerably enhanced the political importance of the archbishop;

and, on the king's going abroad, he, together with his friend, Walter Langton, bishop of Lichfield and Lord Chancellor, who had loaned Greenfield 500 marks to help pay off his debts, became regents of the whole country.

The archbishop's influence was further increased during the next reign; although, despite Edward II's wishes, he found himself unable to crown that monarch owing to the hostility of Canterbury and the pope. In the north he threw himself whole-heartedly into the Scottish war, entertained the defeated king at York after the defeat of Bannockburn, and rallied the demoralised English. In 1314 and 1315 he summoned the northern magnates and great ecclesiastics to meet him in York 'to provide for the safety of the kingdom'. He also made use of his own powers to excommunicate the rebel bishop of Glasgow, whilst at the same time upholding the loyal bishop of Whithorn and inspiring the Dominican friars to preach against the Scots.

Clement V was now leading the campaign against the Templars, and he commissioned Greenfield to examine the charges against them in England. Then, to papal annoyance, he proved unexpectedly tolerant and generous, declining altogether to act in the southern province, and in the north, after conscientiously examining the evidence, pronounced no more severe sentences on the guilty than a penance within a monastery. Furthermore he absolved those whom he thought had been unjustly excommunicated and supplied them with food and other necessities. He was, however, in general agreement with the papacy that the Order ought to be dissolved, and sat near the pope at the Council of Vienne, where this was accomplished.

In his own diocese, which had been sadly disturbed by the Scottish wars, he energetically sought to correct clerical abuses, visited the monasteries and drastically reformed his own household, thereby once again restoring law and order in the northern Church. In 1306 he had issued a series of constitutions; then again in 1311 promulgated statutes revising the procedure of his consistory court, disciplining its officials, and regulating the functions of its proctors. He was urgent in pressing upon the papacy the need to canonise his friend, Robert Grosseteste, bishop of Lincoln, but without any success. He died at Cawood on 6 December 1315, and was buried in the Minster, where his monument still exists. Edward I once said of him to the pope that he was a man 'of wisdom in council, industry, literary knowledge, and much usefulness to the State'.

William Melton was elected to the archbishopric in his stead on 21 January 1316 by a unanimous vote of the York chapter, which was endorsed by the king, who then recommended his appointment to the pope. But, owing to an interregnum in the papacy from the death of Clement V to the election of John XXII, it was not until 25 September 1317 that Melton received consecration from the latter at Avignon together with the pallium. His temporalities were restored the following October.

The new archbishop was of humble birth, who had first come into prominence as an employee of Edward II whilst still Prince of Wales. From then onwards his rise was a rapid one, accumulating a variety of clerical and political preferments, including prebends at York, Southwell and Lincoln, the deanery of St. Martin-le-Grand in London and the archdeaconry of Barnstable, besides becoming keeper of the privy seal, commissioner for the Cinque Ports and protector of the Scottish marches. Now, as archbishop, he found himself facing a Scottish invasion, and when he and other ecclesiastical dignitaries of the north engaged this traditional enemy in battle at Myton-on-Swale, they were soundly defeated. Melton and his fellow clergy indeed barely escaped with their lives; for, as Barbour wrote:

The Chapter of Mytoun for thar
Shame as many prestis war.

Later Edward II employed the archbishop as one of his commissioners in treating for peace with the Scots. As the king's loyal servant he sided with the Dispensers against Thomas of Lancaster, and, after the latter's death, prohibited his worship as a martyr; but is also on record as protecting another of the rebels, Adam Orleton, bishop of Hereford, from prosecution. The archbishop then became justiciar of Nottingham and in 1325 Treasurer of England, a post he retained until Edward III overthrew the government of Roger Mortimer and Queen Isabella; but he was quick to change sides, officiated at the marriage of Edward with Philippa of Hainault, and, being acquitted of any involvement in Edward of Woodstock's plot, was re-appointed Treasurer and made justiciar for enforcing the Scots truce. He opened the parliamentary session at York in 1333, and the following year became keeper of the great seal during the temporary absence of John de Stratford. That was the end of his political career, and six years later he died at Cawood Manor on 3 April 1340 and was buried in the Minster.

In ecclesiastical as opposed to secular politics he was by no means so successful, continually quarrelling with the York chapter and with Beaumont, bishop of Durham, whom he excommunicated. Then, on rashly consecrating Robert de Graystanes as the new bishop in the face of royal and papal opposition, he had the mortification of seeing his candidate compelled to resign from that office. None the less he was devoted to his diocese, from which he was never absent for long, and where he worked extremely hard to improve its spiritual life in a period of war, devastation and general unrest. A good example of this can be seen from his visitations of the archdeaconry of Richmond. Most archdeacons were dependent upon their bishop, who gave them their instructions and could overrule their decisions; but the archdeaconry of Richmond was unique in that here the rôles of the diocesan and the archdeacon were reversed. For apart from such episcopal functions as ordination and confirmation, the archdeacon, whose appointment lay in the hands of the

59

papacy and not in that of the archbishop, wielded all the powers of an Ordinary. Only during a vacancy could the archbishop visit, exercise his powers as 'keeper of the spiritualities', and appoint his own officials for the archdeaconry. This archdeaconry was very large, covering some eight deaneries, consisting mainly of wild country, and suffering greatly from Scottish raids. Moreover communications were not only poor but often non-existent. The papal nominees, who were frequently absentees, appeared often to be more interested in the income they could derive from this office than in its conscientious discharge. Melton, unlike his predecessors, was determined to visit it, and first made an attempt to do so during a vacancy in 1332. This was prevented by a Scots invasion; although he did succeed in sending his commissaries, Richard Cave and the dean of Furness and Copeland, to act on his behalf in the five rural deaneries 'across the moors'.

Another chance for a personal visitation occurred in 1328, but again was let slip. However, in 1331 Melton came to an arrangement with the then archdeacon, Robert of Woodhouse, an Englishman, whereby he was given permission to visit, to hold enquiries, and rectify abuses. Consequently the archbishop was able to visit the whole of this archdeaconry in person that year, a visitation described as 'a very thorough one especially in the wilder western deaneries across the moors'.

His second and final visitation took place in 1337, when, however, only the three eastern deaneries were covered. Unfortunately the records of these visitations are lost; but from his register we can deduce the kind of problems Melton had to face: dilapidated churches, neglected churchyards and other ecclesiastical properties, absentee and misbehaving clergy, laymen who would not pay their tithes or other church dues, monasteries ruined by the Scottish raids, and a general collapse of moral and spiritual values. It must have been a tough and exhausting job that entailed endless hours on horseback riding over rough tracts, often infested with robber bands, putting up in poor lodgings, and continuously engaged in conducting exacting interviews and enquiries. Melton apparently stood up to it well, as indeed he did in all his other diocesan activities. Professor Burrows wrote of him: 'a good and kindly archbishop, who possessed physical toughness, but also moral courage, since the duties of his office, which he took very seriously, involved him in an unending round of hard and exacting work.' Melton left a very full register behind him, and from it we glean that he continued with the rebuilding of the Minster, restored St. William's tomb, and gave £700 out of his own pocket towards the completion of the nave. A final aspect of Melton's character still remains recorded: as a financier and business man. Thomas Stubbs wrote of this archbishop:

> . . . severe in correcting rebels, kept a large household and
> clothed it in livery twice a year, often cancelled amercements

imposed on his tenants by his bailiffs, and remitted to the needy the farms and debts they owed him. Above all he assisted Kings Edward II and Edward III and the nobles by loans and gifts. An ardent promoter of his servants and all his kinsmen.

From the evidence of his register we find that Melton made 388 loans to institutions and individuals, including knights, barons, the Yorkshire abbeys and priories, the secular clergy, and the citizens of Hull, Beverley and Ripon, which totalled some £23,551—18—1½. A number of these were to the nobility outside the diocese. In at least 210 cases the archbishop received no interest, but in others he demanded a bond, pledge, or recognisance; and if the debt were not repaid he might seize the debtor's lands. It was not uncommon for borrowers to deposit silver plate with him as a safeguard against defaultment. The Scottish wars had depleted the resources of the barons and other gentry, whilst the monasteries had suffered greviously from the same cause. Consequently they were all in dire need of hard cash and could ill afford to quarrel with the archbishop's terms.

As regards the monarchy, Melton made at least one gift of money to his friend, Edward II, and some silver to the younger Dispenser and his wife. Edward III received loans of up to £3,336—13—4; and his queen and the Earl of Cornwall borrowed small sums. Much of this last was never recovered; and in addition the archbishop had to make gifts to the queen, pension a royal trumpeter, and supply the royal household with loads of wheat from his Southwell manor. There were also some financial dealings with his fellow bishops. The then archbishop of Canterbury, for example, borrowed 100 marks on which he had to pay interest, despite the Church's prohibition against usury. But in his transactions with his own inferior clergy, Melton could be most generous. In all he loaned them £1,691—13—4; but very often remitted the debt when they could not pay, as also with the Yorkshire monks, believing that it was his duty as their diocesan to help them after the Scottish raids.

Where did the archbishop get his money from, since he had inherited no private fortune? He had no doubt done very well out of his civil service career; and it is of significance that the bulk of his loans were made during his two spells as Treasurer of the Realm. The archbishopric itself brought him in a lot of money; for even in lean years like those of the Scottish raids his income never dropped below £2,500 per annum, a very large sum for that period. From such sources, together with the gains he made from his loans, Melton built up a large fortune, which, as a sound business man, he wisely invested in the purchase of private estates, ranging from Yorkshire and Nottinghamshire to Hampshire and Devon. This wealth he lavished on his kinsfolk. He sent substantial gifts of money to his brother Henry and his family, paid for the childrens' education, and supplied them with household goods. Indeed, in the long run he was responsible for founding a knightly family, since his heir, Henry's eldest son, William, used the

61

archbishop's inheritance to obtain a knighthood for himself; and the Meltons were to flourish for centuries at Aston on the archbishop's lands. The younger sons were found rich clerical posts in the York diocese, and their sister, Joan, married the heir of Sir Richard Conyers in 1333. Other kinsmen were employed in Melton's household, or acted for him in the business world as his links with the Bardi and Peruzzi bankers, through whom the archbishop financed his dealings with Avignon. Finally he founded a chantry for his parents at his native Melton. The archbishop never got into debt, like so many of his contemporaries, and sometimes actually made loans to his bankers. Perhaps this was his greatest achievement, that he always remained solvent. Stubbs described him as 'charitable and pious, parsimonious to himself, bountiful to the needy, and above all to the religious as well as mendicants and others'. Another historian wrote: 'he was a man faithful in all that was entrusted to him, and not corrupted by his long intercourse with the court'.

William de la Zouche, Melton's successor, was likewise an Oxford graduate, who had been one of the king's clerks. An able politician he became in quick succession Keeper of the Privy Seal, Treasurer of the Exchequer and, in 1338, Treasurer of England. Neither did he lack ecclesiastical appointments, including a number of canonries, livings and archdeaconries, ending with his nomination to the deanery of York in 1336. Four years later in a fiercely contested election opposed to the royal nominee, William de Kildesby, another of Edward III's clerks, he was chosen archbishop by twelve votes to Kildesby's five. The king was furious and promptly relieved him of the treasurership besides appealing to Rome against his election. Zouche undismayed, first got himself installed and then set out for Avignon to plead his own cause. The archbishop of Canterbury tried to stop him by pronouncing his excommunication; and then, when that failed, another attempt was made by brigands, who set upon Zouche at Geneva, robbing and imprisoning him. This latest effort to prevent the archbishop arriving proved too much for Pope Benedict XII. He not only compelled his captors to release Zouche, but excommunicated and then subjected them to an humiliating penance.

However, Benedict himself died before he could decide between the rival claimants, and Zouche had to wait for two years before his successor, Clement VI, declared his election valid, consecrated him and delivered over the pallium. Furthermore he allowed the new archbishop to hold on to some of his previous preferments for the time being in order to cover the heavy expenses he had incurred whilst awaiting the papal verdict. Edward III, accepting the inevitable, issued letters patent for his safe return home, and then restored the temporalities. Zouche was enthroned with much pomp and ceremony in the Minster on 8 December 1342, but once finally installed he changed sides and supported Edward's candidate, Philip de Weston, for the now vacant deanery against the pope's nominee,

Talleyrand de Perigord, in which action he received the strong backing of the York chapter. Clement replied by excommunicating both the archbishop and Weston, besides quashing the latter's appointment. Talleyrand took over the deanery, but, in order to try and pour oil on troubled waters, persuaded the pope to remove the excommunications.

Once entrenched in his see and province, Zouche largely forsook politics, resided almost exclusively in the north, and busied himself in its ecclesiastical affairs. This did not, however, prevent him from playing an active role in the renewed Scottish war, when, followed by his clergy into battle, he commanded a division at the battle of Neville's Cross. During the period of the Black Death the archbishop courageously stood his ground, leading processions of intercession, visiting his flock, and consecrating new burial grounds★. Because of the dearth of clergy, numbers of whom had either died or fled the plague, Zouche obtained permission from the pope to replace them by ordaining at uncanonical seasons, by issuing indulgences, and even by admitting illegitimate men to holy orders. But the strain was too great; he himself contracted an incurable disease, and realising that the end was near, started to build a chantry in the Minster, where his body could be laid. But before it could be completed Zouche died at his manor of Cawood on 19 July 1352, and was buried instead in another part of the Minster, where no monument to him remains.

His successor, Thoresby, swept away the unfinished chantry whilst rebuilding the choir. This was unfortunate as Zouche had been a zealous builder of chantries, and completed some beautiful ones, notably at Lubberthorpe in Leicestershire, and Clipsham in Rutland. A holy man, who strove to instill beauty not only into architecture, but also into worship, along with peace and reverence, he wrote the following lines in 1349 that could well serve as his memorial:

> For both the Old and New Testaments teach us that holiness becomes the House of the Lord as befits a place erected under His Authority. His worship there should be performed peacefully and with due reverence. No-one should make any noise there and no-one should incite or take part in any sort of disturbance . . . Nothing in fact should happen there to disturb the divine office or offend the eye of the divine Majesty.

★ On the other hand Philip Ziegler in his recent book, *The Black Death*, published in 1969, has asserted that, apart from this archbishop issuing a warning against the plague on 28 July, 1348, when he ascribed the visitation to the anger of God over 'the sins of men who, made complacent by their prosperity, forget the bounty of the most high Giver'; and prescribing processions, litanies, prayers and penances, he himself retired to one or other of his rural manors, leaving it to his suffragan, Archbishop Hugh of Damascus, an Austin friar, courageously to visit the sick, head the processions, encourage the healthy, and consecrate new churchyards for the victims.

John Thoresby, yet another Oxford graduate, Zouche's successor, had begun his career as a private domestic chaplain to Archbishop Melton, through whose patronage he obtained a canonry at Southwell. He then entered the royal service and was sent on various missions to Rome and elsewhere, for which he was rewarded with a number of prebends, including one at York. In 1341 he became Master of the Rolls, and two years later was put in charge of the great seal, in which latter capacity he acted as one of the commissioners appointed to treat with France in 1346. The next step was his elevation to the episcopal bench as bishop of St. David's, when he attended Edward III at the siege of Calais, and was shortly afterwards nominated Lord Chancellor and bishop of Worcester. On Zouche's death, and with the king's recommendation, Thoresby was elected to the archbishopric, in August 1352, being provided and confirmed in that office by Pope Clement VI the following October. The temporalities were restored on 8 February 1353, and he was enthroned in September the same year. Retaining for the time being the Lord Chancellorship, he proved for the next three years to be an absentee archbishop, leaving the affairs of the see in the hands of his vicar-general, William-de-la-Mare, whilst he busied himself in politics. He became Guardian of the Kingdom during Edward's prolonged absence in France but in 1356 resigned the chancellorship, and henceforth devoted himself entirely to his northern province, where he sought to treat with the Scots over the ransom of their king, David, and made the completion of the Minster a prime objective. For this latter purpose he provided stone from his archiepiscopal manors and substantial sums out of his own pocket. In this work he is especially credited with the completion of the choir and the building of the Lady Chapel, where he interred six of his predecessors and endowed a chantry priest.

None the less, possibly his greatest claim to fame is as a 'peace-maker', when he finally settled the dispute with Canterbury over the primacy. However, in his relations with the mendicant friars he was less conciliatory, being the supposed author of a book against them entitled *Processus contra Fratres Mendicantes*, although this work has also been attributed to his nephew, John de Thoresby. Other writings of the archbishop include commentaries on the Creed, the Lord's Prayer and the Ten Commandments. He died in the autumn of 1373 at Bishopthorpe, and was buried in his new Lady Chapel at the Minster★.

★ During the Black Death new churchyards, usually, for health reasons, sited outside the boundaries of the parish, had been consecrated for temporary use only. But now that the plague was over Thoresby forbade further burials there, sternly condemning those parishes that continued to use them, as 'taking an empty delight in novelty'. 'They must resort,' he said, 'once more to their own traditional churchyards'.

CHAPTER IV

The Later Medieval Archbishops of York

During the next 30 years three archbishops, **Alexander Neville**, **Thomas Arundel** and **Robert Waldby** all played an important part in the troubled politics of the late fourteenth and early fifteenth centuries, being allied to one party or another in the struggles of the great barons for power. None of them had much time to spare for their archdiocese, and two of them were driven into exile and both translated to the see of St. Andrews *in partibus schismatorium*. Robert Waldby, who had passed through three bishoprics in 10 years, was never even enthroned. **Richard-le-Scrope**, their successor, indeed took more interest in his archbishopric; but he too became immersed in politics and died on the scaffold.

These men were followed by a series of mainly ministerial prelates: **Henry Bowet**, **John Kempe**, **William** and **Lawrence Booth** and **George Neville**, who proved themselves useful servants of the state, but largely absentees from the diocese. The last of them, Neville, however, was much more than just a civil servant, being something of a statesman and Rennaissance scholar. He made his mark during the Wars of the Roses, and is remembered today as the patron who fostered the revival of Greek letters in England, and as the saviour of Lincoln College, Oxford.

His successor, **Thomas Rotherham**, was also a learned man, the benefactor of both universities, and the founder of a school in his native town of Rotherham. All these archbishops were university graduates and men of high birth, with the exception of Waldby and Rotherham, the first an Austin canon and the second the son of a knight. Five of them, Arundel, Kempe, Neville, Laurence Booth and Rotherham, became chancellors of England, and all were very much involved in the turbulent politics of the age; so much so indeed that it sometimes led to their exile, imprisonment and even death. Unlike the earlier medieval archbishops they tended to distance themselves from the business of their see and province, none of them had been a dignitary of the Minster, and only four had held prebends there. Consequently the influence of the York chapter over their appointment or subsequent careers sank to zero. They were translated from other dioceses for political purposes, and knew little of the ecclesiastical affairs of the north.

On the other hand their enthronements were often of a spectacular nature, and being wealthy men most of them remembered their cathedral handsomely in their wills. On the whole they were not unpopular, with the exception of Alexander Neville, who was not forgiven for his aggressive assertion of authority at York, Ripon, Beverley and Durham. His conduct in this respect made his successors much more cautious in their relationships with the canons, both by curtailing their visitations and adopting a low profile in exercising their authority over the minsters. Indeed at York they even permitted the canons to usurp their powers over parish churches, who promptly appropriated many of them either to individual dignitaries and prebends or else for the benefit of the Minster's common funds. Certainly both chapter and cathedral flourished exceedingly during this period. There were now five dignitaries and 36 canons, each with his own fine house; and the Minster itself had become a popular centre for the visits of the nobility and gentry, even occasionally of royalty. Richard III, for example, had his son invested there as Prince of Wales in August 1483. Tourists arrived in large numbers, especially members of the numerous gilds, coming as pilgrims to the tomb of Archbishop Scrope or simply as sightseers. For much popular enthusiasm had been aroused, particularly locally, for what became known as 'the glory of York: the loyal martyr'.

Lancastrian hostility prevented Richard Scrope's canonisation, although the very fact that he had been a rebel against the crown and was executed for open rebellion, would have mitigated against the claim to maryrdom. However, the firm belief of the Yorkists that he had died at a tyrant's hands ensured his veneration; and nothing could stop the enormous visiting crowds right up to 1500 and beyond. But from 1500, for the next 30 years, York was rarely visited by an archbishop until the time of Edmund Lee in the 1530's; yet despite such absenteeism, diocesan administration did not deteriorate. Archbishops were not then pastoral fathers-in-God, for too much of their time was taken up in the royal service, attending parliament and convocation, in visits to Rome, and in managing the great archiepiscopal estates from which their income was derived, for more than mechanised and formal functions. Unlike men such as Archbishop Wulfstan or Richard of Chichester, they were no longer leaders, teachers, or spiritual inspirers of their flock, but rather their censors and judges, correcting and punishing canonical faults or doctrinal lapses. So, in the archbishop's absence, his place could be competently filled by two administrators: the official principal and the vicar-general. The first took over the judicial powers of the primate in regard to such matters as the correction of public offenders, matrimonial cases and the probate of wills. His judgment was final, and there could be no appeal to the archbishop. The second acted in the spiritual field, dealing with institutions to benefices, the issuing of licences and commissions, and in visitations. Indeed by Wolsey's time the latter had taken over the whole of the archbishop's spiritual jurisdiction. Normally he was a clerk or a canon from the York chapter, who had been legally trained; but he was not in episcopal orders, and hence other acts like ordination, confirmation and consecration were performed by suffragans, who had usually been consecrated and appointed to purely titular sees in the Middle East, *in partibus infidelium*. These men indeed continued to carry out such duties even when the primate was in residence. In fact it was an uncommon thing for the archbishop to perform ordinations and confirmations himself, although apparently Wolsey, during his brief five months' visit to his archdiocese, did so.

Thus, throughout all the turmoils of the fifteenth and early sixteenth centuries, the York diocesan machinery continued to function smoothly and the archbishop was rarely missed, and probably chiefly remembered for the scandalous way in which he often diverted much of the archiepiscopal revenues into personal, non-spiritual and most unworthy channels. During this period the York chapter itself contained a large number of distinguished men, who, if no saints or evangelists, were highly competent both as financiers and lawyers. They, aided indeed by substantial gifts and legacies from some archbishops, were primarily responsible for the steady growth of the Minster in beauty and grandeur, until in its fabric and furnishings it yielded to no other cathedral in Europe.

We conclude this introduction with a word about the archiepiscopal registers: these began with the rolls of Archbishop Grey, which were written both on front and back, institutions of livings being recorded on the former and charters relating to the property of the see on the latter. The registers of the next two archbishops have been lost; but from 1266 onwards they became continuous, developing from a roll into a proper register, an elaborate account of the archiepiscopal activities, under subheadings. Archbishop Melton's register covered some 700 pages, and those of his successors down to Thoresby were equally voluminous. But, with the coming of the more absentee primates, they tail off into little more than a record of institutions to benefices, and these are mostly the work of vicar-generals. The majority, however, also contain wills. At no time, of course, did they cover all the archbishop's correspondence, and accounts of visitations of religious houses only appear here and there. Against this background we now turn to the individual stories of the later medieval archbishops of York.

Alexander Neville, born about 1332, was a younger son of Ralph Neville, Lord of Raby. The Nevilles, an important northern family, were linked with others such as the Percies and Scropes, the Lumleys and the Cliffords. Neville's eldest brother, John, became, through service in the

67

royal household and his close connection with John of Gaunt, closely associated with the leading personalities of the day; whilst his nephew, another Ralph, was created Earl of Northumberland in 1397. So as a young clerk Alexander received swift promotion in the Church, being, whilst still at Oxford, granted a dispensation from the papacy to hold a benefice with cure, the rectory of Kirby Misperton and Aysgarth, on the petition of King David of Scotland. He was instituted in 1351, and 10 years later, through family influence, obtained the mastership of St. Thomas' Hospital, Bolton-in-Allendale, and prebends at York, Darlington and Howden. These preferments had been procured for him by his uncle, the archdeacon of Durham, and, after the latter's death, no further promotions came this ambitious young cleric's way for some years. Indeed he blotted his own copy-book by his brazen attempt to secure the archdeaconry of Cornwell for himself in opposition to the royal candidate, Nicholas de Newton, by prosecuting his suit in the papal court. This led to his arrest, the case was dropped, Newton succeeded to the archdeaconry, and Alexander left England for Avignon, where he could both escape from the royal wrath and be assured of papal sympathy. At the papal court he made use of his unofficial position to promote suits for Englishmen, associating himself in this task with Dr. Walter Shirlaw, the erstwhile secretary of Archbishop Thoresby, who had befriended him in the past. Such work, he hoped, together with the influence that his brother John could exert at home, would secure not only his forgiveness but future promotions. In this he was not disappointed, being appointed to the York prebend of Bole in 1370; and then, on his uncle's death, to the archdeaconry of Durham. Moreover, owing to the senility of Edward III, the illness of the Black Prince, and the military disasters in France, the papal influence over episcopal appointments in England was much increased, with the great magnates turning more and more to the pope in order to secure the advancement of their own candidates.

So, when Archbishop Thoresby died in November 1393, he was succeeded by Alexander. A number of factors contributed to such a startling promotion: papal influence, the intrigues of his brother John, the powerful championship of the great northern magnates, especially the Percies to whom the Nevilles were allied, the support of Archbishop Thoresby's family, and the acquiescence of the York chapter itself, who preferred a local cleric, whom they could 'freely' elect, rather than having a royal nominee forced upon them. It was, of course, very much of a gamble, since none of those responsible for his appointment really knew much about Alexander; and in the event it proved a disaster. The new archbishop was a forceful character, but one who lacked experience either in political or ecclesiastical affairs, at a time when the episcopate was expected to play a dominant rôle in both Church and State.

Alexander spent the first 10 years of his archiepiscopate almost exclusively in the north, residing at Cawood Castle, which he largely rebuilt, and where, unlike his predecessors, who were continuously on the move from one of their manors to another, he spent most of his time, apart from occasional forays into his diocese and province, feuding with the canons of Beverley or wrangling with the bishop and priory of Durham. His one extensive journey was his primary visitation of 1375, in the course of which he visited York, Howdenshire (a Durham peculiar) and the great archdeaconry of Cleveland. This last received a very thorough investigation, with the archbishop travelling some 400 miles and covering every corner of the archdeaconry. But Neville's excursion into the see of Durham, especially into its peculiars of Howdenshire and Allerton, besides the hospital of St. James in Northallerton, aroused the wrath of both the bishop and cathedral, and caused a great deal of trouble. There is no record of the archbishop ever visiting any of the other archdeaconries; although it is possible that the following year he inspected the monasteries of Kirkstall, Nostell and Pontefract, together with their immediate localities. Claiming that he had now covered the major part of his own diocese, Alexander again enraged Bishop Hatfield of Durham by threatening once more to invade his see. In 1348 Hatfield had secured a papal bull exempting Durham from all archiepiscopal visitations; but now Alexander, through his influence at the curia, obtained another that overrode it. Hatfield immediately appealed to Edward III, who wrote to the archbishop reminding him 'that the defence of the realm was bound up in the privileges of Durham', and consequently his action in proposing a visitation was both 'unheard of and unusual'. So Neville bided his time until Edward was dead, and then tried again; but only to find that Richard II's government was equally on the side of Durham, confirming the late king's decision. So here the matter ended; although it is only fair to add that Neville was perfectly within his rights in endeavouring to exercise his lawful, customary and metropolitan authority in seeking to visit his entire province. The point of the whole matter was, of course, that at this particular moment it was neither prudent nor expedient to do so.

Unfortunately too this rebuff was to influence his maladroit handling of the vacancy in the bishopric of Durham that occured in 1381, when, instead of administering the see under the *jure diocesano* agreement of 1286, he insisted high-handedly in doing so *jure metropolitico*. Against this the monks of Durham strongly protested, and the matter was still under debate when the new bishop, John Fordham, arrived. Yet not content with antagonising his formidable suffragan see of Durham and the greatest religious house in the north, Neville must now, a year later, engage himself in an even more bitter struggle with the canons of Beverley. This famous controversy can only be dealt with briefly here*. Again the Archbishop proposed a visitation, claiming at the same time, on very doubtful authority, that he himself was a prebendary of the chapter. The canons, led by Richard and John Ravenser, leading clerics in the royal

---

* See, *A Clerical Strike at Beverley Minster in the fourteenth century* (Archaeologia, 1896).

chancery, stoutly resisted him; whereupon the Archbishop seized the revenues of the church, overrode its statutes, and substituted six vicars choral from York for half-a-dozen Beverley vicars. But in so doing he quickly found not only the king and parliament, but even the pope, against him; and in 1388 the Beverley vicars had to be replaced.

At York Neville quarrelled fiercely with both the dean and chapter, where, not surprisingly, the brothers Ravenser, who were also canons of York, were especially hostile, Richard referring to the archbishop as his 'mortal enemy'. The treasurer, John Clifford, was another bitter foe; and eventually Neville found the whole chapter united against him. He replied by moving his consistory court from York to Beverley. The citizens of York were equally opposed to him, and petitioned the king to redress their grievances. This Richard was prepared to do, but not to involve himself in the purely ecclesiastical quarrels. Neville, in fact, had raised up for himself a hornets' nest in the north, being accused among other things of making over-lavish use of the weapons of suspension and excommunication, of being an extortioner, and even of physical assault. On one occasion he actually became engaged in a fight with the Mayor of Hull, who, in retaliation, wrested the archbishop's crozier out of his hands, and attacked his retinue with it. These quarrels, especially with the canons and citizens of York, may well account for the fact that during his primacy all work on the Minster came to a halt. Not that Neville himself had been ungenerous to the cathedral. At his consecration he presented it with two massive silver-gilt candlesticks, and later contributed 100 marks to the fabric fund out of his own pocket, besides a cope adorned with gold and precious stones. But most of his money was reserved for Cawood Castle, where he built two new towers and presented two bells for its chapel. These last were later cast into one large bell, named Alexander.

On the political front Neville played his part in defending the March against the Scots, when he became closely associated with John of Gaunt, who was seeking to create a strong royal influence in the north. Both of them were commissioned to treat with the Scots in 1380; and, when later fighting recommenced in 1383 and 1384, the archbishop, together with other northern magnates, was very active in repelling the invaders. Then, after Gaunt gave up his lieutenancy of the north, which was taken over by the Percies and John Neville, the archbishop in order to assist his brother, left Cawood and began for the first time to move round the diocese from manor to manor.

His connection with Richard II began in August 1385, when he accompanied the king on a military expedition into Scotland, and a strong friendship sprang up between them. This led to the archbishop suddenly quitting Yorkshire altogether, leaving Robert Dalton to act as his vicar-general until the end of his archiepiscopate, and taking up his residence in London, where he began to play an important part in politics. By April 1386 he was 'one of the king's council', arousing the fears of Archbishop

Courtenay of Canterbury that his influence with Richard might re-open the old controversy over the primacy. The Wonderful Parliament named Neville as one of the commissioners set up in the autumn of 1386 to supervise the constitutional arrangements it had inaugurated; but, when the archbishop learned that Richard was strongly opposed to them, he withdrew with the king from London, and accompanied him on his procession through the kingdom. As a result he became one of the main targets of the magnates hostile to the crown, being accused of inciting Richard to leave the capital, and of advising him to join Robert de Vere, Duke of Rutland, in Wales. Indeed he was considered the most militant of all the king's supporters, and of advising him to place his case against the commission before the judges at Shrewsbury and Nottingham, who declared that the regency council, consisting of 11 lords, together with the commission of supervision the Wonderful Parliament had set up, were illegal and treasonable. Neville, or so it was said, had even suggested that the Duke of Gloucester and Earl of Arundel should be surprised and arrested. When finally Richard returned to London the archbishop of York headed the procession as it entered the capital with his cross erect.

But his triumph was short-lived. Gloucester and Arundel were advancing on London with a large army, and their envoy, Archbishop Courtenay, demanded that Neville, Michael de la Pole and others of the king's friends should be punished as traitors. Richard was compelled to agree to their appearing before parliament to answer for their acts; but the archbishop, seeing all was lost, did not wait to be tried. He fled northwards and went into hiding, only to be captured whilst attempting to cross the north sea in June 1388. He was committed to the custody of the Mayor of Newcastle; but the following November, probably with the connivance of his enemies, who were too wise to make a martyr of him, he escaped and found his way to Flanders. Meanwhile the Merciless Parliament that met in February 1388 had declared him guilty of treason, describing Neville as *'vir inutiles'*, 'a predo, a thief, a traytor, both to godde and to his Kynge'. His temporalities were forfeited and he was outlawed; but, unlike his fellow traitors, not sentenced to death, his fate as an ecclesiastic being left in the hands of the Lords Spiritual. The pope, Urban VI, agreed to translate Neville to the titular archbishopric of St. Andrews, titular since the Scots recognised the rival pope, Clement VII, and thus inaccessive to the archbishop.

Thomas Arundel, then chancellor of England and a brother of the Appellant Earl of Arundel, took his place as the York primate. From Flanders Neville found his way to Paris in August 1389, where his fellow exile, the Earl of Suffolk, was on his death-bed. From him, or so it is believed, the archbishop inherited some £20,000. He then went on to Rome to plead his cause with the papacy, and wrote home to his English friends declaring that the pope had promised to restore him. The new pope, Benedict IX, was indeed at that time estranged from England owing

71

to the enactment of the Statute of Provisors; and no doubt he was also aware of King Richard's secret attachment to Neville. However, in view of the implacable hostility of the royal council to the archbishop, any such restoration was impracticable; so finally Neville gave up hope, moved to Brabant, where he served as a parish priest in Louvain, and here he died in 1392. He had throughout his career, rightly or wrongly, enjoyed a consistently bad reputation. In many ways he was simply typical of all too many prelates of the day; but his own strong and quarrelsome character made him more conspicuous than others.

Neville's two successors are quickly described: **Thomas Arundel**, elder brother of the Lord Appelant, and bishop of Ely, was provided archbishop of York by Pope Urban VI immediately after Neville had been translated to St. Andrews in 1388. Caught up in the political turmoil of the time he had been dismissed as chancellor in 1389, but was reinstated two years later. As archbishop of York he took a very much greater interest in his cathedral than his predecessor, seeking to promote its importance by transferring to York the courts of the King's Bench and Exchequer*, by showering it with magnificent gifts, and greatly increasing the endowments of the vicars choral. In the diocese as a whole he attempted to pour oil on troubled waters, especially in his relations with Beverley, where he issued new statutes, restoring peace and order to that troubled Minster. Restored to the chancery and Richard's favour he devoted himself to combating the Lollard threat, and on one occasion actually persuaded the king to return from Ireland, 'since', he said, 'Richard's presence was needed so that they "might better withstand the attacks of the lollards, who aimed at the complete disendowment of the Church"'. In 1396 Arundel was promoted to Canterbury, and his subsequent turbulent career, during which he was sent into exile, does not concern us here.

He was briefly followed by **Robert Waldby**, a Yorkshire man and an Austin canon, who had been educated abroad, where he became both a doctor of divinity and medicine, being 'recommended at once as a physician and a divine.' Furthermore he was said to be *'expertus'* in *'quoris Jure'*. As a favourite of King Richard he passed rapidly through three sees, Aire in Germany, Dublin, where he was also chancellor of Ireland, and Chichester, before being translated and provided to York by the pope, with Richard's blessing on 5 October 1396, his temporalities being restored the following March. But Waldby did not long enjoy the primateship, dying on 6 January 1398. Like his predecessor he had been a zealous persecutor of lollards, but unlike him remained a loyal supporter of Richard throughout his entire career. The king had him buried in Westminster Abbey, where, as Dean Stanley wrote, 'he was the first representative of literature in the Abbey'. Waldby himself is credited with a number of scholastic manuals, besides a learned treatise against the

---

* The courts were, however, moved back to their usual haunts in 1392.

lollards. The York chronicler, however, accuses him of simony, a practice not uncommon among the bishops of the day*.

Yet another favourite of the king's succeeded to the archbishopric, **Richard le Scrope**, the fourth son of Henry, Baron Scrope of Masham, and the godson of Richard, Lord Scrope of Bolton. The Scropes were important Yorkshire magnates, great benefactors of the Minster, and intimately connected with its rebuilding. A member of such a family, who took holy orders, was immediately assured of swift promotion, so Richard, even before he had been made a deacon, had been preferred to the Yorkshire rectory of Audenby Steeple. A graduate of arts at Oxford and of law at Cambridge, where he also became a doctor of civil and common law, his rise in the Church was a spectacular one even for that age: chancellor of Cambridge University, dean of Chichester and an advocate at the papal court, he quickly rose to the episcopal bench, first as bishop of Chichester and then to the more lucrative see of Coventry and Lichfield. Here he was enthroned magnificently in the presence of Richard II himself during 1387, before being sent on two important diplomatic missions, to Scotland and Rome, where he endeavoured unsuccessfully to secure the canonisation of Edward II. Then, shortly after his return from this last journey, whilst staying with the king at Lichfield, news arrived of the death of Archbishop Waldby; whereupon the king immediately appointed Scrope to the vacant archbishopric. Accordingly he was provided and translated by the pope on 27 February 1398, but against the wishes of the chapter; his temporalities were restored the following June, and he was enthroned a month later.

More than any of his immediate predecessors Scrope was to devote himself to his diocese and province, which is borne out by his register. He moved rapidly about from one archiepiscopal residence to another, making his presence felt in the immediate localities; and his ordinations were held not in the Minster as was customary, but in a variety of different places. Curiously enough, however, the 37 ordinations performed during the seven years of his archiepiscopate were in every case taken by his suffragan bishop, Fr. Willelmus episcopus Pharlusis, the titular bishop of Pharos. Scrope for his part presided over the eight provincial convocations held during his primacy. The national finances were at that time in a chronic state, and these convocations were largely concerned with voting subsidies for the Government. Indeed, the demands became so heavy that in 1404 the proctors rebelled, refusing not only to vote 'new subsidies', but also declining to pay those already voted.

The archbishop, as we have seen, was a great favourite of Richard II, yet he did not hesitate to do a 'Vicar of Bray' in 1399, when he not merely consented to the Revolution, but actually served on the commission that

---

* But owing to a delay in the transmission of his pallium, he died in London before he could visit York for his enthronement.

accepted Richard's surrender of the crown; and later joined with the archbishop of Canterbury in enthroning Henry IV. But his conscience must have been ill at ease; and when during Henry's Scottish campaign he made contact with the Percies, his thoughts began to turn towards rebellion. As Harding was to write: 'the rising of 1403 had been entered upon by the good advice and counsel of Master Richard Scrope'. None the less he was not himself actively involved in that conspiracy, and so far from suspecting him of disloyalty Henry IV was actually present at the high mass celebrated by the archbishop in the Minster at Northumberland's submission.

At the 'Unlearned Parliament' of October 1404 Scrope made himself conspicuous by his vigorous opposition to lollard demands for despoiling the Church; but at the same time was making use of his presence in London to continue his intrigues with the northern lords to overthrow the Lancastrian monarchy. So, when the Percies renewed their rebellion in 1405, whilst Henry was in Wales, the archbishop, together with the Earl Marshal, Thomas Mowbray, issued at York a strong manifesto demanding the redress of grievances. 'The estates of the realm' they said, 'and particularly of the clergy were to be treated with less injustice, the nobles to be freed from the fear of destruction, and the heavy burden of taxation to be lightened by greater economy and the suppression of malversation'. But, according to the chronicles, the archbishop also advocated the deposition of 'a perjured king' and the restoration of 'the rightful line'. Whether this last accusation was true or not, it is certain that Scrope expounded his manifesto at great length in the Minster, while the Yorkshire clergy did the same in their churches, plastering their parishes with notices calling their people to arms. The citizens of York rose en masse, and were reinforced by armed men, 'gentle, simple, priests and villeins', who flocked into the city from the surrounding countryside. The archbishop himself appeared in full armour, promising indulgences and full remission of sins for all those who might fall in battle. The plan was to join forces with Northumberland; but the swift action of the royal army under Prince John of Lancaster and the Earl of Westmorland upset all the rebels' calculations. On 27 May Scrope, Mowbray and Sir William Plumpton led out their men, described as 'a priestly rout', numbering some 8,000, under the banner of the five wounds of Christ, to join the other insurgents at Topcliffe. But they no sooner reached Slipton than they found themselves facing the royalists. The latter were heavily out-numbered, so fearing a battle Westmorland resorted to trickery in order to gain his ends. He asked to see the manifesto, assumed that Scrope wanted peace rather than war, and pretended to approve its contents. He then suggested a conference to see how best they could get Henry to agree to the rebels' demands. Scrope fell into the trap and was persuaded to disband his army, whereupon he and his friends were immediately arrested and sent under escort to Pontefract. Henry, who had now arrived on the scene from Wales, quickly made up his mind that Scrope and his fellow conspirators must die, *pour encourager les autres*. He refused to see them; and sent Sir Thomas Beaufort to seize Scrope's crozier, which was only accomplished after a struggle.

A commission was then set up to try them at Bishopthorpe. The archbishop of Canterbury, fearing the worst, hurried north to withstall any illegal treatment of his fellow metropolitan; but was side-tracked by an assurance from the king that nothing would be done without his co-operation and approval. But, while Canterbury 'rested', Henry acted. Chief Justice Gascoigne declined to pass judgment on a prelate, whereupon another member of the commission, Sir William Fulthorpe, was told to take his place, who, although no judge, but with the unanimous approval of the rest of the members, immediately pronounced Scrope, Mowbray and Plumpton to be guilty of treason and sentenced them to death, despite Scrope's denial that they had had any intention of either injuring the king or the realm. However, when he saw that his plea had fallen on deaf ears, the archbishop prayed aloud that no divine vengeance would engulf the royal house. He was brought to York clad in a scarlet cloak and hood, riding on a bare-backed collier's horse, 'hardly worth forty pence', and singing Psalm 17. Arriving under the walls of the city the cavalcade turned aside into a barley field belonging to the Clementhorpe nuns, and here the executions took place. Scrope throughout behaved in the very best traditions of martyrdom, exhorting his fellow victims to be of good cheer, telling the York citizens, who had flocked to the scene, that he died for the laws and good government of England, and kissing and forgiving the headsman, whilst at the same time asking him to administer five strokes of his sword in memory of the five wounds of Christ. Finally, having commended his soul to God, he died with a smile on his face. His body was immediately and reverently conveyed to the Minster by four vicars choral and interred in the Lady Chapel, with the decapitated head placed between the left arm and the body.

Almost at once the martyr's tomb became a centre of pilgrimage, miracles were said to have been wrought there, and a shrine was erected over it to receive the votive offerings that arrived in great abundance. At first the Government did its best to stop all this, by erecting a barricade and covering the shrine itself with logs, whilst a prohibition was issued against any further offerings. Henry was excommunicated by the pope; but as Godwin wrote: 'The pope who had excommunicated the authors of the prelate's death was easily persuaded upon to absolve them after a short time'. Actually this was not the pope, Innocent VII, who had pronounced the excommunication, but his successor, Gregory XII, uneasily aware of his rival at Avignon and not wishing permanently to estrange the English. For the same reason Scrope was never canonised, although strenuous attempts to obtain this were made by the northern convocation in 1462. None the less locally he was regarded as a saint, and once the prohibition

75

had been lifted, the shrine became a very gorgeous affair, a place of pilgrimage, and one of the holiest places in the north. The money offerings that poured in were devoted to the rebuilding of the choir that Thoresby had begun and Scrope continued. Some money too was used for the reconstruction of the great tower. The altar at the east end of the north choir-aisle became known as the Scrope Chapel, and here the Lords Scrope of Masham later endowed a chantry. A Scrope window was also inserted opposite the shrine.

The veneration of the archbishop increased rather than diminished during the whole of the fifteenth and well into the sixteenth century; but with the coming of the Reformation the pilgrimages ceased and the offerings came to an end. The shrine itself was pillaged and destroyed, the altar was removed, and the chantry suppressed. It was even suggested that Scrope had never been executed at all, a canard exploded when the tomb was opened in 1829. His mazer, originally belonging to the Gild of Corpus Christi, and dedicated by the archbishop himself, is still one of the Minster's treasured possessions. There is a portrait of Scrope in the British Museum and a print taken from it hangs in the dining room of Bishopthorpe Palace, with an inscription beneath added by Archbishop Maclagan in 1905. Scrope certainly impressed his contemporaries with his high moral character, his pleasant manners, and simple way of life. Walsingham wrote that he possessed an 'incomparable knowledge of literature', and the late Professor M. D. Knowles declared that he had a reputation for 'gentleness and piety'.

Thomas Langley, a long-standing loyal servant of the House of Lancaster, then dean of York and chancellor of England, was nominated by Henry to the vacant archbishopric, and, on receiving the royal licence, the York chapter duly proceeded to elect him. The king then asked the pope for his confirmation, and at the same time in order to try and placate the papacy over Scrope's execution, conceded that the cardinals of Naples and Florence might hold English benefices, and also agreed to the papal candidate, Roger Walden, becoming bishop of London, a see previously designed for Langley. But Innocent VII was not so easily won over. He had been deeply offended by the archbishop's death, and excommunicated all those who had taken part in it; so now, rejecting Langley's election, he instead provided Robert Hallum, a York prebendary, who was also archdeacon of Canterbury and chancellor of Oxford University, with the archbishopric. Henry was furious. He promptly forbade both the proclamation of the sentence of excommunication and Hallum's provision. Consequently the archbishopric remained vacant, and relations with the curia very strained, until Innocent's successor, Gregory XII, sought to pour oil on troubled waters by offering absolution; and the matter of the archbishopric was settled amicably between king and pope. Langley was provided with the see of Durham by a papal bull of 10 May 1406; Hallum, who had retired to Rome after his rejection by Henry, received the bishopric of Salisbury the following year; and the vacancy at York was at last filled when **Henry Bowet** was translated there by papal provision on 7 October 1407, his temporalities being restored by the king in December.

Bowet sprang from a knightly family that had emigrated from the north to East Anglia; and his career, prior to his York election, had been both distinguished and exciting. He had practised in the ecclesiastical courts as a doctor of civil and canon law, accompanied Bishop Spencer of Norwich on his crusade, and acted as secret agent for Richard II in the Roman curia of Pope Urban VI. Refused pardon by the Merciless Parliament as a known favourite of Richard's, he was protected by John of Gaunt and continued to serve the king's interests abroad: negotiating with the king of Castile, serving as chief justiciar in the court of Aquitaine, and finally being appointed Constable of Bordeaux at the time of Henry Bolingbroke's exile. Bowet now proceeded to act as Henry's agent and negotiated a promise from Richard that in the event of John of Gaunt's death his son would receive his inheritance through a proxy. But, when John died in January 1399, the king broke his promise, seized the estates, and, furious at the part Bowet had played in procuring it, caused him to be condemned to death as a traitor, a sentence later commuted to perpetual banishment in consideration of his clerical status. At the same time he was deprived of all his preferments, clerical and secular. But Bowet had chosen wisely; and, on his return to England with Henry, benefited largely from the Revolution, being awarded not only a number of prebends but by being made regent of all the English possessions in France. Elected by royal command to the see of Bath and Wells, he found himself confronted by the papal nominee, Richard Clifford, keeper of the privy seal. Henry forbade Clifford to accept the papal provision, and persuaded Pope Benedict IX to change his mind. Bowet received Bath and Wells, whilst Clifford went to the diocese of Worcester.

The new bishop, however, spent little time in his see, leaving its duties to a suffragan, whilst he continued to serve the king in a variety of ways. He was treasurer for a time, then served on important embassies to France and Denmark, became a member of the privy council and a trier of petitions, and finally, after escorting Princess Philippa to her marriage with Eric, king of Denmark, Henry rewarded him in 1407 with the archbishopric of York. He was enthroned in the Minster on 8 December that same year.

From henceforth his political career came to an end, and he devoted his considerable energies to his northern province, where he acquired a reputation for diligence and efficiency. His well-kept register discloses that under his leadership the diocese flourished. The York chapter contained some outstanding canons such as Stephen Scrope, archdeacon of Richmond, and the two successive treasurers, Robert Wolveden and Thomas Haxey; and clerics for any office were chosen with care.

Inevitably, however, like all the prelates of the day, he was something of a nepotist. One nephew, Henry Bowet, was provided with prebends at York, Ripon and Southwell; whilst another was appointed archdeacon of Richmond on Stephen Scrope's death. A third Robert Bowet, became archdeacon of Nottingham. All these relations, like their uncle, were lawyers; and no doubt contributed to the fine library of law books that the archbishop left behind him after his death.

Bowet's reputation for magnificence and hospitality were notorious even in this age of princely prelates. His own household, it was said, consumed some eight cases of red wine a year. Like his predecessors he was a great builder, being responsible for the hall at Cawood Castle, the kitchens at Ottley, and his own splendid tomb that fills the eastern arch on the south side of the Lady Chapel in the Minster, of which he was also a generous benefactor.

Outside his diocese he clashed with the archbishop of Canterbury over the right to visit Queen's College, Oxford; but joined hands with him in the zealous persecution of the lollards, assisting at Badby's trial. He also wrote in strong terms to Henry IV about another heretic, John Taylor. He could always be certain of a sympathetic royal ear, since he had lent the crown substantial sums of money.

During Henry V's absence in Normandy during 1417, Bowet organised the defence of the north against the Scots, being carried everywhere in a litter during the entire campaign, accompanied by many of his clergy, for he was now old and infirm. None the less it was his energy, courage and patriotism that largely contributed to the English success. He died on 20 October 1423, rich in honour, but also in worldly goods. His will provided £100 for his funeral, £20 for 1,000 masses to be said within a month of his death, and £20 to be distributed among the poor. Large sums were left to the Minster fabric funds, and for the endowment of the York chapter and the vicars choral. To his old cathedral of Wells he bequeathed a complete set of vestments. Gascoigne narrates the following story about him: 'Why', Henry IV once asked Archbishop Bowet, 'is it that bishops in our days are not translated after their death, on account of their notable miracles, as they once were?' Bowet replied that there were four reasons: 'firstly, at one time, God chose holy men to be bishops, now they are chosen by kings and manipulated by them; secondly, men were originally persuaded to be bishops out of zeal for souls, but that no longer applies; thirdly, prelates were once too conscientiously devoted to their dioceses to desire translation, but now they pass readily from see to see in search of wealth; finally, all too often today they "buy translation" at such a price that they deserve neither miracles nor canonisation afterwards'.

Such comments whether spoken by Bowet or not, certainly mirror the career of his successor, **John Kempe**, whose long reign at York for 35 years was mainly devoted to diplomacy and politics. His appointment, however, was preceded by a long and bitter struggle involving the chapter, the crown, and the pope. At first everything appeared to go smoothly with the chapter electing Philip Morgan, bishop of Worcester as their archbishop, a choice to which Henry VI's regency council gave its consent on 25 January 1424. But rivals in the persons of John Kempe of London and Richard Fleming of Lincoln quickly threw their hats into the ring. The dean of York, William Carey, then at the Council of Pavia and a personal friend of the pope, favoured Fleming, who had already commended himself to the curia at the Councils of Siena and Constance. So on 14 February 1424 Pope Martin V set aside Morgan's election, and, on his own responsibility, translated Fleming from Lincoln to York.

Meanwhile Kempe had not been idle, sending money to his proctor at the curia, William Swan, with instructions to distribute it as Swan thought fit; whilst he himself wrote to the pope and friendly cardinals urging his claims to the archbishopric. Fleming had been supporting the papal demand for the repeal of the Statute of Provisors, and this naturally aroused hostility against him in the English Council; so, on his return to England in May 1424 he found himself summarily deprived of the primacy. Nicholas Bildeston was then sent to Rome to complain about Fleming's translation; and Kempe, who was an active member of the all-powerful Beaufort faction on the Council, now saw his prospects brightening, since Bishop Henry Beaufort of Winchester had just succeeded Langley as chancellor on 6 July. By October Fleming had thrown in the sponge and resigned his claims to York on the understanding that he had never really accepted it and so would not be subject to any penalties under the Statutes of Provisors and Praemunire. This would enable him to return to Lincoln either through a papal declaration or a fresh translation; in return for which he promised to assist the Duke of Gloucester's matrimonial case then before the curia, paying all the fees himself.

Fleming disposed of, a majority on the Council still favoured Morgan's translation to York, although their attention was distracted for the moment by the growing hostility between Henry Beaufort and the Duke of Gloucester. Martin V, who was reluctant to disown Fleming and promote Morgan, bided his time; there was a period of silence, and the solution, when it finally arrived, stemmed from France rather than England. The Duke of Bedford, Kempe's friend, brought pressure to bear upon the pope, whereby it was arranged that Kempe should go to York, Fleming back to Lincoln, and, as a sop to the York chapter, its dean, William Carey, should have the bishopric of London, vacated by Kempe's promotion. Martin announced this agreement on 20 July 1425, and, after some hesitation, the English Council acquiesced. Both Bishop Beaufort and the Duke of Gloucester congratulated Kempe; and at a Council meeting in Westminster on 14 January 1426, which was presided over by the Duke of Bedford, the whole matter was finally settled, Morgan being consoled with the vacant see of Ely. Kempe had his temporalities restored on 22 April 1426.

Gascoigne sums up Kempe's archiepiscopate as follows:

For about twenty-seven years he was wholly absent from his diocese, dwelling in London or in Kent, or in some other distant part of England, save that once in ten or twelve years he stayed for two or three weeks in his diocese. He stayed at York little or not at all, and in his time the palace of York was dilapidated and almost fell to the ground, and was not repaired while he was archbishop. And at his departure from York when Henry VI and Edward, duke of Somerset, made him archbishop of Canterbury, he left the church of York in great confusion without remedy.

Gascoigne was prejudiced; but there is little doubt that Kempe's political activities left him little time for his see. Even his primary visitation, for example, was interrupted by public business. Gascoigne's final remark about leaving York in confusion probably referred to a disputed deanery election, when Kempe, backed by both king and pope, forced a minority candidate upon the chapter in 1452. John Kempe was the son of a Kentish gentleman, and his first love was always with that county, his seat being at Olantigh near Ashford, where he founded a college of chantry priests in Wye church and endowed a grammar school whose provost and fellows were always to be drawn from his old Oxford College of Merton. Here he had been a fellow and doctor of law, and began his clerical career by practising in the ecclesiastical courts, when he assisted at the trial of Sir John Oldcastle. He then became dean of Arches and vicar-general to Archbishop Chichele, before being appointed dean of Durham and passing through three bishoprics, Rochester, Gloucester and London, before reaching the archbishopric. Henry V employed him on a variety of diplomatic missions, and at one time he was that king's chancellor of Normandy.

Under Henry VI he played an important part on the regency council; and, as the right-hand man of Cardinal Beaufort, became deeply involved in the peace negotiations with France. These brought him into conflict with the Duke of Gloucester and the war party, especially after he himself became chancellor. At the Congress of Arras in 1435 and again at the Conference of Oye four years later he acted as Beaufort's spokesman, and, together with his leader, was savagely attacked by Gloucester in 1440 for their failure. But Gloucester was a spent force; and Kempe, who had been made a cardinal in 1439 by Pope Eugenius IV, continued to enjoy the royal favour. In 1441 he replied to Gloucester's attacks by presiding as one of the judges over the trial of the duke's wife, Eleanor Cobham, when she was condemned for witchcraft; and zealously advocated the marriage of Henry VI to Margaret of Anjou, which the duke had bitterly opposed. Then, after Beaufort's final retirement, Kempe again became chancellor, helped to engineer the Duke of Suffolk's fall, and himself emerged as the king's chief minister. Despite age and growing infirmity he was largely responsible for crushing Jack Cade's rebellion, presiding in person at the trial of the Kentish leaders of that insurrection. Closely allied to the queen and the Duke of Somerset he strongly opposed the Yorkist party; and as a reward, despite his age, Somerset, backed by the crown, secured his translation to Canterbury in 1452.

The high esteem in which he was held by his contemporaries is to be seen in his appointment as executor to the wills both of the Duke of Bedford and Cardinal Beaufort; whilst Henry VI once spoke of him as 'one of the wisest lords in the land', and told the pope how much he had appreciated: 'his holiness of life, purity, abundance of knowledge, ripeness of counsel, experience in business, wisdom, eloquence, and dignity of person'. But in his northern diocese he was by no means so popular. He continued the building tradition of his predecessor by reconstructing Cawood Castle, rebuilding the hall at Southwell Manor, and financing the painting of the Minster nave. His register discloses that he visited the archdeaconry of Richmond, but also that he left the bulk of the routine work of the see to officials, who were well trained and efficient; and his episcopal acts to a suffragan. But when himself in residence his autocratic methods aroused much opposition. In 1441, for example, over a dispute between his own tenants at Ripon and those of the Forest of Knaresborough, the archbishop used force to maintain his claims, keeping 'his town of Ripon like a town of war with hired soldiers' and despatching 300 of these mercenaries to compel the Knaresborough men to pay the tolls. Two years later, infuriated by Kempe's high-handed proceedings against some of the laity, and egged on by the Earl of Northumberland, rioters attacked his palace at Southwell; for which offence the Royal Council compelled the Earl to pay damages. At the same time the Justices of the peace in the three ridings of Yorkshire were ordered to prevent any further such attacks on the archbishop.

Yet another of Kempe's despotic acts was his demand at a synod held in York during 1442 that the smaller monasteries should refrain from alienating any of their properties without his permission. However, in the province at large he was more conciliatory; and, taking warning from the mistakes of Alexander, administered the see of Durham during a vacancy under the customary *jure decesano*, and thereby encountered no opposition. Outside Yorkshire he founded a grammar school at Wye which was attached to his College of secular priests, and placed under the care of Battle Abbey; all of these were suppressed by Henry VIII.

William Booth, the first of two half-brothers to become chancellors to Queen Margaret and then archbishops of York, was a doctor of law, who had studied at Gray's Inn and Pembroke College, Cambridge; although Gascoigne denied that he had any kind of degree and referred to him as 'the unworthy bishop of Chester', i.e. Lichfield and Coventry. 'He was', he said, 'neither a good grammarian, nor knowing, nor reputed virtuous, nor a graduate of either university.' As a staunch ally of Queen Margaret, Booth backed first the Duke of Suffolk and then the Duke of Somerset. His championship of the former got him into trouble with the House of Commons, who demanded his banishment, and also in his own diocese of Lichfield where there were demonstrations against him. Jack Cade's rebels, supporting the Yorkist cause, actually composed a poem attacking the Duke of Suffolk, Booth and the queen: but the queen made sure that her clerical friends all got suitable promotion. Booth became bishop of Lichfield and Coventry in 1447, and some five years later, through the influence of Margaret and Somerset, was translated to York. But he was not prepared, after the Battle of Towton, to risk either his life or his archbishopric for the sake of the defeated queen; and readily accepted Edward IV as king, even assisting at his coronation.

Henceforth he played little part in public affairs, but instead devoted himself to his diocese. The Yorkshire chronicler praises his generosity, mentioning in particular his appropriation of churches for the endowment of the York vicars-choral and those at Southwell, where he chiefly resided; and here he built a chapel on the south side of the Minster. He is likewise remembered as an active and industrious primate, a fact borne out by his register. Despite the Wars of the Roses being waged bloodily in his diocese, he visited his people and worked hard to promote their interests, both clerical and lay, during a chaotic situation. It should be recalled that both the Battles of Wakefield and Towton were fought within a relatively short distance of York; and it was only with the greatest difficulty that Edward IV was prevented from sacking the city itself because of the Yorkists' heads displayed on its gates.

Gascoigne had complained that Booth was appointed to the archbishopric by king and pope over the heads of the chapter; and this was even truer of the next archbishop, **George Neville**, the youngest brother of Richard Earl of Warwick, the kingmaker. Due to his aristocratic connections Neville was able to take his B.A. and M.A. degrees at Balliol College Oxford, without having to complete his academic course, and then became a fellow excused from all teaching and administrative duties. In 1453 he was appointed chancellor of the university; and even before he had been priested received prebends at St. Paul's, Lincoln and Ripon, and was made archdeacon of Northamptonshire. When in 1454 the Duke of York was Protector of the realm during Henry VI's illness, George's father, the Earl of Salisbury, persuaded the Council to recommend his son for a bishopric on the grounds of 'blood, virtue and cunning he is of'. George had now been priested, but was still under the canonical age for a bishopric; but none the less the Council bullied Pope Calixtus III into dropping his own candidate for the vacant see of Exeter and providing Neville instead, despite the fact that the chapter had already elected John Hales, archdeacon of Norwich. However, the pope stipulated that George could not be consecrated until his 27th birthday, and so meanwhile would remain bishop-elect. Gascoigne commented sarcastically, 'of all the political preferments of the age that of the brother of the Earl of Warwick was the most conspicuous'.

But George was no fool, for, despite his easy Oxford career, he is remembered as something of a Renaissance scholar, to whom learned scholars dedicated their works, and of whose learning John Paston spoke with enthusiasm. Furthermore he was to display statesmanship of a high order. Professor Hamilton Thompson wrote: 'Since Arundel . . . there had been no archbishop who combined rank with statesmanship, and . . . the latter quality was something more than the official competence of a busy clerk like Kempe'. Although no more than a bishop-elect, Neville was summoned to the Council as one of the episcopate, and began to play a prominent part in ecclesiastical affairs. For instance he was one of the examiners of the heretical bishop, Reginald Peacock, hotly reproaching him for 'impeaching the truth of the writings of St. Jerome and other saints'. His consecration took place on 3 December 1458; and his spectacular political career began the following year.

He wisely avoided being compromised in the fiasco of the Yorkist rebellion of 1459, that resulted in the hasty flight of its leaders from Ludlow Castle, declaring himself 'full worshipfully to the king's pleasure'. But, on the return of Salisbury and Warwick from Calais in 1460, the bishop boldly threw in his lot with them, was present at the Battle of Northampton, and afterwards received the great seal as chancellor. None the less, hedging his bets, and along with the archbishop of Canterbury, he took the oath of allegiance to Henry VI.

After the defeat at the second Battle of St. Albans, in which George was involved, he finally decided to sever his connection with the Lancastrians, accepted Edward IV as king, and defended that monarch's title to the throne in an eloquent sermon at St. Paul's Cross. Apparently he did not accompany the army to the field of Towton, and the terrible slaughter that took place there evidently preyed on his mind, judging from a letter he sent after the battle to the papal legate in Flanders, Coppini, to whom he bewailed the horrors of civil war: 'O luckless race', he cried, 'alas, we are a race deserving of pity, even from the French'.

As chancellor, Neville opened Edward IV's first parliament on 4 November with an address from a text of Jeremiah VII.3. 'Amend your ways and your doings and I will cause you to dwell in this place'; and again opened the second parliament nearly two years later with an equally eloquent sermon. Edward now sent him on an important diplomatic mission to a Conference at St. Omer, later transferred to Hesdon, where he was successful in detaching the Duke of Burgundy from the Lancastrian cause; and this was followed by another to York to conclude a 15 year truce with the Scots.

But this honeymoon period with the king came to an abrupt end when Edward married Elizabeth Woodville, which caused bitter resentment in the Neville clan of brothers. None the less George's claim to the archbishopric of York on the death of William Booth could not be ignored, and accordingly the papal bull providing him with the primacy was published in the Minster on 4 June 1465, his enthronement following five days later. This last was a most elaborate affair, financially crippling the new archbishop, but displaying the power of the Nevilles, who turned out in force to honour the occasion. On the other hand Edward was conspicuous by his absence, being represented by his brother, the Duke of Gloucester, then a fervent admirer of the kingmaker.

The struggle between the Nevilles and the crown came to a head in the summer of 1467, when George was made the scapegoat by being summarily deprived of the great seal by the king in person; and for a moment it looked like civil war. Then the archbishop met the queen's brother, Earl Rivers, at Nottingham, a reconciliation was patched up and the Nevilles returned to court, with George hopeful of once again becoming chancellor. But it was not to be. There was a quarrel with the Duke of Norfolk over the Pastons' property, who were clients of the archbishop, when George went so far as to say that 'rather than the land should go to the duke, he would come and dwell there himself', with Warwick backing his brother, and the Crown Norfolk. The truce between the Nevilles and the king broke down; George crossed to Calais, where Warwick was captain, and, against Edward's express prohibition, married his brother's elder daughter, Isabel, to the Duke of Clarence, who was the heir apparent. Warwick and Clarence then issued a manifesto repeating their grievances, crossed to England, and at the battle of Edgecote defeated the Yorkists. It was the archbishop himself who captured Edward in the little Buckinghamshire village of Olney, and conveyed him prisoner to Warwick Castle, from which he was later transferred to the great Neville stronghold in the north, Middleham Castle in Yorkshire. Public opinion, however, was hostile; and George, sensing which way the wind was blowing, connived at Edward's escape in return for promises of pardon and reconciliation. But he did not accompany the king all the way to London, dropping out at The Moor, his favourite manor house in Hertfordshire. He then experienced a shock, since on attempting later to travel south, he was peremptorily ordered by Edward to stay where he was. But the Nevilles were finally pardoned, and an uneasy lull followed, while the king waited for Warwick again to overreach himself. This happened in the spring of 1470, when a Neville rising was crushed in Lincolnshire and Warwick and Clarence fled to France.

George took no part in this rebellion, but was forced to take a solemn oath of loyalty to the crown and confined to The Moor, 'with divers of the king's servants' until he should be sent for. His other brother, John, although angered by being deprived of the Earldom of Northumberland, remained loyal. Then, with French help, Warwick returned to England in September, both his brothers rallied to his side, and Edward only escaped by the skin of his teeth to Burgundy. George became chancellor again and opened parliament on 26 November in the name of Henry VI, with a discourse on the text; *Rivertimini ad me filii revertentes ego enim vir vester*; and as a reward for his eloquence Warwick presented him with the manor of Woodstock.

At the same time he had the satisfaction of compelling the Duke of Norfolk to surrender Caister Castle to the Pastons. But the Neville triumph was short lived. Edward landed in Yorkshire during March 1471; and, after Warwick had marched north to meet him, George was left in charge of London and Henry VI. So in order to try and whip up a little enthusiasm for this bedraggled monarch the archbishop paraded him through the streets, to little or no effect. Edward's army by-passed Warwick, and, on his reaching St. Albans, George knew that the game was up. He opened London's gates, refused to allow Henry to take refuge in the Westminster Sanctuary, and instead surrendered himself and that unfortunate king to Edward. The archbishop went to the Tower, but was released within a few weeks and pardoned; but as part of the bargain he had to swear allegiance to Edward's newly born son, the luckless Edward V.

After the Battles of Barnet and Tewkesbury, to all appearances, George was restored to favour. He entertained John Paston at The Moor for Christmas in princely style, who recorded that 'he had had great cheer and had been as welcome as he could devise'; hunted with the king at Windsor; and was promised a royal visit. But Edward still harboured suspicions of this wily prelate; and when it was discovered that the archbishop had been in correspondence with the exiled Lancastrian, the Earl of Oxford, the king ordered his arrest, just as he was making the most lavish preparations for Edward's entertainment. Secretly conveyed to Calais and imprisoned in Ham Castle, all Neville's personal possessions were seized, including The Moor. His jewelled mitre was actually broken up to make an additional crown out of its stones, and the archiepiscopal temporalities were put into sequestration.

His fall from grace was gleefully seized upon by his enemies as an opportunity to revile him. Warkworth, for example, wrote: 'Such goods as were gathered with sin, were lost with sorrow'. The secret of his imprisonment was so closely guarded that the rumour grew that he had been murdered; but Neville still had some friends, and Richard, Duke of Gloucester, who had married Anne, Warwick's younger daughter, at length succeeded in securing his release. Broken in health the archbishop returned to England, but only to die at Blyth in Northumberland on 8 June 1476, in his 44th year.

As might well be expected George had not been especially active in his archiepiscopal diocese; and his register, compared with those of his predecessors, is sparse. But he was lavish with his benefactions, founding a college at York dedicated to St. William, which was sited in the close at the east end of the Minster and contained some 23 chantry priests; but it was at Oxford that he is chiefly remembered. His gifts to Balliol College are carefully recorded in a window of its library, and Lincoln College recalls how he saved it from confiscation by Edward IV. This college had been a Lancastrian foundation, and its Visitor, Bishop Chedworth of Lincoln, a protégé of Henry VI, greatly feared that the Yorkist victory might lead to its dissolution. So he appealed to the scholarly-minded George Neville to use his influence with the king on the college's behalf. As a result a royal charter was promulgated on 9 February 1462, confirming the foundation of the college; and in the following January another document was issued providing a royal pardon for 'all transgressions' up to 4 November 1461, and releasing all fines to 5 March 1462. Finally letters patent were issued on 20 April 1463 under the great seal ratifying, with parliamentary consent, all that had gone before.

The college wrote to Neville thanking him for having saved their society '*ab avidis canum latratribus at manibus diripientium*', assuring that he and his family would have a place in their prayers 'in no inferior to that of its other founders and benefactors'. His orbit was linked with that of Cardinal Beaufort; but after his dramatic fall from grace his name was quietly allowed to drop out of sight. The archbishop also lavished much money on his favourite residence, The Moor, where 'he builded right commodiously and pleasantly'.

Lawrence Booth, Archbishop William Booth's half-brother, was translated from Durham to York and provided by the pope on 31 July 1476. A lawyer and graduate of Pembroke Hall, Cambridge, of which he became Master and ultimately Chancellor of the University, when he made himself responsible for the building of the arts and law school, Lawrence had followed in his brother's footsteps as Queen Margaret's chancellor, who loaded him with ecclesiastical preferments, culminating in the bishopric of Durham, when he was consecrated by his brother. In the political field he became keeper of the privy seal in 1456, helped to arrange the Scottish truce, and was made tutor to the Prince of Wales.

At first he remained steadfastly loyal to the Lancastrian cause, and was actually rewarded with some of Warwick's forfeited estates; but, after the Battle of Towton, he changed sides, and swore fealty to Edward IV. But his ties with Queen Margaret were still strong; he was discovered assisting her invasion of the north, had his temporalities seized, and, although not officially deprived, became generally known as 'the late Bishop of Durham'. However, in 1464 Edward restored him to his bishopric, where he wisely remained quiet during the stormy years that followed. Consequently in 1471 he was fully restored to favour, swore a new oath of fealty, and returned to his parliamentary duties, when he was made a trier of petitions. He even got back the forfeited Warwick estates in the Palatinate. By 1473 he was coining his own money at Durham; and Edward, who valued his legalistic abilities appointed him chancellor, when Bishop Stillington had to retire through illness.

Booth now showed himself extremely energetic in raising funds for the coming war with France, 'exhorting the Commons to deal liberally with the king'; and he continued to enjoy the royal favour even after relinquishing the chancellorship to Bishop Rotherham. So, within 10 days of Neville's death, he was given the custody of the archiepiscopal temporalities; and then, with the joint agreement of king and pope, elevated to the archiepiscopal throne. But his tenure of the see was very brief, for he died four years later on 11 May 1480.

Both the Booth brothers made their residence at Southwell Manor, and here Lawrence completed the chapel that William had begun, in which they lie buried. At Durham he reconstructed the gates of Auckland Castle and built some neighbouring houses; and, when archbishop, purchased the Manor of Chelsea for the see, where he erected a sumptuous residence. As Master of Pembroke Hall, Cambridge which he had held in conjunction with the archbishopric, he became one of its most liberal benefactors.

Two final items of interest may be added: he was the first bishop of Durham to become archbishop of York; and as he had married a niece of the Earl of Westmorland, he continued the long Neville connection with the archbishopric.

Thomas Rotherham,* the last of the fifteenth century archbishops, is sometimes given the alternative name of Scott. This was not, as has sometimes been supposed, because he was the illegitimate son of one of the Scotts of Barn Hall, Ecclesfield; but due to the fact that his father, Sir Thomas Rotherham, who was a Scott, had adopted the name of the town in which he was born. The future archbishop was educated by 'a teacher of Grammar' in Rotherham, and possibly at Eton, before becoming a scholar of King's College, Cambridge, where he remained for some 14 years, being elected a fellow and taking his B.D. degree in 1446.

The then archbishop of Canterbury, Bouchier, secured his appointment as chaplain to the Earl of Oxford, and also the provostship of Wingham in Kent, together with the post of legal adviser to the prior and convent of Canterbury.

The de Veres, as stout Lancastrians, suffered grievously during the Wars of the Roses; but Rotherham himself, after the execution of the Earl and his son following the Battle of Towton, changed sides and became an ardent Yorkist. From 1461-5 he was rector of Ripple in Worcestershire, which he held in *commendam* with Wingham, secured a number of prebends and the important London living of St. Vedast in Foster Lane.

* See page 65.

Then he was made archdeacon of Canterbury and introduced to royalty when Edward, recognising his legalistic abilities, appointed him keeper of the privy seal and made him one of his chaplains.

The road was now wide open to promotion, and in 1468 he was raised to the episcopal bench, and employed on a number of important missions abroad to France and Burgundy. From the see of Rochester he was then translated to the more important diocese of Lincoln, became Chancellor of Cambridge University and replaced Lawrence Booth as Lord Chancellor, since Edward needed a stronger man than either Stillington or Booth now that the war with France was beginning.

Rotherham had more than proved his loyalty during Warwick's brief tenure of power, by taking sanctuary with the queen at Westminster; and was regarded as the greatest equity lawyer of the age, a man renowned for his uprightness, humanity and courage. A close friend of the king, he never became his creature. His eloquence, in persuading parliament to grant liberal supplies for the war, so impressed Edward that he not only decided to take the chancellor with him on the campaign, but named him in the deed of enfeoffment providing for the king's possible death. Bishop Alcock took over his duties at home but Rotherham continued to control all affairs connected with the war. He was present at Picquighy, when Edward and Louis met on the bridge over the Somme, prophesying, according to Philip de Commines, that 'at this spot a mighty peace between France and England was in course of accomplishment'. Later, with many others, he partook of the bribes dealt out by the French king.

Once more at home Rotherham resumed his full duties, but apparently made no direct effort to save the Duke of Clarence from his fate, yet none the less refused to preside over the attainder 'as being an affair of blood', his place being taken by the Duke of Buckingham. In 1478 his two terms as the Cambridge Chancellor expired; but on the death of Archbishop Booth, was appointed by the king to the archbishopric of York, when he was also re-elected Master of Pembroke Hall. Provided by the pope and translated on 1 July 1480 to York, the following September he was made a legate of the apostolic see and the temporalities were restored. At the same time Edward granted him a general pardon in order to safe-guard the new archbishop against any possible accusations in the future.

In January 1483, on opening the parliamentary session Rotherham again pleaded eloquently for ample supplies in view of the prospect of renewed war with France; but the king's death put an end to any such preparations. As Edward's chaplain the archbishop heard his last confession, and was present at his death bed when Edward exacted a promise from the members of his council to be loyal to his young heir. He celebrated the funeral mass in Westminster Abbey, helped cense* the corpse at the gates of Windsor Castle, and sang the requiem mass.

* Perfume with incense.

Afterwards he firmly supported the queen in her bid to control the Government and prevent Richard, Duke of Gloucester, from becoming Protector. Then, when the news of Richard's coup at Northampton arrived, and Elizabeth fled to sanctuary, Lord Hastings sent a message to Rotherham in the middle of the night informing him that 'he should do nothing for all should be well'. To which the archbishop retorted: 'be it as it will, it will never be as well as we have seen it'.

He hastened to Westminster and comforted the queen 'in the best manner he could', telling her that if anything happened to Edward V, 'and if they crown any other king than your son, whom we now have, we shall on the morrow crown his brother, whom you have with you'. As a further proof of his devotion he left the great seal with her, 'for the use of your son'. But of this last act he quickly repented, and the very next day demanded and received it back.

Not unnaturally Richard took a dim view of these proceedings, and at the council meeting that appointed him Protector, deprived Rotherham of the chancellorship, entrusting the great seal instead to Bishop Russell of London. In revenge the archbishop joined the conspiracy of the Woodvilles, led by John Morton, bishop of Ely, and Lord Hastings, to overthrow Richard, once they had learned that he intended to claim the throne for himself on the grounds of the illegitimacy of his nephews. This led to the dramatic confrontation in the Tower, when Lord Hastings' head was struck off on the Green, and the other conspirators were imprisoned for longer or shorter periods. Rotherham was lodged in the Tower, and so could not, as Sir Thomas More alleges, have assisted the archbishop of Canterbury in persuading the queen to surrender her younger son on 16 June 1483. Cambridge petitioned Richard to release their ex-chancellor, and it appears he was set free after the new king's coronation; but was notably absent from the splendid reception of Richard and Anne at York, when they lodged in the archiepiscopal palace, and the bishop of Durham officiated at the ceremony of installing their son, Edward, as Prince of Wales.

Indeed from now on Rotherham took little part in politics, although apparently restored to favour. His name appears among the triers of petitions in Richard's only parliament of January 1484, and again among the lords assembled at Nottingham the following September to consider a possible Scottish royal marriage, and he attended the court. Here, according to Polydore Vergil, Richard confided in him complaints about the queen that 'she brought forth no children'; and it was even suggested that Richard made use of the archbishop to promote a plan for marrying his niece Elizabeth. Both of these stories are highly suspect.

Then, after the Battle of Bosworth, Rotherham again took office for a brief period as Lord Treasurer, before being superseded by Lord Dynham. However, he remained a trier of petitions, and was one of the feoffees named by Henry VII for executing his Will when the king was contemplating another invasion of France. In Yorkshire he helped to enquire into the unrest that had led to the Earl of Northumberland's violent death, and later appeared both at the installations of Arthur as Prince of Wales, and the future Henry VIII as Duke of York. But he took no part in either ceremony, and at the latter is described as being '*not in pontificalibus*'.

In his rôle as archbishop, Professor Thompson declared that Rotherham was 'the most zealous tenant of the see since the time of Thoresby'. Two complete registers of Rotherham's still exist, which show him to have been a most active visitor, either in person or through a deputy. Inevitably owing to his political duties and attendance at court, the archbishop himself was often an absentee, and consequently the visitations were in the hands of his vicar-general; whilst ordinations and confirmations were performed by his suffragan, William, bishop of Dromore. None the less the archbishop acquired a thorough knowledge of his diocese; the religious houses, hitherto neglected, received a complete overhaul; and after each visitation injunctions were issued.

Like other archbishops Rotherham displayed a particular interest in his native place: he helped build the church at Rotherham, gave and dedicated an altar in the name of Jesus, and founded a Jesus chantry. This last was described by Leland as being 'very fair . . . sumptuously builded of brike', and consisted of a provost and three fellows, who were to teach grammar, writing and song to six poor resident boys from Rotherham. The college was open to all stipendiary or chantry priests 'of good fame and honest conversation'. The archbishop provided a large capital sum out of his own purse and appropriated to it the benefices of Almonbury and Laxton. Other buildings for which he was responsible included: the chapel of Our Lady on the Bridge, the tower at Buckden, the kitchens at York Place in London, and those at the manors of Southwell and Bishopthorpe. At Southwell he created a park of some 300 acres, which was later used by one of his successors, Savage, for hunting. Both universities benefited from his generosity. He contributed largely to the building of St. Catharine's College at Cambridge, gave £100 for work on King's College, and another £100 to the church of Great St. Mary's, where his arms are carved on its tower. He helped finance the building of the Cambridge School, and in particular its noble gateway and library, which he endowed with 200 volumes. Consequently his name is still commemorated as one of Cambridge's benefactors.

Lincoln College, Oxford, again fell on evil days in 1471, to whose financial plight the then rector drew Rotherham's attention, who not only secured a further royal confirmation of its charter, but added a magnificent endowment in the shape of the appropriation of the two parish churches of Twyford and Combe Longa, together with two houses in Oxford itself. He also released the college from its annual payment of £4 for the already appropriated churches of St. Michael and All Saints in Oxford, including the incorporation of St. Anne's chantry at All Saints into the college. Then out of his own pocket he contributed an annual pension of £5 during his life. The number of Lincoln fellows was increased from seven to twelve, and the quadrangle completed; whilst Rotherham put the coping stone on his achievements by having a new body of statutes drawn up, in which fellowships were allocated to regions, one of which must include a native from Rotherham. Lincoln dubbed him their second founder and his portrait hangs in the college hall.

The archbishop apparently died of plague whilst in residence at Cawood Castle and lies buried in the Minster, where his monument, damaged by fire in 1829, was restored and enriched by Lincoln College. His Will showered bequests not only on his own family and household, but on every benefice and bishopric he had served. York Minster received a mitre worth £500, a statue of St. Margaret and £100 for the vicars-choral. Anxious to escape from purgatory, he left the residue of his estate as masses for his soul. The Will ends with a solemn profession of faith: 'I bear witness that in the passion of Christ and in the Sacraments of the Church which draw their virtue therefrom, I place the salvation of my soul'.

The last three medieval archbishops of York were all notorious absentees. **Thomas Savage**, son of Sir John Savage of Clifton in Cheshire, was a Cambridge doctor of law, and a favourite of Henry VII, who had employed him on various important missions abroad, and rewarded him with first the see of Rochester and then with that of London. Finally in 1501 king and pope agreed on his elevation to the archbishopric of York, being provided on 18 January and having his temporalities restored the following April. But he was never enthroned; although it is said that he angered the diocese by sending a deputy to Beverley Minster to be enthroned in his place, together with a fool to amuse his household. He spent most of his time at the royal court, where he attended all the important ceremonies of the day, living like a secular nobleman, 'with a household of tall servants'. A keen sportsman, and passionately fond of hunting, he made good use of the park that his predecessor had created at Southwell. He died at Cawood Castle on 3 September 1507, and was buried in York Minster under a fine tomb; but his heart went to Macclesfield, where he had intended to found a college. He does not appear to have played any notable part in the ecclesiastical affairs of either his diocese or province, apart from repairing some of the manor houses of the see, especially at Cawood and Scrooby.

His successor, **Christopher Bainbridge**, a member of a well-known Westmorland family, was educated both in Italy and at Queen's College, Oxford, of which he later became provost, endowing it with two Oxford manors for 'fynding of the scolers'. Like his predecessor he was awarded a doctorate in both civil and canon law; and, thanks to the patronage of a distinguished uncle, Thomas Langton, bishop of Winchester, quickly became loaded with ecclesiastical preferments. Then his ability as a lawyer gained him a place in Henry VII's council, where he voted for the execution of Perkin Warbeck and Edward Warwick. In 1504 he was appointed Master of the Rolls and received the twin deaneries of York and Windsor, which three years later led to the bishopric of Durham and six months afterwards to the archbishopric, that had stood vacant since Savage's death. He was probably chosen for the primacy because as an outstanding lawyer and an able administrator, the friend and favourite of Lady Margaret Beaufort, the then High Commissioner of the North, he would co-operate with her in averting a possible Scottish invasion, and in building up the defences of the border on which a quarter of the palatine revenues were to be spent. But the new archbishop had little time to spare for organising his diocese, since in 1509 he quitted England for Italy never to return, its affairs being left in the very capable hands of John Carver his vicar-general, and John Hutton the suffragan.

Bainbridge, who along with Lady Margaret was an executor of Henry VII's Will, attended Henry VIII's coronation on 21 June 1509, before being commissioned the following September as the king's orator and proctor to undertake all the negotiations in the court of Rome that concerned the Crown and other English interests. Before his departure he set up a commission, which included the bishops of Winchester and Norwich, with full powers to administer the York diocese in his absence. He exacted a promise from them that his officers and servants would not be oppressed; and later, when this was not observed, persuaded the Pope to order an investigation; whilst at the same time revoking a statute forbidding the York canons to reside during their first term of office, that had led to a serious diminution of the Minster's services. This interference in the internal affairs of the York diocese from abroad was strongly resented; and his successor, Wolsey, later claimed that Bainbridge had left the see in a sadly dilapidated state, making it an excuse for seizing his money.

Archbishop Bainbridge with his legalistically-trained mind, and Italian background, was ideally situated for serving Henry's interests at the curia. He worked hard, reconciling Pope Julius II to the Republic of Venice, and helping to form the Holy League against France. Julius, anxious to drive the French out of Italy, made Bainbridge a cardinal in February 1511 and appointed him as his cardinal-legate to attack Ferrara, an expedition that not only failed, but led to the French capture of Bologna and a setting up of a council of rebel cardinals under the patronage of Louis XII. In reply Bainbridge achieved his greatest triumph by persuading England to join the Holy League, with a promise from Julius to crown Henry as king of France in Paris and transfer to him the title of Most Christian King.

Unfortunately however, the campaign against France both in Italy and Guienne went badly, Julius died, and the new pope, Leo X, although continuing to favour Bainbridge (who was the first English cardinal to attend the conclave of cardinals to elect a pope) became reconciled to France; and the Holy League was disbanded. Bainbridge had hoped that he would have been sent to England as *legate-à-latere* to bestow on Henry the title of Most Christian King, to arrange an alliance between England, the pope and the emperor, and procure a marriage between the Emperor's son, Prince Charles, and Princess Mary; but found himself left in the lurch. Truces were arranged between France, Spain, England and the Emperor. The archbishop had served Henry loyally, but, with the all-powerful Wolsey at home hostile, distrusting Bainbridge's aggressive policies and fearing his return to England as *legate-à-latere*, the latter saw himself isolated. Furthermore Wolsey now had his own agent in Rome, Silvester de Giglis, bishop of Worcester, who sent back reports on Bainbridge's activities. The archbishop had done much for English interests at Rome, especially by raising the status of the English Hospice and increasing its income; but he had also made some powerful enemies among the cardinals. In 1514 he was appointed Chamberlain of the College, and aroused resentment by his arrogant behaviour; so it was not altogether surprising when he died suddenly in the night of 14 July under very suspicious circumstances. One of his chaplains, Raynaldo da Modena, was accused of poisoning him, confessing under torture that he had bought poison in Spoleto and put it in Bainbridge's soup. Furthermore he said that he had done so at the instigation of Giglis, who once employed him in England, and used him now as his spy in Bainbridge's household. Giglis, of course, stoutly denied the charge; and, after Raynaldo committed suicide 'with a small knife', declared that he had retracted that part of his confession that involved Giglis himself, in the presence of his surgeon before he died. This was hard to believe, as Raynaldo had no personal grievance against the cardinal, who had greatly befriended him, and referred to his chaplain as 'dear and familiar'. Richard Pace, Bainbridge's Secretary, was convinced that Giglis promoted the murder, and pressed hard that he should be arrested, imprisoned and tortured in order to reveal the truth. He wrote both to Henry VIII and Wolsey urging this course, and adding that Giglis had even denigrated the cardinal after his death, 'with false and untrue things'. But Giglis, like his fellow bishop, Cardinal Hadrian of Bath and Wells (neither of whom had ever set foot in England, but received their sees in return for helping to promote Henry's interests with the papacy), claimed diplomatic immunity. Giglis also used his money 'to escape correction'; and, although his chamberlain was interrogated, nothing damaging could be extracted from him. No request came from England for Giglis's arrest; and, despite Leo X's promise that the whole matter would be thoroughly investigated, it was in fact hushed up, and the bishop absolved.

There is little doubt, however, that Giglis was guilty. He gained enormously from the murder, becoming sole English ambassador and orator at the Roman court, and earning the good-will of Wolsey. Indeed, it is more than possible that Wolsey himself was behind the assassination; since he had always been intensely jealous of Bainbridge, coveting both his archbishopric and cardinalate. The cardinal had been allowed to make a Will exempting his goods from being forfeited to the papacy after his death; but now Wolsey sequestered this wealth for himself on the grounds of alleged dilapidations in the diocese of York. He even wanted Bainbridge's vestments, cloth and tapestries as well, but these Giglis kept for himself. The murderers had done well for themselves. However, they did not entirely escape retribution. The rumour spread widely that the poison had been sent from England, 'by a certain prelate hostile to the cardinal, to be administered unto him by his cook'; and the fact that Wolsey made no attempt to have the investigations pursued only heightened the suspicions. A letter he wrote to Giglis made matters even worse. 'As glad as I am of your honourable acquittal', he said, 'in the slander of the great malice laid to your charge as though the same had touched me. And with like ardent mind shall I persecute those that thus maliciously hath accused you as though they had similarly laid the same thing to my charge'. As indeed it ultimately was, when, after Wolsey's fall in 1529, it formed part of the indictment against him.

Bainbridge was given a splendid funeral costing 1,400 ducats, and buried at the English Hospice. Both popes had lavished riches, preferments and titles upon him, and he died a very wealthy man. He has been accused of living a life of magnificence and luxury unbecoming a cleric, of practising numerous vices and possessing an ungovernable temper; but he is also remembered as a patron of literature and learning, of having founded a school at Bologna, and promoting the careers of a number of distinguished Englishmen. Above all, as a loyal servant of Henry VIII, he faithfully and untiringly defended England's interests at Rome, sometimes indeed when no-one else dared to do so.

The long line of medieval archbishops ends with the best known of them all, **Thomas Wolsey**. Wolsey, the son of an Ipswich butcher, graduated B.A. from Magdalen College, Oxford, at the early age of 15, being nicknamed 'the boy bachelor'. Later he took his M.A. degree, but was never either a doctor or even a bachelor of divinity. As bursar of his college he raised funds for the building of its famous tower, which may well have wetted his appetite for the more ambitious edifices he was to initiate in the future. His story is of course so well known that it would be pointless to repeat all the details here. It is sufficient to note that through such useful patrons as the Marquis of Dorset, Henry Deane, archbishop of Canterbury, and Richard Foxe, bishop of Winchester, Wolsey eventually came to the notice of the king and began to be employed on diplomatic missions. In December 1509 he was appointed the king's almoner and henceforth his rise to power was phenomenal. He became Henry's closest adviser, and soon began to dominate the affairs of Church and State alike until his fall, much as Richelieu was to do in France during the reign of Louis XIII. At the time of Bainbridge's death Wolsey was bishop of Lincoln, and immediately the king pressed the pope both to create Wolsey a cardinal and issue bulls translating him to the archbishopric of York, together with the usual dispensation for non-residence. Leo X issued the bull in September 1514, after some haggling over annates, but declined to create Wolsey 'a cardinal sole' as Henry had desired. Instead he had to wait for his hat until the next batch of cardinals were nominated.

Certainly the dispensation for non-residence was needed, since Wolsey spent less than five months out of more than 16 years as primate within the boundaries of his diocese, and never actually visited York. His archiepiscopal functions were all performed through deputies. His position of dominance in England was quickly recognised on the continent, and everywhere he went he was received with all the splendour usually only accorded to royalty. His love of magnificence became a byword; and indeed it was only towards the end of his life, conscious that worldly power was slipping from him, that he began seriously to think of his spiritual welfare, donning a hair shirt and attending regularly to his religious duties.

His chief residences were York Place and Hampton Court. The former he had inherited, but acquired the latter on a long lease in 1514 from the prior of St. John of Jerusalem, and enlarged it into a magnificent palace containing 280 rooms, manned by a staff of 500 servants. He also possessed two country residences, The Moor and Tyttenhanger; and had the use of suites of rooms in all the royal palaces. In 1525 he handed over the lease of Hampton Court to Henry VIII, but continued to live there. As cardinal, *legate-à-latere* and Lord Chancellor he completely dwarfed Warham, the then archbishop of Canterbury, even to the extent of overruling the decisions of the ecclesiastical courts in the southern province, and taking precedence over his fellow metropolitan by presiding in Convocation. Taking advantage of his position he engrossed an enormous number of ecclesiastical preferments, including several bishoprics and abbotships both at home and abroad; and was even able to bestow others on his illegitimate son, Thomas Winter, for whom he obtained a dispensation from the pope to hold them, despite his birth and being under the canonical age, *in absentia*. Winter actually lived in Paris on the proceeds; but, after his father's fall from grace, was compelled to relinquish them all.

As a builder Wolsey outshone his predecessors, although none of his work was to be found in the York diocese. For apart from turning Hampton Court into a magnificent palace, he built another at York Place, founded Christ Church, Oxford, originally known as Cardinal College, and began another at his native Ipswich. Christ Church continued to rise after his fall; but all work at Ipswich immediately ceased. Probably Wolsey's most important contribution to the future course of the Church of England, far more so than his fervent yet largely futile persecution of heretics, was his systematic suppression of a number of monasteries, providing a precedent that the king, in alliance with the cardinal's erstwhile collaborator, Thomas Cromwell, eagerly copied. Monasteries had occasionally, but very spasmodically, been suppressed in the past, when usually the confiscated property had been used for religious, educational or charitable purposes. Under Wolsey this process took a very much more sinister shape; for as soon as he became papal legate he procured a bull from the pope authorising him to reform the monasteries; and in 1524 he secured yet another bull which entitled him to suppress at least 21 religious houses, whose revenues might then be used for erecting his colleges at Oxford and Ipswich.

Actually Wolsey made no attempt to reform these monasteries, some of which were quite large, and with little in their histories either moral or financial to warrant their destruction, but simply dissolved them out of hand because he needed their money. In order to carry out his purpose Wolsey adopted methods, later copied by Henry, of first denigrating his victims as corrupt and decayed, and then instituting a so-called enquiry that inevitably recommended dissolution. Prior to his fall he had composed a further list, which in the event he was unable to implement.

Wolsey's disgrace appeared as sudden and dramatic as his rise to power had been. In June 1529 the archbishop was sitting in state with Campeggio, the papal legate, in his legatine court, judging between the king and queen, and to all outward appearance still the ruler of England. But the following October he was charged with treason, pleaded guilty, and on conviction deprived of all his property, which was forfeited to the crown. Then, in November, when parliament met, a bill of attainder was passed against him; and, in view of the length of the charges, the Commons urged Henry to make an example of the cardinal. Wolsey, aware of his danger did his utmost to negotiate the best possible terms for himself by distributing bribes in all directions. He was kept in suspense during the winter of 1529/30; but in the end the sentence was not unfavourable: he received back all his archiepiscopal estates, apart from York Place, and the financial arrangements were not ungenerous; while he was allowed to take up residence in Richmond Palace.

But his enemies, especially the Duke of Norfolk and Anne Boleyn, would not leave him in peace. He was ordered to go to York to carry out his duties as archbishop, Henry allowing him 2,000 marks out of the cardinal's Winchester bishopric's revenues to cover the cost of his journey. Accordingly Wolsey set out on 5 April, 1530, escorted by a large retinue, and followed by 12 carts of luggage. During this leisurely journey he was treated with the greatest respect wherever he stayed, arriving eventually at Southwell. Here he lived in grand style in one of the canon's houses, whilst he set about turning the dilapidated manor house into a magnificent palace. Then in October he moved to Cawood, planning to enter York in state for his enthronement; but 48 hours before he was due to leave, the Earl of Northumberland arrived and Wolsey was put under arrest. They set off for London; but at Sheffield Park, the home of the Earl of Salisbury, the archbishop was handed over to Sir Anthony Kingston, Constable of the Tower. Here he began to develop alarming symptoms of diarrhoea and vomiting; and by the time they reached Leicester Abbey on 25 November Wolsey was dying. He said to the abbot on arrival: 'I am come hither to leave my bones among you'.

The charge against him was that of treason, plotting with France; and although he was told Henry still favoured him, the archbishop knew well that he would not long survive once he had reached London. So it is possible that he committed suicide by taking poison, or even that the king, wishing to avoid any damaging revelations emerging from his trial, had him assassinated. But all the indications are that he died a natural death on 29 November 1530, after receiving extreme unction from the abbot. Some of his last words to Kingston show how clearly he realised his position:

> I see the matter against me how it is framed. But if I had served God as diligently as I have done the king, He would not have given me over in my grey hairs. Howbeit this is the just reward that I must receive for my worldly diligence and pains that I have had to do him service only to satisfy his vain pleasures, not regarding my godly duty.

He was buried the same day with full honours in the abbey.

In concluding this chapter it is of interest to note that throughout this period, and long before the Reformation, the claims of the papacy to nominate the bishoprics had become little more than a formality in England. The power of the crown over such appointments was absolute; and should the pope attempt to exercise his right of provision without the royal sanction he quickly met with a rebuff. Bishops, for example, were granted the enjoyment of their temporalities even before the papal bull formally restoring them had been issued. Such was the case at York after the appointment of George Neville, Lawrence Booth, Thomas Rotherham and Thomas Wolsey.

The Arms of Archbishops Neville, Booth, Rotherham and Wolsey. See also page 187

CHAPTER V

The Archbishops of York in an Age of Reformation

Thomas Gascoigne wrote in the middle of the fifteenth century:

> There are three things today that make a man a bishop in England, the will of the king, the will of the pope or the court of Rome, or the money paid in large quantities to that court.

As we have seen, however, the papal influence had declined as the century went on; and, of course, after the break with Rome, ceased altogether, leaving the monarchy all-powerful. For in an age of change and turmoil in religious affairs, it was essential that men should be promoted to bishoprics who could be relied upon to carry out the royal policy whatever that happened to be at the moment. Consequently the monarch's choice must not be gainsaid, and so the election of prelates by their respective chapters became even more of a formality than it had been in the fifteenth and early sixteenth century. It is indeed of interest to note that, when in the reigns of Edward VI and Elizabeth I some archbishops of York were pronounced puritans, their calvinist theology was always expected to be conformist, and they even became persecutors of protestant extremists.

Wolsey's successor, **Edward Lee**, had long been a favourite of Henry VIII. A native of Kent and a graduate of both Oxford and Cambridge, he sprang into prominence over a bitter controversy with Erasmus, in which he was supported by the king, who then sent him abroad on a number of diplomatic missions where his oratory helped to promote the royal policies. Loaded with ecclesiastical preferments, and awarded an Oxford doctorate of divinity he then began to make himself very useful in the matter of the king's divorce, particularly by using his eloquence to try and persuade Queen Catherine of Aragon to forego her rights, withdraw her cause from Rome and submit to the decision of the bishops and doctors. In September 1531 Henry asked the pope to provide Lee with the archbishopric of York; and Clement, anxious no doubt to appease Henry, readily agreed and issued the necessary bull on 30 October. Lee was accordingly consecrated on 10 December and enthroned in York Minster by deputy seven days later.

Apart from Nicholas Heath in the Reign of Mary I, he was the last archbishop to be provided by the papacy. His heavy expenses in connection with the sudden elevation to the archbishopric, especially the large sums of money payable to the Roman court, coupled with the disastrous state into which the archiepiscopal properties had declined since the death of the disgraced Wolsey, made Lee all the more determined to keep on good terms with the king and his chief minister, Thomas Cromwell. But there were problems, since Henry and Cromwell were now pursuing religious policies of which the archbishop could not approve. This led to some curious vacillations: in 1533 he offered to sign the declaration that Queen Catherine's marriage had been void from the beginning; but then was induced to persuade the York convocation to oppose the divorce. He disapproved personally of the Act of succession, yet went out of his way to try and convince Houghton, the prior of the London Charter House, and Bishop Fisher of Rochester that this was a matter not worth dying for. He disliked the royal supremacy, but informed Henry that the pope had no greater power in England than any other foreign bishop, promising to obey him instead. Yet he refused to publish the new title in the Minster or to command his clergy to do likewise in their parishes. For this he was sharply rebuked, and instantly recanted, himself preaching in the cathedral on the injuries the pope had done to the king. Then, urged by Archbishop Cranmer, he told his clergy to do the same, rejecting the papal supremacy and putting that of the crown in its place; whilst at the same time they were to defend Henry's divorce and remarriage. He was opposed to the dissolution of the monasteries and argued in Convocation for the retention of catholic customs. When the Pilgrimage of Grace got under way he at first supported and then condemned it! All this shilly-shallying rendered him suspect at court; and one of Cromwell's commissioners sent to enquire into the monasteries, Robert Layton, then dean of York, subjected the archbishop to a lengthy interrogation on the subject of the royal supremacy.

But Lee, like bishops Gardiner and Tunstall, retained no real affection for the papacy; and since, as long as Henry lived, there was no substantial change either in doctrine or church order, he was content to submit and do as he was told. Cromwell remained Lee's firm friend, and the king enjoyed his sermons.

In May 1538 he helped to draw up the bill for the famous Six Articles, and defended it in parliament; and a year later he served on a commission dealing with the doctrines and ceremonies that were to be retained by the church. In his visitation of York Minster in 1534 he ordered the canons to reside, admonished them for allowing immoral women into the close, and for not making bequests, as the statutes decreed, to the Minster at death. He also told them to provide pensions for the vicars serving their cures.

He was reluctant, however, to carry out the drastic reforms that Cranmer was demanding from all cathedrals, but had to toe the line. In

1530 there had been some 36 York prebends, but by 1550 six of them had been abolished, and much of the wealth confiscated from the remainder; the treasurership disappeared and the cathedral statutes were revised. Then in 1541, under pressure from Dean Layton, and prompted by the privy council, Lee agreed that the monuments associated with papacy should be destroyed, including the shrine of St. William. The clergy were again ordered publicly to deny the authority of the papacy and to proclaim that the king was the head of the Church. But generally speaking, catholic worship and doctrine survived, although the worship was now in English and the bible could be read in that language.

Under royal pressure Lee began to alienate some archiepiscopal estates to the crown, a practice that his successor, Robert Holgate, continued. In 1542 he handed over the manors of Beverley and Southwell, together with other lesser properties, in exchange for some forfeited monastic lands, of little value; and this systematic robbery of the archbishopric was to continue.

Lollardy had not been unknown in the York diocese during the primateships of Bainbridge and Wolsey; and Lee now became their active persecutor. Thomas Fuller accuses him of excessive cruelty towards Valentine Freez and his wife, who were burned at York in 1540; and he was known as a strong opponent of the New Learning, who had composed a number of books against Erasmus. But he was also remembered as a holy man, frugal in his habits and of considerable learning, the supposed author of the translations of the lives of the saints. He was the last archbishop of York to coin his own money. Lee died on 13 September 1544, aged 62 years, and lies buried in the Minster.

He was followed by a much more full-blooded protestant: **Robert Holgate**, a Yorkshireman from Hemsworth, who had a long and distinguished Cambridge career at the Gilbertine House of Studies near Peterhouse. Here he met some leading protestants of the day like Cranmer, Latimer, Ridley, Salcot, Hilsey, Hooper and Holbeach, who were to prove useful friends in the future. In 1529 Holgate became prior of St. Catharine's without Lincoln, when he had a lawsuit filed against him by Sir Francis Ayscough, which brought him to London and to the notice of the king. Later, as President of the North, Holgate helped Ayscough win another lawsuit, saying: 'that he was more obliged to Sir Francis than to any other man in England; for if it had not been for his pushing him to London, he had lived a poor priest all his life'. Consequently he received in quick succession the Mastership of St. Gilbert's, Sempringham, the priory of Watton in East Yorkshire, and finally the bishopric of Llandaff in 1537, through the good offices of Thomas Cromwell, to whom his old Cambridge friend, John Hilsey, now bishop of Rochester had introduced him.

At the outset of the Pilgrimage of Grace Holgate wisely withdrew from Watton; but there is no truth in the story that he decamped with the priory funds. His enemies certainly accused him of being Cromwell's creature, who had acquiesced all too readily in the dissolution of the monasteries, surrendering Watton in return for an enormous pension, together with most of its lands and the benefices in its patronage. Through Cromwell he now became a member of the Council of the North, set up by Henry VIII in the aftermath of the Pilgrimage in order to strengthen and re-organise the royal government in that region. Bishop Tunstall, another Cambridge friend, was its president, and he soon found Holgate's help invaluable. 'Surely', Tunstall wrote to Cromwell, 'he is a man very meet to serve the king in these parts'. By 1538 Holgate was himself President, an office he held for 11 years, with his headquarters at the King's Manor in York. Despite Cromwell's fall, he continued to enjoy the king's favour, who needed him. The north, traditionally conservative and restless, where feudalism was strong, communications poor, poverty rife and government hitherto weak, craved for a man like Holgate to bring back law, order and justice. And here, undoubtedly, he was a great success, reducing the province to conformity, taking over the estates of the Nevilles and Percies as crown lands, and replacing their feudal councils by that of an all-embracing Council of the North.

His services did not go unrewarded, for, on the death of Lee, Henry nominated him to the vacant archbishopric in January 1545. At his confirmation Holgate took the oaths renouncing the papacy and accepting the royal supremacy, receiving his pallium from Archbishop Cranmer at a special service held in Lambeth Chapel. Now, indeed, both as President of the North and archbishop of York he wielded supreme power north of the Trent. His principal tasks entailed repressing papalism and conspiracy, keeping the Scots at bay, and dispensing impartial justice. At the end of his term of office he boasted that no man could complain 'for lack of justice'. During his presidency he suppressed two rebellions, the Wakefield conspiracy of 1542, and the Seamer rebellion of 1549; organised campaigns against the Scots; provided defences for the east coast; established a network of intelligence agents in Scotland; collected taxes; and, after the suppression of the chantries, sent their silver to London.

Such activities meant that Holgate was always on the move, riding from one archiepiscopal manor to another, at one moment finding himself on the Scottish borders, and the next galloping up to London, where he was always regular in attending the parliamentary sessions and important ceremonial occasions.

When the Admiral of France visited Henry in 1546, the archbishop assisted the young Prince Edward to receive the distinguished guest at Hampton Court, and boasted that he had brought with him from the north some 70 horsemen and spent the large sum of £1,000. From his own pocket he also laid out £4,000 on the Scots' wars, and much more on various obligations and charities connected with his office. For the Tudors believed in making their servants bear all the financial burdens of which they were capable.

Under Edward VI and Protector Somerset, Holgate continued to flourish; but with the rise of the Duke of Northumberland his star waned. 'He put me forth from the room of President' the archbishop complained, 'and could lay no offence to my charge'. But Dudley was determined to remove all Somerset's supporters, and the Earl of Shrewsbury took over the Presidency of the north in February 1550.

The fact that Holgate was the first bishop to accept the royal supremacy and renounce Rome, did not save him from having to surrender to the crown the remaining feudal jurisdictional franchises belonging to the see of York, together with some 30 manors, in return for a mere 33 impropriations and advowsons that had previously been the property of dissolved monasteries. This deal greatly impoverished the archbishopric of York, although Holgate himself remained a very wealthy man. Henry wanted money for his wars and was none too scrupulous as to how he obtained it. Neither were his son's advisers. The archbishop served on the Yorkshire chantries commission, but had no control over the lands and money seized; although he did manage to save the schools (one of which bears his name in York to this day). Neither he nor any of his clergy, moreover, were members of that other commission that confiscated 'surplus' church goods.

Holgate supported the Edwardian prayer book of 1552, and indeed helped Convocation to revise it; but in his attitude towards the communion service he took a conservative stand, telling Cranmer: 'the oblation and sacrifice of Christ at the mass, is the presenting of the very body and blood of Christ to the Heavenly Father, under the form of bread and wine, in remembrance of his passion,' to which he added: 'the Gospel should be taught at the time of the mass, and it were convenient to use such speech in the mass, as the people might well understand.' In the injunctions issued after his primary visitation of 1547, he roundly condemned the lack of a preaching ministry; condemned the York prebendaries for neglecting their parishes; and accused all the canons and dignitaries of non-attendance at the Minster services, or, even when they did so, of too much 'confabulation'. The cathedral, he declared, had decayed because of their neglect.

The royal visitation and Edward VI's Chantry Act wrought great changes in the Minster: two bibles were installed in the choir, and two others in the nave; the library was 'modernised' to contain the works of Erasmus, Calvin, Bullinger and other protestant reformers; the 'hours' were abandoned and only one communion celebrated a day; 50 chantries disappeared; and the clergy were ordered to abstain from hunting, hawking and other sports. The confiscation of plate and vestments, begun under Henry VIII, was intensified under his son, even those in the private possession of the prebendaries.

Holgate's second visitation of 1552 produced other drastic injunctions: the space over the high altar, where the tabernacles had stood, was now to be painted over with scriptural texts; a theological lecture established in the Minster was to be attended by all the cathedral clergy, to which they must give 'a diligent ear', and upon which they would be examined. The vicars-choral under 40 years of age must learn by heart a chapter from St. Paul's Epistles in Latin, the older men reading and memorising its main points; while the choir boys were expected to learn a chapter of St. Matthew's Gospel. To make sure that such orders were obeyed they were all examined: the vicars-choral by Holgate himself, and the boys by their master. Each vicar was expected to possess a bible and read a chapter after dinner and supper, and any deacons who refused to study would be expelled. As regards the prebendaries they must 'prepare themselves effectuously' for communion, preach in the Minster on at least one Sunday in the year and use the 1552 prayer book only. No music was to be allowed except plainsong; organ playing was strictly prohibited; and the vicars-choral must sing the services 'distinctly'. The underlying plan behind these injunctions being 'so that which shall be sung or read may be well heard and understood of the lay and ignorant people'. No cleric should shave his crown, and both dignitaries and prebendaries must subscribe to the 42 articles of religion.

Holgate founded three schools: at York, Hemsworth and Old Maldon. These were secondary schools, a nursery for the New Learning; and the Masters were to have 'an understanding of the Hebrew, Greek and Latin tongues'. The schools were free, being financed from the archbishop's own lands, but no boy would be accepted who could not already read, and all the pupils must attend the Sunday services either at the Minster or in their local churches. The York school, however, was not simply for boys, since newly ordained deacons were expected to attend it regularly. But apart from these three schools, Holgate founded at least two others in the diocese, at East Retford and Sedbergh, and helped to refound yet another at Pocklington. He is also reputed to have been a generous benefactor to Kirby Ravensworth School and Hospital. In such educational ventures he was assisted by St. John's College, Cambridge.

To complete this section we should record that he was a liberal contributor to both universities, and likewise to the Minster fabric fund. In the latter connection he was especially concerned with excluding the pigeons who were fouling its interior. But his main task was to 'turn the Minster into an institution for the education of young men for the Protestant ministry'; and in this he was largely successful. Holgate's register is very scrappy; but it shows that he made much use of suffragan bishops, vicar-generals, official principals, notaries and apparitors for the routine business of the see. However, judging from what is written into it by the notaries, the archbishop made sure that such matters as ordinations, confirmations, institutions, the holding of church courts, the proving of wills, and the imposing of penances, were all carefully carried out.

After the downfall of the Duke of Somerset, Dudley not only had

Holgate ejected from the Presidency of the North, but attempted 'in a greate rage' to force him into surrendering his Watton lands in exchange for a see farm. The archbishop stood firm, and, after some tough negotiations, he agreed to a compromise whereby he leased the Watton lands to the crown, receiving instead the manor of Scrooby, a Nottinghamshire residence, and a large group of advowsons previously taken from the archbishopric.

On Edward VI's unexpected death, and the failure of Lady Jane Grey to usurp the throne, Holgate was committed to the Tower on 4 October 1553 by Queen Mary, 'upon the pretence of Treason or great crimes'; and all his wealth was seized, including his houses at Cawood, Battersea and elsewhere. On the 16 March 1554 he was deprived of the archbishopric, along with three other bishops, also ex-religious, for being married. One of his judges happened to be his old friend, Bishop Tunstall, but that did not save him. They were all deprived for 'their grave and enormous crimes and sins, especially marriage, after express profession of chastity'.

Holgate's marriage had been unfortunate in more ways than one. He had married Barbara, the daughter of Roger Wentworth Esq., of Hamswaite near Aswick-le-Street, at Bishopthorpe on 15 January 1549/50, although it was alleged that they had been secretly married before; and, moreover, that Barbara was already wedded to a certain Anthony Norman, a gentleman of Arksey. This former marriage, had taken place when the bride was five and the bridegroom seven years old, and they lived together in her father's house. But at the age of 12 Barbara brought a suit of nullity against Anthony on the grounds that the marriage had never been consummated and 'she could not find it in her heart to love him'. She was examined by her relatives and found to be a virgin; whilst, according to canon law, infant marriages were regarded as null unless the participants gave their consent at the age of discretion, 12 for a girl and 14 for a boy. Anthony vainly tried to prove that they had lived together, but the case went against him; and Holgate's marriage was pronounced valid. However, two years later Anthony re-opened the case before the Privy Council, not desiring Barbara back, but hoping for substantial damages from the rich Holgate. Again he lost; but in the conservative north the archbishop's marriage continued to be regarded as a scandal; and Holgate found himself compelled to deprive a young deacon, John Houseman, of his stipend for heading an anti-clerical marriage party in the diocese. Now in prison Holgate wrote a dignified Apology to Queen Mary, in which, whilst admitting that his marriage was wrong, and possibly a divine judgment because of his original oath of chastity, sought to excuse it on the grounds that it had been forced upon him by the Duke of Somerset:

> . . . that he being of the aige of three score and eight years married a gentlewoman called Barbara Wentworth by the councell of Edwarde then Duke of Somersett and for feare of the laite Duke of Northumberland using to call him papaste, and he thought

veryelye then that he myght have done soo by Godes Lawes and the Kinges.

This may well have been true, since Northumberland resented Holgate's comparatively moderate protestantism and his toleration of Roman Catholics. In the event Barbara was now restored to Anthony Norman, and Houseman, who had petitioned the Marian Government for damages against Holgate for persecuting him for his views, received compensation.

In addition to this repudiation of his marriage, the Apology also contained a promise to obey the queen's laws, and pointed out that his supposed offences were slight in comparison with those of the other imprisoned bishops, 'they being much further gone amiss in religion than he was, and with obstinacie.' But the main object of the Apology was to recover his properties and thus both save his schools and be in a position to found a hospital at his native Hemsworth. Finally, as a bribe, he offered the queen £1,000. Whether it was the money or his eloquent appeal that turned the scale, Holgate did secure his release, together with some other prisoners, on 18 January 1555, when 'there was a great shottying of guns'. He was bound over by the Privy Council for 2,000 marks, 'to good abearing, ordre and fyne at pleasure'. Moreover he got his estates back; and in April 1555, whilst living at the Master of Sempringham's 'headhouse', Cow Lane, in the parish of St. Sepulchre's, London, he drew up the deeds for the hospital at Hemsworth for 20 men and women over 60, especially those who were either blind or lame, to be financed out of his properties. The Master was to be a priest and the Earl of Arundel was appointed to supervise the work. His wishes were faithfully honoured and the hospital still exists.

He died on 15 November 1555 and was buried in St. Sepulchre's 'without worldlie pompe, pride or vanitie'. He left nothing in his Will to either his wife or the two children she had borne him. Holgate was never a great churchman, but had a zeal for learning, charity and justice; and, whilst lacking any firmly rooted principles or deep spiritual convictions, yet displayed great abilities and industry as an administrator.

Queen Mary's archbishop of York, **Nicholas Heath**, was born at Apsley near Tamworth, and educated at both universities, obtaining the Cambridge D.D. Whilst archdeacon of Stafford he had taken part in Henry VIII's negotiations with the German princes of the Smalcaldic League, and here he met and was greatly influenced by Philip Melanchon. On his return to England, he became first bishop of Rochester, and then in December 1543 succeeded Hugh Latimer as bishop of Worcester. During Edward VI's reign, whilst appearing to conform to the new Protestantism, he kept a low profile; but secretly corresponded with the exiled Reginald Pole and Princess Mary, devising schemes for re-unification with the papacy. He was honest enough to refuse to sign a new form of ordination, which he and the other bishops had been bidden to draw up, but compromised his stand by saying it was 'good and godly', and promising to use it himself. This did not satisfy the king and his council, who suspected his catholicism; and, when he went further and declared that he would never agree to the taking down of the altars and replacing them with tables in the churches, he was deprived of his bishopric and committed to the Tower. Then, when released, he was put into the custody of Nicholas Ridley, bishop of London, a man whom Heath greatly admired as 'the best learned of the party'. But the advent of Queen Mary quickly brought him back to favour, and he was restored to Worcester in place of the deprived Hooper.

When Holgate's expulsion from the archbishopric followed soon after, a *conge d'elire* was issued to the York chapter for electing Heath, which took place on 19 February 1555, being immediately confirmed by Pope Paul IV, who granted him the pallium during October. Heath was to prove, like his fifteenth century predecessors, very much of an absentee archbishop, since he also held the offices of President of Wales and Lord Chancellor, which necessarily took up most of his time. Yet in one respect at least the see is greatly indebted to him; for the manors that Holgate had alienated to the crown, were, at Heath's request, restored with Mary's blessing, including Ripon and seven others in Yorkshire, the one at Southwell, and five more in Nottinghamshire. Indeed it can be said that the archbishopric owes a third of its possessions to this archbishop.

He was also responsible for using the money from the sale of Suffolk Place, London, which was a gift from the queen, for building a new York House in the Strand. At the Minster seven prebendaries were dismissed on account of their marriages, and three vicars-choral lost their posts for the same reason; although one of these last regained his place after doing a penance. Catholic services and ceremonies were swiftly restored, with scarcely any opposition from the remaining prebendaries and vicars; whilst the citizens of York apparently welcomed their return. Slowly the cathedral rebuilt its stock of vestments, ornaments and plate. Nicholas Wotton, who had succeeded Layton as dean, calmly accepted the catholic reaction, as indeed he was later to do that of the Elizabethan Settlement; so in neither case was he disturbed. However, it should be noted that these catholic services were largely conducted by deputies, since neither the dean nor most of the prebendaries remained in residence, allowing their houses to fall into decay and the pigeons once again to foul the Minster.

Heath's most important act in Yorkshire was to refound the cathedral school with the express purpose of propagating catholicism and fighting protestantism. It consisted of some 50 pupils housed in the old Horsefair Hospital. This school was to survive, but in the next reign under a protestant regime.

Heath was still Lord Chancellor when Mary died, and he immediately did Elizabeth a service she never forgot by proclaiming her succession at once in the House of Lords. He told the peers: 'It would have been a much more sorrowful loss to them, if there had not been a successor that was the next and undisputed heir to the crown, of whose right and title none could question.' He continued in office for a while; and, in a disputation between catholic and protestant divines at Westminster, actually rebuked his own side for their 'disorderly conduct'. None the less when the bill came before the Lords to establish the queen's supremacy over the Church, Heath made a long speech against it; and later, summoned before Elizabeth herself to take the oath in accordance with the supremacy act, he declared that such an oath was against the word of God, and begged the queen not only to repudiate the supremacy but to keep her sister's covenant with Rome and suppress heresy. Consequently with other bishops he was deprived and committed to the Tower, where he was well treated, quickly released, and allowed to retire to his estate at Cobham in Surrey, after promising 'not to interrupt the laws of the Church and State or to meddle with the affairs of the realm'. Here Elizabeth paid him a visit, was royally received, and they parted on the best of terms. For the queen was not only grateful to him for his swift proclamation of her succession, but hoped that his attitude as a leading Marian prelate would influence other Romanists towards her.

He died in his late 70s and was buried under a plain black stone in Cobham church. The disposition of his property, as laid down in his Will, was scrupulously respected.

Actually the Marian reaction in the diocese of York had had little impact. Some married clergy were disciplined and there was a certain reshuffle of livings and other clerical offices, but most clerics were prepared to conform at least outwardly in the belief that at a time of rapid change the important thing was to cling to their clerical way of life to which they were accustomed, whatever the official forms might take. The north had always been conservative, but the Reformation had brought to that region tranquillity and justice under such able administrators as Holgate, Gargrave and Rokeby, whilst the gentry and middle classes were determined to retain the possessions they had acquired after the dissolution of the monasteries. So its loyalty to the Marian Government largely depended upon its acquiescence in the status quo. They were not pro-protestant, but afraid to see the precarious newly found social stability upset. Consequently the church courts moved very cautiously, and little was done either to restore church lands, or, apart from the marriage question, to persecute the clergy simply because they had been ordained under the Edwardian ordinal, or even for heresy. Heath himself was mild and tolerant, the Earl of Shrewsbury, Mary's adviser on northern affairs, showed himself reluctant to press matters too far, and the protestants themselves were unheroic and submissive, giving little trouble. Consequently the Marian reaction, lacking a positive religious policy, failing to enter the mission field, deficient in great teachers or divines, and centring round a catholic queen and extremists like Cardinal Pole and Bishop Bonner of London, never really got off the ground in the north, its most fertile field for re-Romanisation; and thus killed once and for all the chance of England accepting the Counter Reformation.

With the advent of Elizabeth the York prebendaries had now to make up their minds whether or not they would accept the royal supremacy. Nicholas Wotton, the dean, and Ralph Rokeby, the precentor, promptly did so, and were followed by a number of others; but Robert Pursglove, the suffragan bishop, Geoffrey Davies, the chancellor and about half the chapter refused to comply and were deprived, 'a displacement of canons such as the chapter had never experienced before'.

Owing to the death of her first candidate for the vacant archbishopric Elizabeth did not appoint a new primate until the beginning of 1561, when her choice fell upon **Thomas Young**. In the meanwhile the still conservative Ralph Rokeby carried on the administration, and made few changes. Young, a Welshman and an Oxford graduate, had been accused in 1547, when precentor of St. David's Cathedral, of robbing the cathedral's plate; but this turned out to be no more than an excess of protestant zeal. During Mary's reign he 'lived in obscurity' abroad; but on his return to England was appointed by Elizabeth to the see of St. David's in place of the deprived Bishop Morgan Phillips in 1560. A friend of the new archbishop of Canterbury, Matthew Parker, he was recommended barely a year later for the archbishopric of York, being translated to that see by the end of February 1561. His primary task, of course, was to seek to pacify the north and bring that very conservative region back into the fold of the Reformation Church; and so, for that purpose, he was also created President of the Council of the North. But he soon found that like Agag he must tread very delicately indeed. Wotton, Rokeby and other surviving canons from the Marian era were bitterly opposed to any drastic changes; and so, until they left or died, progress was necessarily slow.

However, progress there was; and when in 1561 Richard Barnes replaced Downes as chancellor, and six years later Matthew Hutton became dean, reforms were accelerated. Young ruthlessly removed clergymen who refused to toe the line; and in 1566/7 brought pressure to bear on others, including the dean and canons of Durham, to compel them to wear the surplice, cope and other clerical apparel ordered by the advertisements of 1564. For the archbishop, a conforming calvinist, could be as severe on extreme puritans as on devout Roman catholics, his job being to uphold the Elizabethan Settlement.

Undeterred by Holgate's disastrous marriage Young had two wives. His second, Jane, bore him a son, the later Sir George Young. This reappearance of wives, not only those of the archbishop but of some of the prebendaries as well, aroused considerable hostility in the conservative city of York. So much so indeed that Alderman Allen interrupted

Prebendary Tunstall's sermon defending clerical marriage on the grounds that the apostles themselves were married, thereby causing a brawl in the Minster. For this Tunstall caused him to be summoned before the ecclesiastical court in York. However, hostility was tempered by curiosity when Young brought Jane, the daughter of Thomas Kynaston of Eastwick in Staffordshire, to York in 1561. Apparently she lived down all the opprobrium, surviving her husband for more than 40 years, and dying in 1614. The archbishop earned a reputation for 'a painful forwardness in setting forth the true religion'; and on 30 June 1563 was able to inform the queen that, 'touching ministers and administration of the sacraments they [the Yorkshire clergy] are now thoroughly agreed in these parts according to law'. But his zeal for reform sometimes outran his discretion, taking it upon himself even to rebuke Elizabeth herself and the archbishop of Canterbury. 'I thought well', he boasted on one occasion, 'to admonish and counsel the queen with regard to her method of life and conduct'. On yet another, we are told, Elizabeth and his old friend Parker were observed leaving his presence 'very crestfallen'.

This outspokeness did him no harm with the queen and archbishop, who asked him to help draw up the Articles of 1561; but Sir John Harrington accused him of staining 'the reputation of learning and religion'; whilst others condemned him for granting long leases on archiepiscopal estates to the crown, and pulling down part of York Palace for its lead. On the other hand he earned high praise for his thorough reformation of Manchester College. In 1566 a suffragan bishop of Nottingham was appointed to assist Young, who by then was very old and infirm. He died two years later at Sheffield and lies buried in the Minster where his monument still stands at the east end of the choir. He may well have been a notable reformer, but his other task of pacifying the north appears to have been less successful, judging from the formidable rising of the north a year after his death.

The savage repression of the rising of the north cowed that region into submission; and it was followed by the sending to York of two men of calvinistic views to seek to accomplish what Young had failed to do: the Earl of Huntingdon as President of the Council of the North, and **Edmund Grindal** as its new archbishop. Grindal, a farmer's son from Cumberland, a Cambridge graduate and its Lady Margaret preacher, became chaplain to Nicholas Ridley, bishop of London, but fled abroad during the Marian regime, when he resided at Strasburg. A noted protestant disputant, who helped to revise the Elizabethan Prayer Book, he was appointed, through the influence of Archbishop Parker, bishop of London in July 1559 in place of the deprived Bonner; but disappointed his patron by his weak vaccilating performance as diocesan of that important see. He had taken an active part in raising funds for the restoration of burnt St. Paul's and played an important part in helping to revise the Articles, for which he was rewarded by the Cambridge D.D.; but he came into conflict with queen and archbishop over the Act of Uniformity, being loath to order the clergy to wear surplices. Also, against the queen's wishes, he defiantly encouraged the puritanical 'exercises' or 'prophecyings'; so Parker made up his mind to get rid of him, declaring that he 'was not resolute and severe enough for the government of London'. However, the only way to get rid of him was to kick Grindal 'upstairs' into the vacant archbishopric of York, where, as a north countryman he might well be acceptable, and as a strong calvinist root out Romish superstitions to his heart's content. Consequently he was nominated and translated to the primacy in April 1570.

Immediately he adopted a firm anti-Roman policy, enforcing it both through the Council of the North and the Court of High Commission. His injunctions, after his primary visitation of 1571, ordered the archdeacons to compel churchwardens to remove all Romish ornaments and furnishings from the churches, and make sure that only the *Book of Common Prayer* was used in their worship. Grindal, reverting to Holgate's educational scheme, further appointed a reader of divinity to lecture twice a week at the Minster, when all the vicars-choral and other cathedral inferior clergy were commanded to attend. There was also to be a weekly sermon; communion should be celebrated there once a month to be attended by all the clergy including dignitaries and prebendaries, who must communicate; and the precentor was made responsible for the education of the choristers in true religion. He caused the Minster statutes to be revised along Protestant lines, made its chapter meetings more representative of the whole capitular body, and compelled the dean and chapter to take a more active part than of yore in the life of the diocese as a whole. But, as his predecessors had found before him, it was almost impossible to make much headway against chapter inertia. Outside in the diocese the archbishop appointed 40 preachers from the universities to educate the church congregations in the reformed faith; whilst at the same time seeking to raise the standards of the parochial clergy themselves, whom he found to be woefully ignorant. They were to be examined; and those who failed to reach a sufficiently high standard, must attend a course of instruction. Neither was he prepared to institute a cleric to a benefice, if, after examination, he found him wanting in learning; although in this respect the archbishop had sometimes to moderate his zeal when he discovered himself up against both powerful patrons and the secular courts. In his injunctions of 1571 the archbishop told his clergy:

> Ye shall daylie read at leaste one chapter of the oulde Testament and another of the New with good advisement, and such of you as be under the degree of maister of arts shall provide and have your owne, according to the queens majesties injunctions, at leaste the New Testament both in latin and Englishe, conferringe the one with the other everye day one chapter thereof at the leaste, so that upon examination by the Archdeacon commissary or their

officers in synods and visitations or any other appointed tymes it may appeare how ye proft in the studye of holeye scripture.

The injunctions of 1571 also forbade the ringing of bells for superstitious purposes, the holding of any prohibited fast or festival, the burning of candles at Candlemass, auricular confession, the worship of images, and many other popish practices. The clergy were to catechise 'every sunday and holyday', not merely the youth of the parish, but 'the servants both menkinde and womenkinde'. Parents and masters, who did not send their children or servants for such instruction, were to be denounced 'to the Ordinarye'. No priest was to communicate, marry or accept as godparents anyone who 'cannot saye by heart at leaste the ten commandments, the articles of the faithe and the Lordes Prayer in English', in addition to the Catechism itself.

Grindal's second visitation of the diocese in 1575 lasted from 27 April until 2 June; after which the apparitors summoned those people presented by their parishes into the correction court at the cathedral, where the sessions were held from 19 August until 18 January 1575/6. This visitation was even more thorough than its predecessor, and the presentments from 506 parishes covered a very wide field. The laity were presented usually for laxity in morals or non-attendance at church; but the clergy for a variety of misdemeanours and misbehaviour. Churchwardens were admonished for the neglect of the church fabric, overgrown churchyards and not providing such items as a prayer book, a register or Jewel's *Apology*. However, this visitation was often hampered in its effectiveness by the intervention of powerful lay impropriators, and consequently large numbers of offenders escaped correction. As in 1571 the archbishop made use of the visitation to examine the clergy in the scriptures and assess their preaching capacity, whilst also enquiring into the methods they employed in catechising, and whether the church registers were kept up to date. Both these visitations in fact were turned into powerful instruments for maintaining the momentum of the Reformation in the north.

As he had previously done in London the archbishop favoured the puritanical 'exercises', provided they were licensed and presided over by the archdeacon or his deputy; a policy that was eventually to lead to his suspension after his translation to Canterbury. This translation took place on 10 January 1576, when, following the death of Archbishop Parker in August 1575, Cecil, whose puritanical leanings corresponded to those of Grindal, persuaded the queen to appoint him Primate of All England.

Edwin Sandys, Grindal's successor in 1577, had imbibed his theology whilst in exile; and consequently became an even more pronounced calvinist than his two predecessors. A Lancashire man, who had been educated at Furness Abbey and then St. John's College, Cambridge, where he gained the M.A. and D.D. degrees, he went on to become Master of St. Catharine's Hall and Vice-Chancellor of that university.

111

A strong supporter of Lady Jane Grey, he was imprisoned by Mary, first in the Tower and then at the Marshalsea prison for about a year. After his release he fled abroad; and, on his return home, was nominated by Elizabeth in 1559 to the bishopric of Worcester. As one of the commissioners for the revision of the liturgy, he objected both to the use of vestments and the cross in baptism, but was overruled; and his pronounced calvinistic views aroused a good deal of hostility. Sir John Bourne was actually committed to the Marshalsea prison for declaring that the bishop was 'no gentleman'.

Meanwhile Sandys went from strength to strength, helping to translate the *Bishop's Bible*, and being created bishop of London in 1570. Here he not only persecuted Romanists, but encouraged the extreme puritans, in particular a certain Dering, reader at St. Paul's, for which he was publicly rebuked by the queen. Like Grindal he supported the puritanical 'prophesyings'; and in consequence for similar reasons was 'kicked upstairs' to York on 19 January 1577, where his strong protestantism might be more usefully employed in the still conservative north.

Here his aggressive methods very soon became evident: he refused to surrender Bishopthorpe to the then President of the Council of the North; embroiled himself with the new bishop of London, Aylmer, over the London revenues and dilapidations; and, during a vacancy at Durham, antagonised its clergy by his visitation, when he became involved in a dispute with the dean, William Whittingham, whom, the archbishop maintained, had never been properly ordained. Worst of all he created a dangerous enemy in the person of Sir Robert Stapleton, by refusing to grant him the leases of certain archiepiscopal lands on easy terms. So, when Sandys was at Doncaster in May 1581, Stapleton, with the connivance of the host, introduced the host's wife into the archbishop's bedroom, Then, the said husband, accompanied by Stapleton, burst into the room and Sandys found himself hopelessly compromised. As a result he was blackmailed into paying money to the husband and handing over the disputed leases to Stapleton, in return for their silence. But, when the blackmail was renewed, Sandys wisely went to the Royal Council with his story, who not merely exonerated him from guilt but severely punished his blackmailers.

Now, in order to restore his tarnished reputation, and safe-guard his authority, rather than from real conviction, the archbishop adopted the role of conformist-reformer, which immediately aroused the anger of the dean of York, Matthew Hutton, who himself favoured the more extreme wing of the puritan movement. His hostility flowered into prominence over Whittingham's trial before the High Commission, when he was accused of only possessing Genevan Orders. Whittingham claimed these orders were valid and was backed by Hutton, who said that they were at least better than papal ones, a shaft, of course, directed at Sandys. Battle was now joined, with the archbishop telling the dean that if he liked the Genevan orders so well, why did he not take them and repudiate his own. Whereupon the latter retorted that his orders were better than Sandys'. 'I will prove it', he said, 'for I was made a minister by the orders of the queen and the laws now established, and your grace a priest after the order of popery'. 'What', roared the archbishop, 'dost thou call me a papist. If I be a papist thou art a puritan'. Sandys then preferred a charge of 13 articles against the dean, who was forced to submit; although he fiercely denied everything except violent language.

Apart from this attack upon his orders the archbishop had been incensed by Hutton's openly expressed objections to his nepotism, filling every diocesan office at his disposal with relatives, regardless either of their age or fitness for the posts to which they were preferred. Another sign of Sandys' now conformist zeal was his patronage of Richard Hooker, who became tutor to his son, later Sir Edwin Sandys, and through the archbishop's interest secured the Mastership of the Temple. His *Laws of Ecclesiastical Polity* was loudly commended by Sandys.

However, it was not easy for the archbishop to walk a precarious tight-rope between his own convictions as a strong calvinist, and the need to act as a conformist prelate upholding the authority of the Elizabethan Settlement. He continued to support the puritan 'exercises', but kept them on a tight rein; and, like Grindal, instituted study groups for the less learned clergy. Non-conformists too, unless they made trouble, were left in peace; for as Archdeacon Lowth remarked: 'the Eye of the Bishop in detecting any irregularity may aptly be described as the Blind Eye'.

Extremists, however, had to be dealt with. These men Sandys described as:

> New orators . . . rising up from among us, foolish young men, who while they despise authority, and admit of no superior, are seeking the complete overthrow and rooting up of our whole ecclesiastical polity.

Such men included firebrands like John Wilson, Alexander Horrocks, vicar of Kildwick, and Robert More, rector of Guiseley, who were prosecuted before the High Commission, when both Wilson and Horrocks were imprisoned. But their real offence amounted to an infringement of the archbishop's authority, and insolence against his person rather than their calvinism. Meanwhile Sandys' crusade against catholicism proceeded unabated, in the course of which he demanded of the dean and chapter of York that they should provide him with the names of all those persons who to their knowledge still attended mass or favoured Rome in any way.

In his visitations the archbishop also continued to follow up the enquiries that Grindal had set on foot concerning papistical practices, ornaments and vestments throughout the diocese. However, he had enough time to spare from such arduous duties, to reject fiercely and successfully any further attempts to deprive the archbishopric of any more of its properties, and in particular the manor of Southwell a few miles west of Newark, which he had made his home for many years. He once commented: 'These be marvellous times. The patrimony of the Church is laid open as a prey unto all the world'. He died at Southwell on 10 July 1588 and is buried in its Minster. Although perhaps best remembered for the hot-tempered and vindictive way in which he pursued his quarrels, Sandys' achievements as scholar and educationalist should not be forgotten. He is credited with founding grammar schools at Hawkeshead and Highgate. Twice married, his second wife, Cicely Wilford, produced seven sons and two daughters of whom three of the sons were knighted and had distinguished careers.

The archiepiscopate of the next primate spanned less than six years. **John Piers**, born at South Hinksey near Oxford, a fellow and doctor of divinity of Magdalen College, was also rector of Quaintain, where he became notorious for tippling in the village alehouse. But, in later life, bitterly regretting his youthful follies, he adopted such a strict teetotalism, that he even refused to take a little wine on his deathbed. Esteemed by both Queen Elizabeth and Archbishop Parker he was swiftly promoted in quick succession to the bishoprics of Rochester and Salisbury, became the queen's almoner and was employed by her in various capacities: as her agent to try and persuade Grindal to resign the archbishopric of Canterbury; as one of her consultants concerning English intervention in the Netherlands; and as the preacher at the thanksgiving service after the defeat of the Armada. Failing to obtain the see of Durham, he was shortly afterwards compensated with the more important archbishopric of York, being nominated and translated there on 15 January 1589.

Piers' short reign as primate was marked by an increased effort to enforce uniformity. He visited the diocese twice, and, after the second visitation of 1594, boasted that he had only found two puritans. His injunctions of 1590 ordered that all non-conformists should be summoned before the archdeacon's court and told to conform; but failure to do so within a given time would mean very harsh penalties. No records remain to show whether or not such methods were successful, but Piers himself had no doubt that they were. He died at Bishopthorpe on 25 September 1594 aged 71, still a bachelor, and lies buried at the east end of the Minster. His funeral sermon, a long eulogy, was preached by his chaplain, John King. He was long remembered as a prelate of very high character, 'a primitive bishop, one of the most grave and reverend prelates of the age'. A scholar of considerable learning, he possessed all the christian virtues: modesty, generosity, kindliness, and, unlike his predecessor, a spirit of meekness and love.

Matthew Hutton, the next archbishop, was another Lancashire man, who had had a most distinguished Cambridge career, as Lady Margaret and Regius professor of divinity, Master of Pembroke Hall, and a doctor of divinity. In 1567 he was sent north as dean of York in order to dispute with the Roman catholics; but his strong arm calvinistic methods, as we have seen, brought him into violent conflict with Archbishop Sandys. However, these self-same principles made him in Archbishop Parker's eyes an unfit candidate for the see of London; but instead, through the influence of the puritanical Lord Burleigh, he was nominated first to the bishopric of Durham, and then, on Sandys death, translated to the archbishopric of York in February 1595. At the same time he was made President of the Council of the North, a post secured for him by his friend the Earl of Essex, but of which he was later deprived after the Earl's execution.

Once in office, however, the new archbishop became remarkably tolerant to Roman catholics as well as extreme puritans. He continued none the less to regard Genevan orders as valid, and generally accepted the Genevan type of religion, discontinuing Piers' persecution of the non-conformists. Then, in order to tighten up the discipline of the laity along protestant lines, the Court of Chancery was kept open throughout the year to receive presentments from churchwardens, a practice that was to cease on Hutton's death. It is typical of Hutton that one of his last acts was to write to Robert Cecil asking for the relaxation of prosecutions against the puritans. He died at Bishopthorpe on 16 January 1605/6, and lies buried in the south aisle of the Minster choir.

Besides being a very learned man, and despite all his strong calvinistic principles, the archbishop was also a very humane one. In 1594 his letter to Lord Burghley not only secured the release of Lady Margaret Neville, who had been implicated in the rebellion of her father, the Earl, but obtained her a pension for life. When Sir Robert Kerr, warden of the Scotch marches, was entrusted to his custody, he treated his prisoner with the utmost courtesy and consideration. An eloquent and fearless preacher, whilst at Cambridge he did not hesitate, when conducting theological disputations before the queen, to rebuke her for her lack of warmth in the protestant cause. Like his predecessor he married twice and had a large family. Two of his sons were knighted, and one of his descendants became both archbishop of York and Canterbury in the eighteenth century.

The archbishops in this age of Reformation were learned, and hard-working prelates, zealous for the reformed faith. But, although most of them accepted the calvinistic theology, they found themselves obliged to uphold an episcopal form of government by virtue of their office, the very type of government that the spiritual republics of Germany and Switzerland sought to destroy as the deadly enemy of their own systems of religion. Consequently, whilst striving to root out all forms of catholic dogma and Roman superstitions, they also, with the possible exception of Hutton, as conformist-calvinists, sought to suppress those non-conformist puritan agitators bitterly opposed to the Elizabethan Settlement. Edwin Sandys, for example, wrote in his Will: protesting against 'all such rude and indigested platforms, as have been more lately and boldly than learnedly or wisely preferred'; and in particular rejected the claims of 'those who would reduce the Church of England to the state of a small private church.'

Archbishop Thomas Wolsey (1514-1530)
Groat incorporating his initials 'T. W.' in the circle close to
the royal arms and with his cardinal's hat below.
See page 94.

Archbishop Edward Lee (1531-1544)
Half-groat incorporating his initials 'E. L.' in the circle
close to the royal arms. This was the last ecclesiastical coin
to be issued from the mint at York, before the right of coinage
was withdrawn when the monasteries were dissolved.
See pages 98-100.

CHAPTER VI

The Archbishops of York in an Age of Revolution

Toby Matthew, who was translated from the bishopric of Durham to succeed Hutton, owed the archbishopric to the favour of James I, being elected by the chapter on 20 July 1606. Born at Bristol in 1544, Matthew had a distinguished career at Oxford, as public orator, President of St. John's College, Dean of Christ Church and Vice-chancellor. A doctor of divinity and a fashionable preacher, the young cleric, seeking further advancement, complained in a sermon before Elizabeth that she had failed to promote those who most deserved it, which earned the retort: 'Well, whosoever have missed their rewards thou has not lost thy labour'. Nor had he, since in 1583 he became dean of Durham. But Matthew's sights were set on a bishopric, which he pursued tirelessly. In 1587, despite the weighty support of Francis Walsingham and the Earls of Huntingdon, Essex and Leicester, he failed to obtain Durham, which went to Matthew Hutton. Then, when London fell vacant in 1594, Fletcher was preferred, although Burghley had promised it to Matthew. But at last fortune smiled upon this ambitious cleric; for, on the death of John Piers, Hutton was elevated to York, and Matthew finally rewarded with Durham.

Here as the royal agent he was expected to track down recusants; but Matthew, although himself a strong protestant and one of the stoutest supporters of the Elizabethan Settlement, was never a persecutor, seeking always to persuade rather than to coerce, provided neither recusant nor extreme puritan seriously menaced that Settlement. Anxious to increase the pastoral efficiency of the clergy, he not only encouraged both the puritanical 'exercises' and more and better preaching (always under careful supervision), but himself set a notable example in the latter capacity. His sermons, witty and plain, carrying their considerable learning very lightly, were in great demand. His diary, which has survived, contains a record of all the sermons he preached over 40 years from his appointment as dean of Durham down to 1622. In all they number 1,992. Many of these were preached in country villages to thin congregations; and on one occasion at least he arrived at his destination to find an empty church, recording ruefully in the diary: 'neither priest nor people'. But apparently it was not his custom to wear a surplice should he find few people in church.

The episode of the empty church, which lay in the East Riding of Yorkshire, occurred after Matthew had become archbishop; and as primate he proved himself an indefatigable visitor, whatever the obstacles in his path. 'I came to Southwell', he once wrote in the diary, 'through high waters and foul roads', and elsewhere he refers to 'a sore blow on my head in the coach', 'sore vexed with the flux', 'an intolerable pain by a corn in thupper part of my middle toe of my left foot', and 'I began to have a pain in my ancles divers days, yet I preached as soon as I could'. In 1625 at the age of 81, according to the then vicar of Leeds, the archbishop 'still preached more sermons in a single year than all the popes in history, from the time of Gregory the Great'.

Matthew insisted on his Yorkshire clergy being resident, learned and able preachers. Nor did he hesitate to suspend or deprive defaulters. Besides his regular visitations, he confirmed personally at least 20 times during his primacy, when the average number was well over 1,000; and ordained at all the regular seasons. In fact he always did his very best to enforce the 1604 Canons. Certainly Matthew's interests lay much more with the diocese than the cathedral, where he interfered very little in the affairs of the Minster, simply re-issuing Sandys' Articles in a summarised form during his visitation of 1615.

In accordance with royal instructions he regularly sent up to London lists of Yorkshire recusants and details of their examinations; but usually only took action against activists, whether papists or puritan extremists such as the Brownists. Recusants who remained quiet were not molested, and conforming puritans were actually encouraged by their archbishop and rewarded. These views of Matthew found expression in a book written by his chaplain, the vicar of Halifax, entitled: *Antiquity Triumphing over Novelty*, which was published in 1619. This advanced the thesis that the Protestant Reformation was only opposed to Roman Catholic novelties, so episcopacy itself remained unaffected. Consequently conformist puritanism became solidly established in the north during Matthew's primacy of more than 20 years; something which the next archbishop, Richard Neile, found almost impossible to destroy.

The one exception to Matthew's tolerance was the Separatists, and his persecution of them was supported by the conformist puritans, since they were stealing their converts. For this purpose the archbishop made use of the High Commission, on the grounds that they were attacking what they called 'the lordly tiranus power of the prelates'. William Bradford, the historian of the Pilgrim Fathers, bitterly complained of this persecution; but, considering the age in which they lived, it is remarkable that the Separatists were allowed to remain active so long and to enjoy a relative immunity.

118

It is indeed worthy of note that whereas the Canons of 1604 required a subscription that the Book of Common Prayer 'contained nothing contrary to the word of God', under Matthew's rule so many clergymen, who conscientiously refused to conform wholly to this book, were permitted to remain in office. The archbishop, a favourite of James I, also played his part in politics. In 1609 he was one of the commissioners for 'examining and determining all controversies in the north'; was a leading figure at the Hampton Court Conference; and was appointed custodian of that highly important political figure, Lady Arabella Stuart, who escaped from his house in 1611. A regular attendant in parliament, until illness and old age prevented him from making the journey, he more than once incurred the wrath of his fellow peers by siding with the Commons against them. On one occasion indeed he was the only bishop to vote for a conference between the Lords and the puritanical Commons, which temporarily lost him the royal favour.

In 1624 he handed over York House to the king for the use of the Duke of Buckingham, in exchange for certain Yorkshire manors, a deal of considerable benefit to the archbishopric in the long run, although at the time it deprived Matthew of his London residence. He married Frances Barlow, the daughter of the Henrician bishop who had consecrated Archbishop Parker and so preserved the episcopal succession. All five of Barlow's daughters married bishops, so, as Frances had previously married Parker's son, her memorial in York Minster stated 'A Bishop was her father, an Archbishop her father-in-law, she had Four Bishops her brethren, and an Archbishop her husband'. Frances herself has been described as 'a prudent and prominent matron'; but she was something of a trial to her second husband, since she did not like the north, and, in the words of the diary: 'was that night crow that ever croaked in mine ear, "For God's sake get us gone hence. Why came we hither? Who but us would any longer tarry here" '. She outlived Matthew, dying in 1629 at the age of 78.

There were three sons of the marriage, the eldest being the brilliant and wayward Sir Tobie Matthew, who turned Roman Catholic and became a Jesuit. Frances also bore two daughters. Archbishop Matthew himself died on 23 March 1628, and lies buried on the south side of the presbytery in the Minster. He was a handsome, witty man of whom Fuller wrote, 'a cheerful spirit without any trespass on episcopal gravity'. His portrait hangs in the hall of Christ Church, Oxford. But it has to be recorded on the debit side that he was one of the best known examples in the Elizabethan Age as a practitioner of simony. For, after being appointed to the see of Durham with Burghley's help, he sent his patron £100 in gold, and other large rewards to Robert Cecil and their secretary, Michael Hicks. He is also known to have made use of church lands and money whilst at York to advance members of his family.

Except for a short visit to York for his enthronement in the summer of 1606, Matthew did not come north to reside in the diocese and hold his primary visitation until a year later. Meanwhile a rumour spread that he had died; and such rumours (encouraged, or so Fuller believed, by the archbishop himself, incredible as that may appear), continued to be resurrected from time to time. Indeed, so persistent was one report in 1616, that the archbishop of Spalato, who was always on the look out for a rich see, actually applied to the king for the archbishopric, which, we are told, 'caused considerable mirth at the expense of the avaricious archbishop'.

The two prelates that followed Matthew need not detain us long. **George Monteigne** previously dean of Westminster, and then successively bishop of Lincoln, London and Durham, was translated to the archbishopric of York on 5 June 1628. The tale is told that whilst Charles I was discussing with Monteigne possible names to succeed Matthew, the bishop, laying his hand on his breast, exclaimed: 'Hadst thou faith as a grain of mustard seed, thou wouldest say unto this mountain be thou cast into that see'. The king, relishing the witticism, immediately ordered the York chapter to elect him. But Monteigne did not long survive his elevation, being, as Fuller wrote, 'scarce warm in his church yet cold in his coffin'. For he died in London, aged 59 years, on the very day, 24 October 1628, when he was enthroned by proxy in the Minster. He lies buried in Cawood church, his native birthplace.

Monteigne had been a court prelate, and his successor, **Samuel Harsnett**, was of the same persuasion. A Colchester baker's son who had had a distinguished Cambridge career, Harsnett became a great favourite of James I, who appointed him in rapid succession to the sees of Chichester and Norwich, despite the fact that his extreme high church views almost verged on papacy. Then Charles I, who was much in sympathy with his strong 'laudianism', secured his election to York. At Norwich his enemies had accused him of excessive harshness in enforcing discipline, of 'setting up images in the church', and of 'using extortions many ways'. Now, as archbishop he set himself to coercing the puritans into submission. But under Matthew Protestantism had consolidated its grip on the north, and during Harsnett's short primacy of less than three years, it proved impossible to break it, try as he would. None the less he did his best. The Act Book of his primary visitation is lost, but evidently he laid great stress on greater reverence and more ceremonial in the churches, besides a much stricter application of the rule that parishoners must attend their own parish church and none other. His injunctions ordered that men should cease to wear hats in church, prohibited the practice of people walking and talking before and after the service there, and forbade the churches to be used for secular and social purposes.

A learned man himself, he founded a Latin and English school at Chigwell, whose statutes, which Harsnett drew up, were entitled: 'The

Principles of the Christian Religion, according to the order of the Book of Common Prayer'. He died at Moreton-in-the-Marsh on 25 May 1631 and is buried in Chigwell church. William Prynne, referring to his persecution of puritans, described him as 'a furious Hildebrand'. Prynne may well have had in mind Harsnett's famous work: *Considerations for the settling of church government*, which Laud pressed upon the king and the then archbishop of Canterbury, George Abbot. On the other hand the archbishop is also remembered as a man of 'great learning, strong parts and a stout spirit'. His library was left to the Colchester Corporation, and now resides in the castle.

During the often prolonged absences of these court-prelates, in Harsnett's case aggravated by chronic ill-health, the York diocese was effectively ruled by three men: the chancellor, William Eastdall, the vice-chairman of the High Commission, Phineas Hodson, and the archdeacon of York, Henry Wickham. The puritans, despite Harsnett, still held their ground, but there were strong indications that the Arminians* were preparing a counter-attack. For instance this triumvirate began to increase the efficiency both of the High Commission and the Chancery Court for disciplinary prosecutions; and the Council of the North, hitherto presided over by puritans, now came under the control of Thomas Wentworth, Charles I's advocate of the policy of 'thorough'.

Richard Neile, archbishop of York from 1632 to 1640, proceeded to take up the task that Harsnett had prematurely laid down. He, in alliance, with the triumvirate, was to prove the hammer of the puritans in the north during the next eight years. The son of a Westminster tallow chandler, he had been enabled to enter St. John's College, Cambridge, through the influence of Mildred, Lady Burleigh, but his university career was not a distinguished one, which meant that he began his working life as no more than an obscure incumbent and clerical schoolmaster. But he was fortunate enough to come to the notice of Richard Bancroft, archbishop of Canterbury, and through him to the king, whose chaplain and favourite he became. Henceforth Neile's rise was a rapid one from the deanery of Westminster to the bishoprics of Coventry and Lichfield, Lincoln and Durham. At Westminster William Laud became his chaplain and a fast friend; so much so indeed that Neile was prepared to sacrifice his rich see of Durham to George Monteigne in order to enable Laud to go to London. Neile himself received the less important bishopric of Winchester; but he did not have to stay there long, being translated to York on 28 February 1631. He had long shown himself to be an uncompromising Arminian and believer in the Divine Right of kings, who was prepared fiercely to defend the royal prerogative against the attacks of the House of Commons. Many complaints were made against him in parliament; and he became

* Adherents of the Dutch protestant Arminius, who attacked the views of Calvin especially on predestination. The so-called English Arminians, however, were anti-puritan high churchmen.

notorious not only as Laud's patron, but also of many other prominent Laudians, including Montagu, Cosin and Sibthorpe, whom he once defended against an onslaught in the Commons from young Oliver Cromwell.

He was more than suspected of popery; and on 13 June 1629 the Commons voted that 'Dr. Neile, bishop of Winchester, and Dr. Laud, bishop of Bath and Wells, be named as those near about the king who are suspected to be Arminians and they are justly suspected to be unsound in their opinions that way'. Among other things he was accused of telling his clergy that 'they must not preach against papists now as they had done formerly'. Neile replied to this canard by a savage persecution of recusants. However, he served regularly on the courts of High Commission and Star Chamber, and in 1612 was a party to the burning of the protestant, Edward Wightman.

Such was the man who now came to York to clean out the Augean stables, when in his 70th year. He summed up his position as 'a great adversary of the Puritan faction . . . which he held himself bound in conscience and duty to God, to King and the most happy Established Church to be'. But obviously at his age he needed some able and vigorous allies to carry out his policies, and he found them in William Eastdall, the Chancellor, and Edward Mottershed, the Advocate General of the North, responsible for prosecuting offenders in the High Commission Court. Neile's primary visitation, which also included the neighbouring diocese of Chester, was conducted by three commissioners. Eastdall, Wickham and Cosin. Its object was to uncover and prohibit all unlawful puritanical activities and enforce the 1604 Canons, through the Chancery Court. Matters specifically dealt with were: the re-edification and repair of parish churches, their adequate furnishing, strict conformity to the Prayer Book, the saying of the weekly services, and the replacement of the afternoon sermon by catechising. This last was aimed at the puritan clergy, who were ardent preachers. At the Minster the archbishop re-issued Matthew's Articles, and personally supervised its rebeautification and the introduction of the laudian services. But in the city itself he came up against the mayor and corporation for the holding of puritanical conventicles, where the Prayer Book was not in use. For these offences they were prosecuted in the archiepiscopal courts. Two of Neile's injunctions were especially obnoxious to the puritans, namely the order to read the *King's Book of Lawful Sports*, and the command to remove the communion table from the nave of the church and place it behind rails at the east end. These reforms, apparently, were so ruthlessly enforced that the next visitation in 1636 showed that very few churches, including the peculiars, had refused to conform.

Neile was always prepared to reason with his puritan clergy, but should they remain obstinate he had no scruple in either suspending or depriving them. Annually the archbishop submitted an official report to the king on the state of his diocese, and these usually contained the words *omnia bene*; but occasionally he would complain of clerics who were not conformable, or of 'too many' of them emigrating to New England. However, the overall picture he painted was one of complete calm, which Neile must have known to be palpably false, unless he was subconsciously deluding himself. For beneath the surface the see was boiling like a cauldron, ready to explode once the moment was ripe. The archbishop might be able to enforce outward conformity, but he was totally incapable of winning either the hearts or minds of the majority of the population. None the less he steadfastly and vigorously pursued his policies, both politically and ecclesiastically, right up to the moment of his death, which took place 'in the manor house belonging to the prebend of Stillington within the close of the church of York' on 31 October 1640. He was buried at the Minster in the chapel of All Saints, but has no monument.

In his Will he left his wife an annuity of £300, but apparently had so little confidence in her business ability that he appointed his son, Sir Paul Neile, as his sole executor. He mentions the sum of £2,000 which he had lent to the king, fearing it will never be repaid; and in the preamble he reaffirms his firm adherence to the 'Articles of the Religion and Faith of the Church of England'. Heylyn described the archbishop as 'a man who very well understood the condition of the Church of England, though otherwise not so eminent in all parts of learning as some other bishops of his time'. He also referred to Neile's 'uncourtly conversation'. Archbishop Laud, on the other hand, was profuse in his praise: 'a man well-known to be as true and as stout for the Church of England Established by law as any man that came to preferment in it'. Not unnaturally the puritans thought otherwise, calling him 'a great enemy to us'. Neile's portrait hangs in Bishopthorpe Palace.

John Williams, the next archbishop, was a very different type and held totally different views. A Welshman of great charm, eloquence and learning, he distinguished himself as a scholar and fellow of St. John's College, Cambridge, became James I's favourite ecclesiastic and was the last cleric to be appointed Lord Keeper of the Great Seal. The Duke of Buckingham, then a Marquis, procured him the deanery of Westminster, which he continued to hold despite every effort of Laud and Charles I to wrest it from him; whilst at the same time acquiring a mass of other ecclesiastical preferments, including the bishopric of Lincoln. The death of James I, and the hostility of Charles and the Duke of Buckingham, who had turned against him, prevented the dean from attending the coronation service; and his arch enemy, William Laud, eventually succeeded in bringing about Williams' downfall. He was accused of tolerating if not actually favouring the puritans, on whose behalf he had written the controversial pamphlet *The Holy Table, Name and Thing*; and in 1637 was committed to the Tower on a charge of treason. He could have bought his release should he have agreed to give up all his preferments and retire to an

Irish bishopric; but he consistently refused to do so. However, when the Long Parliament met Williams was released, and for a brief period became virtually the head of the government, advising the king to sign the Earl of Strafford's death warrant, presiding over the ecclesiastical committee set up to restore order in public worship, and seeking to placate the puritanical House of Commons by ordering the communion table at St. Margaret's, Westminster, to be moved into the nave.

But this flirtation with the Commons was soon over. He spoke against the bishops' exclusion bill in the House of Lords; and Charles, as a reward, translated him to the now vacant archbishopric of York on 4 December 1641. Williams' views expressed during the debate, however, so angered the London mob that he was violently assaulted on his way to the House of Lords some three weeks later. The very next day, 28 December, the London apprentices attacked the Abbey, which the archbishop, still as dean, vigorously defended. During the scuffle that ensued the leader of the attackers was killed; and when Williams, along with other 'too haste' bishops, complained to the Commons that they were now unable to attend parliament for fear of their lives, which, they declared, meant that no Act passed in their absence would be lawful, Pym used these excuses to move their impeachment for treason. Consequently Williams found himself once again in the Tower, where Laud was already incarcerated. The two primates did not meet, but exchanged affectionate greetings, and so the old enmity was healed in the face of their common affliction.

On 5 May 1642 Williams was released on bail, the condition being that 'he would not go to Yorkshire during the distractions there'; but the archbishop immediately jumped his bail and fled north to join the king in York, where he was duly enthroned in the Minster on 27 June. 'But', wrote Hacket, 'God prevented it that he could never settle his household in Yorkshire as he desired'. For, after Charles raised his standard at Nottingham on 22 August and Civil War had begun, the archbishop quickly became a fugitive. At first he fortified Cawood Castle; but, on hearing that the younger Hotham, son of the governor of Hull, was advancing upon him with the declared intention of putting him to death, Williams fled in October to his native Wales, where he took over the command of the royalists in the north of that palatinate, establishing his headquarters at Conway Castle. Here he encouraged the local nobility and gentry to deposit their valuables with him for safe-keeping; and having fortified the castle, devoted his energies to organising and training the northern militia. But he never engaged in any hostilities; and that part of the country remaining quiet, spent the years 1644 and 1645 at Oxford, where he consecrated his successor, Accepted Frewen, as bishop of Lichfield and Coventry in Magdalen College chapel. He also took the opportunity to warn the king against Oliver Cromwell, whom he described as having 'the properties of all evil beasts'. On returning to Wales, however, he found that Sir John Owen had taken over Conway

Castle along with all its contents; and, unable to obtain any redress from Charles, who had been defeated at the Battle of Nazeby in 1645, Williams came to terms with the local parliamentary leader, Mytton, and offered to help him take Conway Castle, on condition that the gentry got their goods back. He justified this action on the grounds that Charles had by then surrendered to the Scots and so further resistance was useless.

He himself retired to 'Gloddaeth' in the parish of Eglwys-Rhos, Carnarvonshire, where he had some property; and spent his last few years in comfort there, unmolested by the victors. He died, probably of pneumonia, on 25 March 1650, aged 68, and was buried 'where his house Pentrin stands' at Llandegai. Here a monument was erected to him. In his life-time he had become notorious for lavish hospitality and ostentatious display, reminiscent of some of his medieval predecessors; and his Will revealed the same characteristics. He founded fellowships and scholarships at St. John's College, Cambridge, besides leaving funds for the building of its library; whilst at Oxford he supplied Lincoln College with new panelling and glass for its windows; provided money for improving Buckden Palace; endowed the Jerusalem Chamber in Westminster Abbey; established charities in his old benefices of Honington and Walgrave; and others for the poor of his old see of Lincoln. There are seven portraits of this archbishop, the most famous being that by Van Dyck at Pengwern near Rhyl. He was something of a latitudinarian in his religious views, sympathising with the puritans, whilst also greatly admiring the Holy Household of the Ferrar family at Little Gidding, which he visited several times. No further archbishop of York was to be appointed until after the Restoration.

York surrendered after the Battle of Marston Moor in 1644; and the Yorkshire Committee of the Northern Association, together with the mayor and city corporation, took over the control of the Minster. Dean Scott was already imprisoned in London for debt; but Archdeacon Marsh now also suffered imprisonment. The Minster itself escaped both looters and iconoclasm, its fabric being kept in good repair by the city. However, the organ and the little altars were removed, and the great brass reading desk in the choir, along with the brass of Becket's shrine and the silver candlesticks were all sold, the proceeds being used for structural repairs. New seating was installed in the nave, and the whole of the cathedral became converted into a great preaching centre. The York corporation petitioned parliament for a grant of £600 a year out of the confiscated dean and chapter lands for this purpose, utilising the money to provide stipends of £150 per annum for four ministers, who would be based on the Minster but also serve the city as a whole. Some of the prebendaries and vicars-choral, like Phineas Hodson and Henry Mace, were given pensions, adapted themselves to the new situation and helped to lead the psalm-singing in the cathedral.

Certainly it appeared that the York citizens found the form of worship established between 1644 and 1660, very satisfactory, and more suited to their taste than anything they had experienced since the Reformation. So much so indeed that after the Restoration they made desperate efforts to retain at least some of these 'godly practices', offering to pay the ministers themselves. Their plea was rejected, the ministers were dismissed, and the new dean, Richard Marsh, and the prebendaries who had returned, set to work with indecent haste both to restore the laudian services in the Minster and to recover their own lands. Indeed, so enthusiastically did they go about the latter task that when Archbishop **Accepted Frewen** held his visitation of the dean and chapter in February 1662/3 he discovered that they had misappropriated some of the Minster's funds as well as recovering their own. He ordered that the cathedral's revenues in the future, as in the past, must be devoted solely to its own needs; but at the same time insisted that 'only grave, orthodox men and licensed preachers should officiate in the cathedral'. Communicants must kneel to receive the sacrament, the laudian worship must be restored, and the plate, furnishings, ornaments and vestments sold, must be recovered.

Minster and Corporation were once again to go their separate ways. Accepted Frewen, the son of a non-conformist rector of Northiam in Sussex, hence his christian name*, had a brilliant Oxford career as fellow and president of Magdalen College, and vice-chancellor of the university. A notable laudian, but the bitter foe of Roman Catholics, he had earned the friendship of Charles I, when that monarch, as Prince of Wales, had been wooing a Spanish Infanta and was brought under strong pressure to become a catholic. Frewen, then chaplain to the English ambassador, had preached a strongly-worded sermon before him from the text: 'How long will ye halt between two opinions? If the Lord be God follow him, but if Baal then follow him'.

At the beginning of the Civil War he sent the Oxford University plate to Charles at York, whilst also lending him £500 out of his own pocket. He himself became notorious in Oxford for causing the puritan preachers to be banished from the city, and setting up an altar in Magdalen College chapel in place of the communion table: 'the First', or so it was said, 'set up in the university since the Reformation'. After the king's defeat, parliament ordered Frewen, now bishop of Lichfield and Coventry, to be arrested; and in 1652 Oliver Cromwell himself offered a reward of £1,000 to anyone who would bring him in 'dead or alive'. Frewen managed to escape abroad; but, when the country became more settled, he returned, living in obscurity and keeping quiet. But at the Restoration he was immediately elected and translated to the vacant archbishopric of York on 22 September 1660. He was enthroned by proxy in the Minster, but

---

* The puritans were fond of giving their children this type of name. 'Accepted' meant favoured by Christ and God.

himself remained in London as chairman of the Savoy Conference, where, according to Richard Baxter, he exerted a moderating influence.

Frewen was now 73, and his appointment to the primacy little more than a stop-gap. None the less he set the ball rolling. Apart from rebuking the dean and prebendaries, three of whom had now returned, for pocketing the profits of the Minster, he also reminded them that a share of the common fund itself must be used for the benefit of the cathedral. The 'preaching ministers', authorised during the Interregnum 'to preach in the cathedral and other churches in York' had gone; the vicars-choral were restored, and the organ reinstated.

Frewen, who represented the old laudian and cavalier tradition, died at Bishopthorpe on 28 March 1664, and is buried under the Minster east window. His sumptuous monument with its recumbent effigy was largely destroyed in 1829, but has since been repaired. Frewen never married; and was apparently so afraid of sex and women in particular that he would not 'suffer a woman servant in his family'. A very wealthy man, the archbishop left most of his fortune to his younger brother, Stephen; but there were also a large number of bequests: £500 to Magdalen College, 'my Mother that gave me my breeding', besides cancelling a debt of £500 he had lent to the College 'in a time of necessity'. Every diocesan bishop received a ring worth 30/-, the bishop of Rochester being given one belonging to Bishop Jewel; 'to every servant a year's wages, besides their due'; and his tenants likewise profited from the Will.

In all Frewen distributed some £15,000 in benefactions. But curiously enough, despite his riches, perhaps because of them, the archbishop himself was a careful spender. In December 1662 he earnestly desired to be excused from attending parliament: 'to prevent (if it may be so) sundry foreseen inconveniences to my purse which must necessarily come with it: the carrier horses for my coach, mine own not being acquainted with such service'.

It is of interest to note that during this period, and indeed throughout the eighteenth century, the archbishop of York possessed the patronage of all 30 prebends at the Minster. Inevitably this was a temptation to nepotism; but also meant, as in Frewen's case, that he was under constant pressure from all sides, crown, fellow bishops, the nobility and gentry, politicians, and even his own parochial clergy, who coveted such rich prizes either for themselves or relations, friends and clients.

Frewen's successor was yet another product of the laudian era, **Richard Sterne**. The son of humble Nottinghamshire parents, after a distinguished university career at both Oxford and Cambridge, in the course of which he acquired the Oxford doctorate of divinity, he became in 1633 one of Archbishop Laud's chaplains. At the beginning of the Civil War he was Master of Jesus College, Cambridge, when very injudiciously he attempted to send large quantities of the college's plate to the king. This design was frustrated by Oliver Cromwell himself, who took over both the town and university on behalf of parliament, arrested Sterne, and caused him to be sent to prison. For the next few years Sterne was incarcerated in a number of places, including an Ipswich coal ship on the Thames, where he suffered great privations. There was even some talk of selling him into slavery. Eventually, at Laud's request, he was allowed to attend his old master in the Tower, composed the final address that Laud delivered from the scaffold, and witnessed his execution. Released at last he maintained himself by teaching in a school at Stevenage, whilst keeping a very low profile. At the Restoration he was not only restored to the Mastership of Jesus College, but created bishop of Carlisle in the autumn of 1660. At the Savoy Conference Baxter was so struck by 'his honest face', that he appealed to him to support his petition to the bishops, 'not to cast out so many of their brethren through the nation, as scrupuled a ceremony, which they confessed indifferent'. Sterne's reply, taunting Baxter for using the words 'in the nation . . . He will not say in the kingdom lest he own a king', expressed his own animosity towards non-conformity to which he later gave vent, when as archbishop of York, he confessed his profound relief that Charles II's Declaration of Indulgence in 1672 had failed to get a bill through parliament granting relief to dissenters. 'The Bill for Indulgence', he exclaimed joyfully, 'is at an end for this time, and that it will never proceed again, if it begin anew'.

After helping to revise the Book of Common Prayer, Sterne was elevated to the archbishopric of York on 7 April 1664; but, according to his enemies, he left the bishopric of Carlisle in a greatly impoverished state, which led to a lawsuit with his successor, Edward Rainbow. Apparently undeterred by such criticism, Sterne continued the same policy at York, judging from the words of Gilbert Burnet, 'he minded chiefly the enriching of his own family'. Then, to the wrath of men like Burnet, he became a strong supporter of the Duke of York, campaigning vigorously on his behalf in parliament during the debates on the Exclusion bill, and bringing down on his own head the charge that he favoured popery.

At York, the task that Frewen had begun of restoring high Anglicanism was enthusiastically carried forward by Sterne during the 19 years of his archiepiscopate. At the Minster the finances were at last put on a sound basis: chests were provided for the fabric fund, St. Peter's portion, and the common fund of the vicars-choral; a strict accounting of all the moneys paid into them was then enforced by public audits and the regular declaration of dividends. Leases were granted only in accordance with the statutes, and the tenths were paid to the choir. Consequently by 1670 all loans had been repaid and the cathedral funds were once again in the black.

At the same time the work of restoring the Minster services and providing new furnishings, ornaments and plate steadily went ahead. In 1670 the chandeliers were refurbished and given fresh chains; and three years later Sterne himself bequeathed 'all my gilt plate commonly used in the said chapel . . . that is to say one gilt basin, two gilt flagons, one gilt paten, one gilt chalice with cover, together with the cases wherein they are commonly laid up.' This was a particularly welcome gift in view of the fact that a recent survey had revealed that the cathedral then only possessed 'one little silver plate gilt, and two silver candlesticks'.

As regards the Minster services: the Wednesday, Friday and Advent services in Latin were restored; the bells were re-hung; and in general the position prior to the Revolution era reinstated. It was, however, a slow business, which became greatly accelerated after the appointment of the energetic Thomas Comber as precentor in 1683. During the Interregnum the townsfolk had become accustomed to occupying the Minster stalls both in choir and nave, from which they were now excluded; although it was still impossible to keep them out of the cathedral altogether. As early as 1632 Archbishop Neile had deplored their 'idle noisy promenades'; and these were to continue into the next century.

Sterne had married Elizabeth Dickinson, daughter of the lord of the manor of Farnborough, who bore him 13 children, one of whom, Simon, became the grandfather of Laurence Sterne, the author of *Tristram Shandy*; so no wonder he felt bound to try and provide for them out of the archiepiscopal patronage. This, as we have seen, called down upon his head the wrath of Gilbert Burnet, who also attacked him for his dependence on the backing of the Roman Catholic Duke of York.

The archbishop died at Bishopthorpe, aged 87, on 18 June 1683, and his monument stands on the inner side of the north choir aisle, surmounted by his recumbent figure, with the head resting on one arm. This work was not by Grindling Gibbons, but is attributed to an unknown member of his workshop. The original iron railings surrounding it have disappeared. In his Will Sterne left substantial legacies both for the rebuilding of St. Paul's after the fire, and to the colleges at Oxford and Cambridge with which he had been associated. Like his predecessor he has been named as the possible author of *The Whole Duty of Man*, but in neither case is this true; although very possibly both of them saw the manuscript before publication and made suggestions for its improvement. Burnet, a prejudiced witness, refers to the archbishop as 'a sour tempered man', and condemned him as a greedy, worldly prelate without conscience or scruple. Others remembered his loyalty to Church and king, and how grievously he had suffered on their behalf; and that however he acquired his wealth, he had shown himself to be extremely generous in his benefactions. A scholar of note, who was partially responsible both for the Prayer Book of 1662 and Walton's Polyglot Bible, he wrote a number of learned works; and no one could deny that he was a good family man, a loving husband and a devoted father. Harsh towards dissent, which was scarcely surprising in view of the trauma occasioned by the Great

Interregnum, he worked ceaselessly during his 19 years' archiepiscopate to rebuild Anglicanism in the north.

The last two archbishops covered by this chapter, **John Dolben** and **Thomas Lamplugh**, together only occupied the archbishopric for scarcely six years, with a year's gap between them. **John Dolben**, a scholar of Westminster School and a student at Christ Church, Oxford, joined the army at the outbreak of the Civil War, and was badly wounded at the Battle of Marston Moor and in the subsequent siege of York. As a royalist he lost his studentship, but remained in Oxford, where he and his friends, Richard Allestree and John Fell, organised secret Prayer Book services at the home of Dr. Thomas Willis. 'Here', we are told, 'most of the loyalists in Oxford, especially scholars ejected in 1648, did daily resort'. All three were ordained by Bishop King of Chichester in 1656; and, after the Restoration, were made canons of Christ Church and awarded the D.D. Dolben's mother was related to the now powerful bishop of London, soon to be archbishop of Canterbury, Gilbert Sheldon, and through this connection he became in swift succession archdeacon of London, dean of Westminster and bishop of Rochester, when he continued to hold his deanery *in commendam*. An outstanding preacher and an eloquent speaker he came to be a power to be reckoned with in the House of Lords, and a great favourite of Charles II, who enjoyed his sermons. Dryden wrote of him in *Absolam and Architophel*:

> Him of the Western Towers, whose mighty sense
> Flows in fit words and heavenly eloquence

At Westminster he is remembered both for the part he played in the Great Fire and Great Plague, marching out his scholars to fight the flames, and courageously serving his flock at the time when 300 inhabitants of Westminster died.

Consequently on Sterne's death he was Charles' candidate for the archbishopric of York, and was elected 'in a very full chapter' on 16 August 1683. He also became the king's Lord High Almoner. Burnet, who owed Dolben a grudge for preventing him from studying in the Cotton library, whilst engaged on his monumental work *The History of the Reformation*, yet paid the new archbishop this tribute: 'an excellent preacher, a man of more parts than discretion, but of a fine conversation, which laid him open to much censure in a vicious court . . . he proved a much better archbishop than a bishop'. Certainly Dolben displayed great vigour and courage during his three brief years at York. 'He was much honoured as a preaching bishop', wrote Thoresby, 'visiting the churches of his diocese and addressing the people in his plain vigorous style'. At the Minster he restored the regular weekly communion services, and tightened up the preaching there. The prebendaries had hitherto been lax in providing substitutes during their absence, so the archbishop ordered that their names should be displayed in a frame hung in the vestry.

Preachers too had now to be found for the Wednesdays and Fridays in Lent. But perhaps Dolben's greatest achievement was to appoint Dr. Comber as Precentor, who was to do so much to revive and restore the Minster's services to their ancient glory, and assist the archbishop in his determination to turn the cathedral into 'a seminary of christian virtue'. In his visitations Dolben exhorted the Yorkshire clergy to be careful to observe all saint's days, pointing out that they in no way represented a Romish superstition; and he was also most conscientious in performing his episcopal duty of confirmation. William Sampson, rector of Clayworth, Nottinghamshire, records in his journal such a service taken by the archbishop at Retford on 16 July 1685, when 33 persons were confirmed, an indication that Dolben was prepared to confirm in quite small parishes.

The diocese on the whole appeared to have been 'very happy with its archbishop'; and no doubt it genuinely mourned his sudden death from smallpox, which he had picked up in an infected bedroom at an inn on his journey back from London to York in the spring of 1688; although it was somewhat improbably suggested by Comber that the archbishop's death had been hastened, not so much by the smallpox, as 'rather to grief at the melancholy prospect of public affairs', i.e. the Romanising policies of James II. He was buried in the south choir aisle of the Minster, and his effigy depicts him half-rising with angels above his head, 'as if awaking to the Last Trump'. In his Will he bequeathed his chapel plate to the cathedral's high altar, and some 376 books to the Minster library. Dolben had always taken a great interest in the latter; and when he discovered that since Holgate's primacy, 'though much increased since that time . . . wholly useless in a place which much needs such a help to good learning', he ordered the books to be properly catalogued, duplicates to be exchanged for new volumes, and three vicars-choral 'to waite by turns two houres every morning and two houres every afternoone, keeping the library open . . . and taking care that the bookes be not purloined or damnified by such as shall pretend there to study'. Dr. Comber was entrusted with supervising this work, which he admirably carried out, noting justly: 'I left the library in good order'.

The diarist Evelyn, speaking of Dolben, lamented the passing of a good friend: 'an inexpressible loss to the whole Church'; while Sir W. Trumwell recalled the archbishop's outstanding record as a speaker in the House of Lords.

Thomas Lamplugh, a fellow of Queen's College, Oxford, had been forced to take the Covenant and resign his post in 1648; but he secretly assisted Bishop Skinner in his ordinations, 'continuing to own the doctrines of the Church of England in the worst of times'. However, at the Restoration he remained suspect as a man liable to change his coat whenever it seemed appropriate to do so. Anthony à Wood maintained, for example, that he had been 'a great cringer to Presbyterians and

Independents, he is now following the same course to prelates and those in authority'. Lamplugh for his part, to prove his loyalty, not only renounced the Covenant, but took an active part in purging Oxford University of dissenters. His conversion was taken at its face value; and in 1676 he became bishop of Exeter, where, when James II succeeded to the throne, he again adapted himself to the policies of the day, posing, in accordance with the king's Declaration of Indulgence, as the friend of non-conformists, refused to sign the petition of the seven bishops against it, and caused it to be read throughout his diocese. Then, on learning of the landing of the Prince of Orange, Lamplugh hastened to London, strongly reaffirmed his loyalty to James, and received as his reward the archbishopric of York, which had been kept vacant for a year and a half by the king in the hope of ultimately appointing a Roman Catholic. James now praised Lamplugh as being 'a genuine old cavalier', and he was translated from Exeter on 8 December 1688, barely two days before the king's flight from England.

Immediately the new archbishop changed sides, was one of the first prelates to swear allegiance to William III, received his temporalities back from that monarch, and assisted at his coronation on 11 April 1689. Appointed a member of the royal commission to consider the Comprehension Bill, Lamplugh wisely absented himself, and instead began a vigorous campaign in his diocese for the refurbishing of parish churches and the rebeautification of the Minster, whilst entertaining his clergy with a lavish hospitality, and spending much of his own money in making gifts to the cathedral. By so doing he hoped to win over his people and get them to forget his unfortunate past. Indeed, during the three brief years of his archiepiscopate he proved himself a most active primate. He visited the Minster in 1690, and afterwards issued injunctions ordering that both dignitaries and prebendaries resident in York should regularly attend the weekly communion, that this service must begin punctually, and that none of the clergy might leave the cathedral before its close. As in the chapel royal, there must always be an epistoler and gospeller besides the celebrant himself; and the vergers must escort the dean and the residentiary to and from their stalls. A sharp watch must be kept to prevent people from walking and talking in the choir during this service. In his visitation of the diocese he made sure that regular sermons were preached in all the parish churches, and held confirmations himself at all suitable centres.

Once again William Sampson records such a service at Retford on 16 May 1690. This, however, proved to be of a far less decorous nature than Dolben's had been. 'There was a confirmation' he wrote in his journal, 'but so confused a thing that I could not see who of my own parish was there'.

Thanks to Dr. Comber's energy and the archbishop's generosity a great deal more was done during this archiepiscopate to rehabilitate the

Minster. It was then that a new organ was purchased, towards which Lamplugh contributed £200, whilst also providing the casing and painting. At his own expense he refitted the altar and sanctuary with a crimson velvet cover, three pieces of tapestry, sanctuary rails, three large prayer books and a bible. finally he caused the whole of the space to be repaved in black and white marble.

In his injunctions Lamplugh had ordered that either a verger, a bellringer or a bedell should be constantly in the nave from 8 a.m. to 6 p.m. to prevent 'the tumultuous playing of boys in the bodye of the church'; and so at last restored at least some reverence and order into the daily life of the cathedral.

He died at Bishopthorpe on 5 May 1691, and lies buried in the south aisle of the Minster choir. His monument is undoubtedly by Grindling Gibbons, who received £100 for it. It contains his standing effigy, wearing a moustache and a small beard, with a glass window nearby bearing the archbishop's arms.

Apart from Toby Matthew and John Williams the archbishops in this Age of Revolution were all professed laudians, most of whom in one form or another suffered for their principles during the Great Interregnum. Matthew had allowed conformist puritanism to consolidate its position in the north, which his successors, with the possible exception of Lamplugh, did their best to eradicate. They were all men of ability, who sprang from comparatively humble homes, and, Neile being the odd man out, first made their mark at the universities. Devoted loyalists they climbed to high office on the shoulders of the monarchy, and were whole-hearted advocates of the royal prerogative and the divine right of kings. Williams alone remained unmarried; but some of the others had large families for whom they did not scruple to use the archiepiscopal office and its patronage for their advancement. Starting with little or no worldly wealth, they grew rich from their preferments, but were generous in their gifts and bequests to enhance the beauty, learning, furnishings and ceremonial of their cathedral. Apart again from Neile they were notable scholars, and all proved themselves able administrators. None however could lay any claim to true saintliness. On the whole they served the archbishopric well in an age that contained much violence, religious acrimony, and produced two Revolutions.

The Arms of Archbishops Matthews, Neile, Williams and Lamplugh. See also page 187

CHAPTER VII

The Archbishops of York
in the Age of Reason

The first primate of this period was undoubtedly the best loved of them all. For, as his correspondence has revealed, **John Sharp** was an exceptionally pastoral prelate, a real father-in-God to his clergy, lending not only a sympathetic ear to, but supplying practical and continuing help in, solving their many problems. Then, whilst in residence at Bishopthorpe, 'the meanest man in the diocese who wore a gown, was as welcome at his table as often as he pleased'. Nor were his acts of benevolence confined to his own diocese. When Samuel Wesley, rector of Epworth in Lincolnshire, lay in jail, his wife Susannah appealed to Sharp for help and not in vain, for, as she records: 'he made me a handsome present, nor did he ever repent of having done so'.

John Sharp, the son of a Bradford salter, a puritan and close friend of Lord Fairfax, but also of a royalist mother, graduated at Christ's College, Cambridge, and, after ordination, became the domestic chaplain of the then Solicitor-General, Sir Heneage Finch, later Earl of Nottingham and Lord Chancellor, through whom he obtained a number of valuable preferments including the rectory of St. Giles-in-the-Fields and the deanery of Norwich. In accordance with a recognised practice of the day, Sharp retained the rectory *in commendam* with the deanery; for which he was severely rebuked by Archbishop Sancroft, who remarked: 'I could never think him fit for that dignity till he could take up his parish of St. Giles and set it down at the gates of Norwich'. Although himself a royal chaplain, Sharp did not hesitate to condemn James II's Romanising policies, and one of his sermons led not only to his own suspension from office but also to that of the bishop of London, Henry Compton, who had refused to take proceedings against him. But after the Revolution of 1688 he was swiftly promoted to the deanery of Canterbury, and then offered one of the sees vacated by the *non-juring* bishops, which his principles forbade him to accept. This refusal angered William III, and it was only with the greatest difficulty that his close friend, John Tillotson, now archbishop of Canterbury, persuaded the king that Sharp was really waiting for York; so he was nominated as Lamplugh's successor and consecrated as primate on 5 July 1691.

He was an ardent advocate of the Comprehension of dissenters, which he constantly hammered home in his sermons, declaring that 'to make a rent in the Body of Christ is directly contrary to preserving the unity of that body'; he strongly supported Tillotson's Comprehension Scheme; and when that failed threw his weight behind the Toleration Act of 1689. In Yorkshire Sharp championed the dissenting Richard Frankland, who had established a flourishing dissenting academy in the north of England, by quashing two indictments against him in 1695 and 1697, the whole matter being settled amicably between them in the archbishop's study, where 'cosily ensconced with a pipe of good tobacco and a glass of good wine they had a most friendly and confidential discussion'.

In his diocese the archbishop was a constant visitor and regularly carried out his confirmations. His charges impressed upon the clergy the paramount importance of leading a blameless life, both in public and private; 'to study good authors and to use the best conversation they could meet with, and to improve themselves in all kinds of knowledge'; to reside on their cures; catechise the youth; and, if possible, say prayers daily in church. He sought to ordain only learned men, who were good preachers; and in this latter respect set a splendid example himself, both in the Minster and throughout the diocese. At All Saints-in-the-Pavement at York he instituted a lecture for preacher training, which urged short, practical, simple christian teaching. Controversy was to be avoided. 'Mr.——', the archbishop once recorded in his diary, 'instead of preaching railed against the dissenters'. At confirmations he made a point of laying hands on one or at most two candidates at a time, a most exhausting task when there were often thousands of them at any particular service.

Like most of his contemporaries Sharp made use of his archiepiscopal patronage to promote relations and friends, such as the Finches; but otherwise resisted pressure from outside, even from the highest quarters, bestowing the prebends on deserving Yorkshire and Nottinghamshire incumbents. Yet for all his kindness, tolerance, sympathy and helpfulness, he was not the man to condone indiscipline. Misbehaving clergymen were sternly rebuked, and should they remain obstinate would be either suspended or deprived. Nor did he hestitate to confront evil-living or evil-minded laymen, however high exhalted. He conducted a vigorous visitation of Southwell Minster, then notorious for its slackness, and affected a thorough reformation there. But when the great fire of 1711 devastated its church, he was the first to put his hand in his pocket to the tune of £200, and urged others to do the same towards the cost of repairs.

The archbishop took a great interest in education, providing schools and seeking to raise the status of the humble clerical schoolmasters; besides encouraging the work of S.P.C.K. and S.P.G. both at home and abroad. As Queen Anne's Lord High Almoner and her very dear friend, he became her closest adviser in political and ecclesiastical affairs alike; and, while endeavouring to be non-partisan, inevitably found himself, in accordance with her wishes, siding more with the tories than the whigs. Sharp played an important part in drawing up the scheme for Queen Anne's bounty in 1704; and did his utmost always to influence the queen not to allow herself to fall into the hands of either party in politics, but to seek to utilise the services of the best men in each. He himself in the House of Lords spoke and voted strictly in accordance with his conscience, regardless of party. This made him oppose the tory Occasional Conformity bill; refuse to vote for the ratification of the Act making Presbyterianism supreme in Scotland, a measure supported by the whigs; and help to defeat another whig scheme to bring the Electress Sophia of Hanover to England, as the heir presumptive.

In the ecclesiastical field he usually favoured the high church tories against the low church whigs, but not invariably so, since he was instrumental in preventing Dean Swift from obtaining a bishopric, warning Queen Anne, 'that her Majesty should be sure that the man, whom she was going to make a bishop, was at least a christian'. But as a good friend, though a bad enemy, he sometimes let his feelings run away with him, as when he backed the highly controversial Dean Francis Atterbury of Carlisle against his bishop, William Nicholson.

The archbishop was certainly no Little Englander, for his interests ranged far and wide. He sought for a closer link between Continental Protestants and the Church of England, declaring himself 'very desirous of seeing the English Church strengthened and the Protestant interest consolidated by a closer union with sympathisers on the Continent'. For this purpose he entered into lengthy negotiations with Leibniz of Hanover and Jablonski of Prussia to try and persuade them both to introduce episcopacy and the English Liturgy into their respective churches. Frederick I of Prussia, who had married the Electress Sophia's daughter, was especially attracted by this scheme, which he hoped might unite the two great German Protestant Churches, the Lutheran and the Reformed. In the end this ambitious project collapsed, partly because the Elector of Hanover became alienated from England over the negotiations leading to the Peace of Utrecht, and partly because the new king of Prussia, Frederick William, had no interest in the ideas of Church Unity.

Sharp also sought to help the hard-pressed Protestants of the Palatinate and the episcopal clergy of Scotland, in an endeavour to relieve their sufferings; while Ireland was another field for his widespread activities, where he advocated the translation of bible and prayer book into Irish, the instruction of the children in the catechism, and a determined effort to convert the papists. Finally he raised funds for the poverty-stricken Churches of the Near East, particularly for that of Egypt, which, he said, was 'afflicted with intolerable calamities'.

No great scholar himself, the archbishop yet showed himself to be a generous patron of authors, even of such eccentrics as William Whiston; and he carried on a correspondence for many years with scholars on the Continent, especially with M. le Clerk at Amsterdam. But Sharp himself made at least one important contribution to scholarship by purchasing the 10 volumes of James Torr's manuscript from his widow. These dealt with the ecclesiastical history of the diocese of York from the earliest times to the end of the seventeenth century; and now the archbishop added an additional three volumes. This work, known as the Sharp Manuscript, was in 1715 presented to the Minster library by his executors. He is also known to have kept a voluminous short-hand diary, which his son, Archdeacon Sharp, later used to compile his father's biography, but which afterwards disappeared.

Mrs. Sharp, a Palmer from Winthorpe in Lincolnshire, bore her husband 14 children, of whom the best remembered were the eldest son, John, who became M.P. for Ripon, and was known in the House of Commons as 'spitfire' on account of his excessive zeal for the Church of England; and his brother, Thomas, Archdeacon of Northumberland, the author of Sharp's biography.

The archbishop had a great love for his Bishopthorpe Palace, compiling a manuscript of its history and architecture, and planting in the grounds an avenue of limes, which still partly exists. Here too he sought to cultivate 'the holy life', with a regular round of worship, prayer and meditation, in a part of the garden he called his 'Temple of Praise'; or sometimes in the neighbouring little village church of Acaster. Sharp died on 2 February 1714 at Bath, and lies buried in the Minster under the east window in the Lady Chapter. His effigy, the work of Francis Bird, displays a recumbent figure about to rise. Damaged by fire in 1829 it was restored by the Sharp family.

Most of his contemporaries had nothing but praise for his 22 years primacy; but inevitably he also had his detractors, the most outspoken being Gilbert Burnet, bishop of Salisbury who wrote:

> Sharp by a great error of Tillotson was made archbishop of York. He has proved an ill-instrument and has set himself at the head of a party, but has suffered much for it in the opinion of many who looked on him before as a man of integrity and simplicity. But few do now retain that opinion, as with regret I confess I do not. I have observed too much art and design in him to be able to think of him as I wish I could do.

This outburst was triggered off by the archbishop's vote against the attainder of Sir John Fenwick; and by the knowledge that, with the accession of Queen Anne, Sharp was to take the place of Archbishop Tenison and Burnet himself as the adviser of royalty in ecclesiastical matters. In a very different context Francis Drake accused the archbishop of practically stealing the Torr manuscript from his widow, declaring 'that there never was a *quantum meruit* paid to the author's relict or his heir for them'. This, as it happened, was quite untrue as Sharp had given her 25 guineas, a very handsome sum for those days.

On the other hand a pamphlet printed after his death, the author being one of his Yorkshire clergy, summed up very fairly what the diocese thought about him:

> In the Government of his Diocese we of the clergy had all the Demonstrations we could wish for, not only of Paternal Affection but even of Brotherly Condescension. As our Superior, upon all occasions, he laid before us, without any unbecoming Reserve, the obligations of our sacred Function; which he might do with the greatest Authority and Earnestness, because he was himself what he admonished us to be. As our Fellow Labourer in the Work of the Ministry he behaved himself with such Meekness, Humanity and Good Nature, as if he had been our equal; never looking supercilious or disdainful upon the meanest of our Order, but kindly admitting them to disclose their grievances and solicit his Assistance, where he was capable of doing them any Justices, or procuring them any reasonable Favour which their Circumstances required. Neither would he confine his Benevolence to those of his own Profession: but to all sorts of People who resorted to him either upon Business or as respectful Visitants, he was easy of Access, affable and courteous, never assuming or morose, but ever pleased and cheerful, allowing and encouraging all innocent Communications in Discourse, which might render Conversation agreeable and useful.

Sharp had long been grooming up **Sir William Dawes** as his successor. Dawes, a wealthy Suffolk landed country baronet, who had been educated at Merchant Taylors' School in London and St. John's College, Oxford, became Master of St. Catharine's Hall, Cambridge, and Vice-Chancellor of that University. His handsome presence, melodious voice, and ability to preach good sermons, secured him the post of chaplain-in-ordinary to William III, and later gained him the favour of Queen Anne, who appreciated his high churchmanship and strong tory principles. As dean of Bocking from 1698 he won the reputation for being a very active country parson; and, with both the queen and Archbishop Sharp as his patrons, was assured of a bishopric sooner rather than later. However, in 1705 William Wake, to Sharp's amazement, was preferred to Lincoln instead of Dawes, when Anne 'refused persons . . . for being tories'. But two years later she relented and chose Dawes for Chester, ignoring other recommendations made by the then whig administration.

At the same time another high tory churchman, Dr. Blackhall went to Exeter, and it was freely asserted by the Duke of Marlborough and his whig friends that these two appointments were purely a manoeuvre to secure two more tory votes in the House of Lords. Then, after Sharp's death, the queen, remembering his wishes, raised Dawes to the northern primacy instead of the very much better qualified John Robinson, bishop of Bristol, who had to be content with London. The new archbishop was translated and elected on 26 February 1714, and confirmed the following 4 March.

In the House of Lords Dawes consistently upheld high church and tory principles, speaking strongly against the repeal of the Occasional and Schism Acts; attacking Benjamin Hoadley, bishop of Bristol, for 'spreading the false theory that dissenters could be attracted back to the Church by indulgence; advocating the retention of the Test and Corporation Acts; and voting for the acquittal of Sir Robert Harley, Earl of Oxford.

After the Jacobite Rebellion of 1715 the archbishop was accused of favouring the Jacobites, which had led to 'the lack of resistance offered to the rebels in his diocese.' This Dawes flatly denied, pointing out that he had voted with the whigs on 5 April 1714 in the debate on whether or no the Protestant Succession was in danger, which had caused Archbishop Wake of Canterbury to describe with amazement, 'the most remarkable circumstances of the debate, that the archbishop of York spoke and voted with the whig lords, drawing after him the whole bench of bishops, three courtiers only excepted'. Indeed, Dawes had been accounted such a dependable Hanoverian that he was appointed one of the regents of the kingdom, pending the arrival of George I. Although no Jacobite, the primate was deeply concerned by the political unrest in the north after the Rebellion, and in 1718 urged the then whig administration to adopt measures of healing, 'lest by what he saw there, in one of the most dutiful parts of his majesty's dominions, they might be in danger of being involved in very great and lasting troubles'. Furthermore he once again made his high church principles very plain in the House of Lords by opposing the bill to allow the Quakers to affirm instead of taking the oaths; and later presented a petition of the clergy against it.

Dawes' 10 years at York were busy but not very distinguished ones. He has been depicted as 'indulgent towards his clergy, with whom he was on the very best of terms'. He visited regularly and issued injunctions urging incumbents to introduce monthly communions in place of the traditional four: at Christmas, Easter, Whitsunday and after Harvest; and at the same time stressing the need for study and regular sermons. As an able scholar himself he was in fact especially anxious to raise the educational standards of all his clergy. A good example of this is to be found in the case of Henry Woods, who in 1722 petitioned the archbishop of Canterbury for a dispensation to hold the rectories of Lambley and Stanford-on-Soar, Nottinghamshire, in plurality, which Dawes would only support on condition that he promised to raise his educational standard, being 'so meanly qualified in respect of learning'.

Like his predecessor the archbishop was lavish in his hospitality, and did much to improve the buildings and amenities of Bishopthorpe Palace. He died of a bowel complaint on 30 April 1724, and was buried next to his wife in the chapel of St. Catharine's Hall, Cambridge, to which he had been a generous benefactor during his life. He was long remembered in the north as 'a Christian bishop . . . a very great ornament to the high station he enjoyed, defending and cherishing the flock committed to his care'. In 1733 his sermons were published in three volumes, together with a brief biography. Apparently he also ranked high enough as a poet to have his name included in Theophilus' *Lives of the Poets*.

The next archbishop of York was a man of a very different character from either Sharp or Dawes; although many of the discreditable stories told about him may well be apocryphal. Yet the very volume of them reflects the opinion held about this gay and witty primate by his contemporaries.

Educated at Winchester and Christ Church, Oxford, where his undergraduate days were wild and unsatisfactory, **Lancelot Blackburne** sailed for the West Indies shortly after his ordination. Here, or so it was believed, he served as chaplain on a pirate ship, taking his share of the booty. Very much later, the story runs, one of the buccaneers returning to England, enquired on arrival what had become of his old chum, Blackburne, only to learn to his amazement that he was now archbishop of York. Blackburne himself on reaching home attached himself to Bishop Trelawny of Exeter and was appointed subdean of that cathedral; but, on becoming involved in the trial of a witch, fell into disgrace for a time. However, the new dean, William Wake, befriended him, making use of his services, during his own prolonged absences, to discipline the chapter. This friendship paid good dividends, for when Wake became bishop of Lincoln, he secured his old deanery for Blackburne, along with the archdeaconry of Cornwall. Moreover, after Wake had been further elevated to the archbishopric of Canterbury, he was able to use his influence to obtain Blackburne the see of Exeter, whilst also bestowing upon him the Lambeth D.D.

That successful promotion to the episcopal bench came about in this way. When George I travelled to Hanover one of his chaplains was selected to go with him, where, if he faithfully discharged his duties, he could be assured of a bishopric on his return. In 1716 Wake chose Blackburne for this office; and sure enough on George again reaching England the archbishop was able to persuade him to nominate Blackburne to Exeter. In the House of Lords, the new bishop as Wake's protégé, inevitably took the whig line, as for instance when he voted for the repeal of the Occasional and Schism Acts; but it was another whig, Edmund Gibson, bishop of London, who suggested his name to the king for the archbishopric of York. George, already gratified by the complacence of the bishop of Exeter in uniting him in marriage with his mistress, readily acceded to Gibson's request. So Blackburne was nominated and translated to York on 19 October 1724, being confirmed in that office the following November.

He had already become notorious as an insatiable seeker after clerical plums. For instance, he had tried to obtain the deanery of St. Paul's, a project not abandoned until his appointment to York; and had asked for a Westminster prebend in 1716 on the grounds 'that he might have a house also to put his head in for parliamentary sessions'; both of which were to be held *in commendam* with his Exeter bishopric. It was even alleged in two ballads printed in 1736 that he had unsuccessfully contended for the archbishopric of Canterbury.

During Blackburne's 19 years' primacy the gossips certainly had much to talk about; and in particular that inveterate 'muck-raker', Horace Walpole, who wrote: 'the jolly old archbishop of York, who had all the manners of a man of quality, though he had been a buccaneer and was a clergyman; retained nothing of his former career except his *seraglio*'. He then went on to imply that both Francis Blackburne, the extreme latitudinarian, who later became archdeacon of Cleveland, and Bishop Hayter of Norwich, afterwards of London, were his natural sons. Other stories in circulation were that he had applauded the conduct of Queen Caroline in not objecting to George II's new mistress; that at Bishopthorpe Dick Turpin was his butler; and, in addition to his loose morals and worldly way of life, he was also a free-thinker if not an agnostic.

After the archbishop's death a poem was published in 1743 entitled: *Priestcraft and Lust or Lancelot to his Ladies, an Epistle from the Shades*. The puritanical diocesan clergy not unnaturally resented their archbishop's unsavoury reputation; and it is reported that after a visitation and confirmation at St. Mary's, Nottingham, when Blackburne asked the vicar, Mr. Disney, to bring some pipes and tobacco into the vestry, 'for his refreshment after the fatigues of confirmation', the latter flatly declined to do so, declaring that 'the vestry should not be turned into a smoking room', and strongly protesting against Blackburne's conduct in general. This story appears unlikely in view of the fact that confirmations were virtually discontinued during Blackburne's primacy, except when Bishop Martin Benson of Gloucester confirmed some 8,922 persons at Halifax and Ripponden in 1737. From 1733 to 1745 there were also no ordinations performed by the archbishop in person, candidates being given letters dismissory 'to any catholic bishop'. Whereupon they betook themselves off to Carlisle, Chester, Lincoln, and even to London. As Blackburne was 74 in 1733, he probably found the journey from London to Bishopthorpe for this purpose too much for his strength; but earlier between 1725 and 1732 he had held 10 ordinations in person, 'in the months of July, August and September, when he was in residence at Bishopthorpe', thus ignoring the canonical embertides. This was due to the fact that he had to be in

London for most of the year in order to attend the parliamentary sessions.

Despite all these failings and the disapproval of his more strait-laced clergy, the archbishop was generally popular in the north. Thomas Hayter, then archdeacon of York, was especially loud in his praises, referring to Blackburne in his charge of 1732 as 'my indulgent benefactor', which was scarcely surprising in view of the many preferments the archbishop had heaped upon him. Yet for all his easy-going ways the primate could be something of a disciplinarian when he felt the need. When, for example, the vicars–choral of Southwell asked him to relax the regulations imposed upon them by Archbishop Sharp, Blackburne, like his predecessor Dawes, gave them a dusty answer. But perhaps he is best remembered today for his ready wit, of which the most notable instance was the reply he made to Queen Caroline's question: whether Joseph Butler, the future dean of St. Paul's and bishop of Durham, the author of *Analogy of Religion* had died? 'No, Madam', replied the archbishop, 'but he is buried', referring to the fact that Butler was then living in obscurity at Stanhope. Whereupon he was quickly resurrected and promoted.

Blackburne had married Catherine Talbot, whose brother, William Talbot, was bishop of Durham. She predeceased her husband, who himself died from the extreme cold of March in the bitter winter of 1743, at the ripe old age of 85. They both lie buried in St. Margaret's, Westminster.

During Blackburne's time, and indeed throughout the rest of the eighteenth century, little or nothing of importance was added to the fabric of the Minster, although some major repairs were done, to which the archbishops subscribed liberally. Nor from the primateship of Dolben down to that of Archbishop Harcourt in 1841 was there any archiepiscopal visitation of the cathedral.

Blackburne was followed by **Thomas Herring**, a son of the parsonage, who had a distinguished career at Cambridge as a fellow of Bennet College and a doctor of divinity, before becoming chaplain to Bishop Fleetwood of Ely, from whom he received a number of livings. He was then fortunate enough to secure the patronage of Sir Philip Yorke, later Lord Hardwicke and Chancellor, who secured his election as preacher at Lincoln's Inn, a chaplaincy-in-ordinary to George I, and the rich living of Bletchingley in Surrey. Herring now established himself as a fashionable preacher of the latitudinarian school; and in 1732 became dean of Rochester, whilst continuing to hold Bletchingley *in commendam*. Then, through the continuing patronage of Hardwicke, he obtained the bishopric of Bangor, a see generally regarded as a stepping stone to something more lucrative. Here he showed himself to be an especially active diocesan not only by his regular visitations, but in more informal tours of his see. This display of energy, along with his devoted loyalty to the whig party and the Hanover dynasty did not go unrewarded; for when

142

Blackburne died in March 1743, the Lord Chancellor again exerted his influence to secure Herring the primacy, after several better qualified bishops had refused it, notably Wilcox of Rochester and Sherlock of Salisbury. Horace Walpole commented: 'Herring of Bangor, the youngest bishop, is named for York. It looks as if the Church were going out of fashion, for two or three of them have refused the mitre.' He was nominated and translated on 6 April 1743, and confirmed in office a fortnight later.

He only held the northern primacy for four years before being translated to Canterbury; and at York he is best remembered for two things. His primary visitation of 1743, when he sent a questionnaire to all the clergy in the diocese, whose returns, published by S. L. Ollard and P. C. Walker in 1929, present us with a very clear and detailed picture of the conditions then existing ecclesiastically in the parishes of Yorkshire and Nottinghamshire; and his stout support of the Hanoverian dynasty and the methods it employed in crushing the Jacobite Rebellion of 1745. Herring's primary visitation was a very thorough one; and writing to his friend, William Duncombe, on 26 November 1743, he boasted: 'I am confident I have confirmed above thirty thousand people'. During this visitation he made a point of calling on the nobility and gentry, a truly exhausting occupation. 'I had much rather', he wrote to Hardwicke, 'confirm three thousand people after a visitation than bear the fatigue of the chat and the bottle among forty or fifty strangers.' But such visits were to pay dividends then and later in the shape of lavish gifts sent to Bishopthorpe, including 'a three-dozen hamper of very fine claret, champagne and burgundy' from the Duke of Norfolk; and when in the General Election of 1747 the archbishop played an important, if indirect, part, he found he had the great magnates behind him.

The questionnaire sent out to the clergy in 1743 contained 11 questions, and was prefaced by the words: 'To God's favour and blessing I heartily commend yourself and your labours in the Church'. The first query asked: 'What number of families have you in your parish. Of these how many are dissenters?' i.e. papists, presbyterians, baptists and quakers. Others demanded to know: the numbers of dissenting meeting houses, schools, hospitals, almshouses, and church properties; whether the incumbent was resident and possessed a curate; how many parishioners were unbaptised or unconfirmed; what services were held, and if the children were catechised; how often communion was celebrated; and finally, 'Do you give often and timely warning of the sacrament, do parishioners send in their names, have you refused the sacrament to anyone, and how has that person behaved?' The very full and detailed Returns to this questionnaire are today of the greatest value to the eighteenth century church historian. They certainly revealed that the Church of England, in the York diocese at any rate, was by no means as lifeless as has sometimes been supposed.

In the course of this same visitation the archbishop also concerned himself with such matters as church repairs, failure to obey the Canons, and the possible corruption of ecclesiastical officials. Summing up these Returns, Canon Ollard remarked: 'On the whole the strong impression left . . . is that of a body of conscientious and dutiful men, trying to do their work according to the standard of the day'.

Herring, acting as the agent of his two patrons, Lord Hardcastle and the Duke of Newcastle, in the north, informed the latter in 1744: 'his majesty's affairs could not be in better hands than Pelham and the Duke of Newcastle, an opinion he was extremely zealous to cultivate'. Consequently he strongly opposed the Young Pretender in 1745. The rebellion broke out just at the time when most English troops were tied up in Hanover, and therefore unavailable, which meant that the situation was critical. Herring did his best to meet it; and told Hardwicke: 'with a little self-conceit an archbishop of York could still fancy himself a kind of Lord President of the North'. Hardwicke replied: 'archbishops of York have before now drawn the secular as well as the spiritual sword, and I hope your Grace will stand between us and Danger. Is it not time for the pulpits to sound the trumpets against Papacy and the Pretender?' Whereupon Herring preached a rousing sermon in the Minster, stirred up Yorkshire into forming an Association for the Defence of the Constitution and Liberties of the Kingdom, and raised some £40,000 in aid of the Government. He himself remained at Bishopthorpe even when York itself was threatened, and flatly rebuffed an appeal from Charles Edward 'to promote his interest in the diocese'.

After the final defeat of the Jacobites at Culloden and 'Butcher' Cumberland's brutal suppression of the highlanders, Herring, far from uttering any protest, welcomed the victor to York with open arms. 'I want', he told the duke, 'to express the fulness of our grateful hearts . . . your conduct, Royal Sir, has been glorious: and though the things you have done for the nation are singularly great, your manner of performing them is still more to be admired . . . Go on as you have begun, Great Sir, in the paths of virtue and glory'. Undoubtedly the archbishop sympathised neither with the jacobites nor the tories; and in 1747 pressed hard for a whig bishop of Chester to counter both. 'Such a man', he told Hardwicke, 'might do good and make a lasting impression on that jacobite and popish country'. He then went on to lament the fact that since 1746 too many tories had been made bishops.

In this same year he conducted another thorough visitation of the diocese, confirming many thousands of candidates. Essentially an Establishment man, Herring was strongly opposed to any kind of reform either in doctrine, discipline or liturgy. 'I think', he said, 'philosophy, Christianity and policy are all against changes'. A known friend of such extreme latitudinarians as Francis Blackburne, Bishop Hoadley and Dr. Samuel Clarke, whose teaching verged on Arianism, Herring's reputation remained high in Government circles; and, after both Gibson of London and Sherlock of Salisbury had refused the primacy, and no doubt in return for the services he had rendered the Hanoverian dynasty in the north, Hardwicke and Newcastle between them persuaded the king to nominate him to Canterbury.

At first the archbishop was reluctant to accept the offer, telling the chancellor: 'I am come to a very firm and most resolved determination not to quit the see of York on any account or on any consideration'. However, he was quickly pressured by the Pelhams into changing his mind, being told: 'It was impossible that a bishop in the vigour of his age, not quite 55, of such a character, so much obliged to the king and so well esteemed and beloved in the world, should decline it'. Accordingly he was translated to the Primacy of All England on 24 November 1747.

A tall, handsome man, Herring yet suffered all his life from delicate health, with a tendency towards asthma. Kind and charitable, he was generally popular with his clergy. 'Few great men', wrote Dr. Jortin, 'passed through this malevolent world better beloved and less censured than he'. A relatively poor man, he yet lavished his money on improving the gardens at Bishopthorpe, and providing the palace itself with a new clock tower. Nichols in his *Literary Anecdotes* wrote effusively of the archbishop: 'his distinguished application to the business of his function, his warm attachment to the Constitution in Church and State, and his pathetic eloquence in the pulpit . . . He was willing to think the best of other peoples' principles and to live the friend of mankind'. Hogarth, indeed, who painted Herring's portrait, was criticised for making it look too severe.

Lovat's features Hogarth might command,
A Herring's features asks a Reynolds' hand.

Herring's reluctance to move to Canterbury would have seemed inexplicable to his intensely ambitious successor at York: **Matthew Hutton**. Hutton, whose ancestor of the same name had been one of Queen Elizabeth's archbishops of York, was born in the family's centuries-old ancestral home at Marske near Richmond, and was educated at Ripon Free School, whose master, Mr. Lloyd, got him admitted to his old college of Jesus, Cambridge, where he took his B.A. degree.

In the eighteenth century it was essential for a young clergyman seeking to rise high in the Church to attach himself to a powerful patron, and Hutton was fortunate enough to discover one in the Duke of Somerset, whose chaplain he became, and from whom he received the valuable livings of Trowbridge in Wiltshire and Spofforth in Yorkshire. In the latter county he caught the eye of Archbishop Blackburne, who procured him one of the Minster prebends and introduced him to the king. The next logical step was a royal chaplaincy, and flowing from this a canonry at Windsor and a prebend at Westminster Abbey. Hutton was

145

now fully launched on the road to a bishopric; and so, when Herring went from Bangor to York, he received the former see, by means of pressure brought to bear on a reluctant George II by his two new patrons, the Duke of Newcastle and the archbishop of Canterbury. He was consecrated in Lambeth chapel on 13 November 1743 by a commission from the then ailing Archbishop Potter, comprised of the bishops of Rochester, Exeter, Worcester and Bristol. He would have liked to have retained his Westminster stall, but on his friends' advice wisely resigned it.

Horace Walpole, for once complimentary, spoke of the new bishop as 'well bred and devoted to the Ministry'. Indeed so closely was he now allied to the whig administration that should Herring have refused to leave York in 1747, Hutton himself would undoubtedly have gone to Canterbury. As it was he became the obvious choice for the northern archbishopric and was translated there from Bangor on 25 November 1747, being confirmed in office at St. Martins-in-the-Fields the following 10 December. York certainly suited him very well; and after his primary visitation of 1748 he wrote to Newcastle expressing his appreciation of what the duke had done to send him there: 'passing through the largest part of my diocese, finding nothing disagreeable in my task or the people with whom I have to do, and resting two or three days in a very pleasant dwelling, I should be ungrateful not to thank you in being the instrument of placing me in so happy a situation'.

This leisurely, comfortable, but reasonably industrious approach to his archiepiscopal duties was to mark his 10 years as primate of the north. 'Everything', he continued, 'easy and the clergy in good temper. The prospect of peace [i.e. the Treaty of Aix-la-Chapelle in 1748 that brought to an end the war of the Austrian Succession] is everywhere agreeable'. A further expression of the duke's goodwill was to persuade George II to appoint Hutton as his lord high almoner; but the archbishop was no sycophant, and when Newcastle requested a York prebend on behalf of a client of his whom the Government wished to please, Hutton courageously refused the demand. 'Can it be thought reasonable', he wrote, 'that I should give the preference to this gentleman before everyone of my own chaplains, friends and relations'. Herring had found himself in a similar dilemma, when he told Hardcastle: 'he wished he knew how to parry his grace, for his friends were somewhat disposed to murmur if not to clamour'. But the requests of patrons, especially as, according to Horace Walpole, Hutton was 'devoted to the Ministry', could not forever be denied, and some three years later the duke's client, Dr. Pyke, became archdeacon of York. Pyke, the archbishop admitted, 'was a stranger to himself and to the diocese, he doubted not his good character would give him the same weight with the clergy of the district that his Grace's recommendation had with himself to collate him to it'.

Hutton's 'devotion to the Ministry' ensured that he always stoutly supported the Government by his vote in the House of Lords; and was an enthusiastic advocate of their policies at home and abroad. For instance he issued a strongly worded instruction to S.P.G. missionaries in America, exhorting them to resist the French, whom he described as 'wicked and barbarous aggressors, who were determined to complete the ruin of the British Settlements and to change the happy condition of our American fellow-subjects under the best of kings for certain tyranny, wretched superstition and Popish idolatry'.

In Yorkshire itself he strove to promote peace and curb any unrest; so successfully that in 1750 he was able to write to Newcastle: 'Nothing in this county has occurred worthy of your grace's notice, unless it be that everything goes well. The gentlemen seem to be in general harmony with one another, and the flourishing state of the woollen trade makes them support the Government'. In his rôle as archbishop he visited regularly and confirmed personally in many centres during 1748 and 1749. A churchman of the latitudinarian school of thought, he was prepared to tolerate some free-thinking in theological matters. Francis Blackburne became first his chaplain, then archdeacon of Cleveland and prebendary of Bolton in York Minster. When he came to Bishopthorpe in July 1750 to be collated into his archdeaconry he found his highly controversial *Apology*, defending Jones of Alconbury's *Free and Candid Disquisitions relating to the Church of England*, on the table in the chaplain's room, and commented: 'I am not a stranger to the Archbishop's liberal notions in ecclesiastical affairs'.

On the other hand Hutton had no sympathy at all with Jacobitism, the Divine Right of Kings, and the Non-Jurors; and very little with the type of enthusiasm displayed by the Methodists and their evangelical sympathisers. He summoned the notorious William Grimshaw, rector of Haworth, to Bishopthorpe Palace; but finding he had increased the number of his communicants from twelve to two or three hundred, reserved judgment until he had paid a visit to Haworth himself. Here he bade Grimshaw preach at two hours notice on a text selected by the archbishop. The rector had made up his mind that he was about to be evicted, so he packed his saddlebags in readiness to ride off and join the Wesleys; but Hutton was so impressed by the sermon and the large and enthusiastic congregation that he publicly announced: 'I would to God that all clergy in my diocese were like this good man'.

On 25 April 1757 Hutton was translated to Canterbury, dying a year later from the effects of a rupture, Of a naturally cheerful and amiable disposition, he yet, we are told, 'never let himself down below the dignity of an archbishop'. There were of course the usual fulsome tributes, described sarcastically by A. W. Rowden as sounding like 'a modern testimonial'. 'This great prelate', wrote Dr. Ducanal, 'had a very extensive knowledge of men and things . . . an excellent scholar . . . a polite and elegant writer . . . few of his predecessors were better qualified for the high and important stations to which it pleased Providence to advance him'. That of his chaplain, Dr. Thomas Wray, was even more laudatory. Among other tributes he referred to the archbishop as 'an affectionate husband, a very tender-hearted parent and a kind master'. Hutton married Mary Lutman from Surrey, who bore him two daughters. In the eighteenth century, as opposed to the Medieval and Reformation periods, a good marriage was considered an almost *sine qua non* for an ambitious cleric. Herring's celibacy indeed earned him a rebuke in 1753 from Count Zanzendorff, leader of the English Moravians, for his 'great omission'; 'and on the archbishop enquiring what such a sin could be, was informed: "the great sin of omission was celibacy".'

The next archbishop only occupied the see for four years, and his primacy was not a memorable one. **John Gilbert**, the son of an Exeter prebendary, succeeded to his father's stall, and then became dean. An Oxford graduate, but with a Lambeth D.D., he was appointed bishop of Llandaff, with which he also held an canonry of Christ Church, Oxford *in commendam*. Like his predecessors he enjoyed the patronage of the Duke of Newcastle, who got him translated to Salisbury in 1749, a much more lucrative see, for which Gilbert duly expressed his thanks. ''Twas a matter of great comfort to himself', he wrote to the duke, 'to be so happily delivered from his present most disagreeable situation'. Llandaff, a very poor bishopric, and the one least coveted by would-be prelates, could none the less be a stepping stone to higher things. But Gilbert's next and ultimate promotion came from the king rather than the duke. Newcastle had pressed George II to nominate Thomas, bishop of Peterborough, to the vacancy at York, but the king, who had grown very fond of Gilbert, then a clerk of the closet and lord high almoner, insisted on rejecting the duke's candidate and nominating his favourite instead, despite the fact that the latter's health was more than suspect. Accordingly he was translated on 29 April 1757, and confirmed in office a month later.

It was unkindly said of Gilbert that, 'he rather languished than lived through a pontificate of four years, when he sunk under a complication of infirmities.' But in actual fact he proved a conscientious and energetic archbishop, regularly carrying out his duties of visitation and confirmation in person whenever possible, and employing other bishops for the latter purpose when unable to do so himself. For example in 1758 Drummond of St. Asaph and Hotham of Clogher each laid hands on some 15,000 candidates. Drummond reported of his visit to the towns of the West Riding: 'everything passed with great ease and order; the persons concerned in the different towns kept great order, the constables and churchwardens all attended and everything was well conducted'. Again, at the very end of his primacy Gilbert engaged the services of the bishops of Chester and Durham. He himself adopted a novel method of confirming. Dr. Thomas Newton wrote:

> This was instead of going round the rail of the Communion Table
> and laying his hands on the heads of two or four persons held close

together and in a low voice repeating the form of prayer over them; he went round the whole rail at once, laid his hands upon the head of every person severally, and when he had gone through the whole then he drew back to the Communion Table and in as audible and solemn a manner as he could, pronounced the prayer over them all.

Like his predecessors he found himself bombarded by his patron, the Duke of Newcastle, for preferments in the archbishop's gift on behalf of his grace's clients, and as far as he was able and certainly more obligingly than either Herring or Hutton, he acquiesced in such demands.

He married Margaret Sherard, sister of the Earl of Harborough, who bore him a daughter, Emma. The latter married George, Baron Mount-Edgcumbe, on 6 April 1761, three days before her father's death at Twickenham. He was buried in a vault at Grosvenor Chapel, South Audley Street, London.

Gilbert was regarded by his contemporaries as a somewhat arrogant disciplinarian. John Newton found him 'inflexible in supporting the rules and canons of the Church'; and Horace Walpole's waspish tongue declared that he was 'composed of that common mixture of ignorance, meanness and arrogance'. Certainly Gilbert could never have claimed to be either a scholar or a theologian; and a good example of his arrogance was seen when, as bishop, he refused to allow the mayor of Salisbury to have his mace carried before him during the processions within the cathedral precincts, maintaining that these possessed a separate jurisdiction. This actually led on one occasion to a physical scuffle between the bishop and the mace-bearer. He published nothing except some sermons.

He was followed by **Robert Hay Drummond**, the son of the Earl of Kinnoull, a very wealthy man, who had been marked out for high office from birth. He attracted the notice of Queen Caroline, whilst still a schoolboy at Westminster, and she remained his patroness until her death.

After the 'grand tour' of Europe, then almost obligatory for the nobility, he took his M.A. degree at Christ Church, Oxford, was ordained, presented to the family living of Bothal in Northumberland, and became a royal chaplain. On inheriting the Perthshire estates from his great grandfather, Viscount Staathallen, he assumed the name and arms of Drummond, and through the favour of George II and the Duke of Newcastle, was consecrated bishop of St. Asaph on 24 April 1748, when he also received the Oxford D.D. Here he spent some of the happiest years of his life, winning the hearts of clergy and laity alike by his industry, generosity and lavish hospitality. The former he described after his primary visitation of 1753 as 'though not learned, were good and able parish priests'; and constantly spoke of the diocese as a whole in terms of 'peculiar affection and delight'.

None the less he was not averse to being translated to the more important see of Salisbury in June 1761; but only occupied that diocese for a few months before accepting the primacy of York the following October. Indeed, as a loyal friend to the then administration, as he informed Newcastle, he would have been prepared, 'to accept a further removal to London *en attendant* a vacancy at York, if this would assist the ministerial shuffling of episcopal personnel'. However, this was not necessary, and Drummond was elected to the archbishopric on 3 October and confirmed in office some three weeks later. Horace Walpole spoke of the new primate as being 'a man of parts and of the world'. George Grenville had once said that he considered bishoprics to be of two kinds, 'bishoprics of business for men of ability, and bishoprics of ease for men of family and fashion'. Drummond was certainly a man of family and fashion, but the archbishopric of York was scarcely a sinecure, and he had no intention of treating it as such.

He was chosen to preach the sermon at George III's coronation; and conditions were soon to change under the new regime. Never a mere lackey of the Duke of Newcastle, he once boldly defended some of his friends, who had been accused of drinking the Pretender's health, and caused an enquiry into their conduct to be heavily defeated. This had annoyed the whigs, although the king had remarked admiringly: 'that Drummond was indeed a man to make a friend of'. The duke was further enraged, when on being dismissed from office, he found many of his old episcopal allies and protégés turning against him, including the archbishop of York. Drummond had made the incautious remark that 'he regarded things and not persons', which invoked the bitter retort from the duke, 'I *simply* carried you from the Duke of Leeds' House to be archbishop of York'. However, the archbishop himself began to feel uncomfortable under the new set-up established by George III, retired from politics altogether and devoted his energies to the northern province. This was hastened by the injudicious attempts of Newcastle and the whig opposition in the Lords to defend the indiscretions of the notorious John Wilkes. Drummond bluntly warned the duke that in his opinion valid opposition in the Lords should be restricted to 'acts definitely unconstitutional'. 'I would', he wrote, 'neither make a random or ineffectual opposition, nor vindicate points or persons which would disgrace the integrity of my intentions'. So from henceforth he concentrated his energies on his diocese, became a most active visitor, and confirmed in all the principal towns.

An account of his tours survives, and shows that in 1763 he confirmed 3,957 persons in Nottinghamshire, and again 8,423 six years later; whilst in Yorkshire he laid hands on 15,827 in the west riding during 1763, and some 17,777 in 1766; 5,827 in the north and east ridings; and 13,300 in 1770. In all, covering vast distances over very rough country, he confirmed as many as 41,600 people.

A wealthy aristocrat, Drummond entertained lavishly, visited all the nobility and gentry of Yorkshire and Nottinghamshire, and stayed for long periods in such stately homes as Castle Howard and Temple Newsam, where, as a territorial magnate himself, he could meet his hosts on their own ground.

The choir roof of the Minster was found in 1773 to be in urgent need of repair, so a subscription list was opened and the archbishop contributed 200 guineas. Archbishop Sharp had obtained permission from the crown to revise the Minster's statutes, reducing the number of residentiaries to five, who must reside for 24 weeks and be in daily attendance at Matins and Evensong. Drummond was now able to reduce that residence to 12 weeks, whilst confirming the power of the dean to nominate the residentiaries. The patronage of the prebends remained in the hands of the archbishop; who was continually being bombarded with applications for these rich prizes, not only from outside the diocese, but also from his own incumbents. There is, for example, a long and interesting letter from a certain William Herring, presumably a relation of his predecessor of that name, who urged the needs of his large and growing family, laid stress on his manifold parochial labours, and assured Drummond of the respect in which he was held by his own people: 'I have', he wrote, 'as great an influence among my parishioners as any clergyman can desire to have'.

The archbishop spent a great deal of money on his manor of Bishopthorpe, remodelling the palace and reconstructing the parish church, where he himself lies buried in the chancel.

In 1749 he had married Henrietta Auriol, the daughter of a wealthy London merchant, and by her had a numerous family, whose education he supervised himself. He was, indeed, an ardent believer in education, even for the masses, and became a strong supporter of the Charity School Movement. Although a liberal patron of the arts, in churchmanship he remained a strong latitudinarian, bitterly opposed to the Methodist Movement, now flourishing in the north of England, and particularly to its Calvinist wing, being a staunch upholder of the status quo in the Church of England. Like Joseph Butler he felt that 'enthusiasm was a very horrid thing', and stoutly defended, 'the decent services and rational doctrine of the Church of England'.

In 1766 he lost a favourite daughter, and four years later his wife died. From these domestic blows he never really recovered and passed away on 10 December 1776. Horace Walpole, no lover of clerics, described him as 'a sensible man', but added as a sting in the tail, 'much addicted to the bottle'. Actually Drummond himself drank sparingly, but benignly tolerated the heavy absorption of alcohol by the clergymen who graced his table. None the less his letters reveal him in other respects as a strict disciplinarian and a very practical man of business. His sermons, based on the Tillotson model, display both learning, clear thinking and much good sense. His portrait was painted by Sir Joshua Reynolds*.

The last of the eighteenth century archbishops of York, **William Markham**, was born in Dublin, the son of a retired major, who kept a school. From Westminster School William proceeded to Christ Church, Oxford, where he acquired the reputation of 'being one of the best scholars of his time'. In 1753 he became headmaster of his old school, and here he was greatly respected both as a scholar and a formidable personality. 'We stood in awe of him', wrote Jeremy Bentham, 'he was an object of adoration'. How formidable was seen when he clashed with that eccentric Westminster prebendary Dr. Thomas Wilson. Markham proposed using some of the property in Dean's Yard for a school boarding house and playground; whereas Wilson wanted it for a garden. The chapter supported Markham; and when Wilson went to law he lost. None the less he got his revenge by publishing a vitriolic pamphlet entitled: *A Review of the Project of Building a New Square at Westminster, said to be for the use of Westminster School*, in which he wrote:

> If we do our best to contrive immorality and injustice, and by the dint of practice inculcate corruption and a love of despotism into our boys at school – they will learn there, when they read the maxims and manners of Antiquity, to despise heroes and philosophers as so many madmen.

But Wilson's was not the only criticism of Markham. He was accused of neglecting the school in order to promote his own clerical career by forming useful social and political contacts. Indeed, through the influence of such patrons as the Duke of Newcastle and the Duke of Bedford, to whom in 1763 he complained of ill-health, which he said made his attendance at school 'very painful', he acquired a string of preferments, including the deaneries of Rochester and Christ Church, Oxford, before being elevated to the episcopal bench as bishop of Durham in February 1771.

Now, through the good offices of yet another patron, Lord Mansfield, he was appointed tutor to the Prince of Wales and Prince Frederick, bishop of Osnaburg, which brought him into contact with royalty. This connection Markham sought zealously to cultivate by using his good offices to promote crown interests. For example, he did his best to obtain the see of Rochester for Dr. John Moore, whose valuable preferments, including the deanery of Canterbury and a Durham prebend, would then automatically have reverted to the crown. Actually Moore got the see of Bangor instead, but the result was the same. The tutor now reaped his reward; for on Drummond's death George III personally intervened, after

---

* When Laurence Sterne published the ninth and last volume of *Tristam Shandy* in 1767, which was coarser and wittier than ever, the archbishop was petitioned from London 'inviting his attention to the scandalous contrast between the indecent tone of Sterne's writings and his sacred vocation'.

Terrick of London had declined it on the score of age, to secure Markham the archbishopric of York. He was nominated and translated on 21 December 1776, when he was also appointed lord high almoner and given a seat on the privy council.

Markham's 38 years at York were not memorable ones. He is recalled as a pompous and bad-tempered primate, who made many enemies; and as a notorious nepotist. He obtained, through his influence, the York deanery for one of his sons, George, and appointed another, Robert, to the York archdeaconry, together with the valuable rectory of Bolton Percy.

Possessing neither the aristocratic connections nor the personal wealth of his predecessor, Markham failed to win the support of the landed gentry; and he was held highly suspect by his diocesan clergy for his unorthodox religious views. Indeed, in May 1777 Markham was attacked in the House of Lords, 'for preaching doctrines subversive of the constitution', to which charge the archbishop replied with some warmth that 'though as a christian and a bishop he ought to bear wrongs, there were injuries which provoke any patience, and he, if insulted, should know how to chastise any petulance'. Then, when Pitt the elder, now Earl of Chatham, rebuked him for 'pernicious doctrines', Markham retorted by voting against the third reading of the Chatham Annuity Bill on 2 June 1778.

He became involved in the Gordon Riots, and was attacked by a protestant mob outside the House of Lords. Undeterred, the archbishop himself rushed to the defence of his friend and patron, Lord Mansfield, when the latter's house was besieged by the rioters. In a letter to his son he gives a very good account of what happened on this occasion. Again he flew to the help of yet another friend, Warren Hastings, whose secretary, one of the archbishop's sons, William, was subjected to a fierce cross-examination by Edmund Burke at Hasting's trial. In most unarchiepiscopal language Markham denounced Burke; for which an attempt was made to censure him in the House of Commons. The archbishop was especially incensed by the manner in which Hastings had been treated, and told Burke that he had been interrogated 'not as if he were a gentleman whose cause is before you, but if you were trying a horse-dealer'.

Curiously enough the two had once been fast friends, when Markham stood as godfather to Burke's son, and had assisted him in his literary works; but later relations soured. The archbishop accused Burke of writing the Junius Letters; and finally broke with him over the Hastings trial. Not unnaturally the primate's warm temper occasioned some unkind comments from his contemporaries: Horace Walpole referred to him as that 'warlike metropolitan archbishop Turpin'; and he was severely dealt with in the *Rolliard* of 1793. Others remarked on his indolence. For if he had proved a negligent headmaster of Westminster, he showed himself equally careless in carrying out his archiepiscopal duties. However, as a scholar of distinction himself, he is remembered as a generous benefactor of the Minster library.

He married Sarah Goddard, the daughter of a Rotterdam merchant, who bore him a large family of sons and daughters; and those of them who either took orders or married clergymen, were sure of obtaining ecclesiastical preferment from their father. Markham died, aged 89, at his house in South Audley Street, London, on 3 November 1807, and was buried in Westminster Abbey on 11 November in the north cloister. Other members of the family are also buried there, including the archbishop's wife, two brothers, two daughters and two daughters-in-law. But in York Minster he is commemorated by an imposing chest-tomb with a black marble top, the work of three men: A. Salvin, the designer, and Charles Haymond and Thomas Willement, who executed it. This apparently is not the original tomb, which was badly damaged in the fire of 1829, but a replacement made after the second fire of 1840. There is no effigy.

William Markham 1777-1807

154

CHAPTER VIII

The Victorian Archbishops of York

Edward Venables Vernon, who took the name of Harcourt by sign manual on 15 January 1831, after inheriting that family's estates in Oxfordshire but subsequently declining a peerage from Lord Melbourne in 1838, was the last great aristocratic archbishop of York. In actual fact some 28 years of his tenure of the primacy were spent before Queen Victoria ascended the throne; although he still had 10 more to run, and died at the ripe old age of 92 in November 1847, having occupied the archbishopric longer than any of his predecessors.

Edward, son of the first Lord Vernon, was born at Sudbury Hall in Derbyshire and educated at Westminster School and Christ Church, Oxford, becoming a fellow of All Souls College and being awarded the degrees of B.C.L. and D.C.L. by that university. After ordination he was instituted to the family living of Sudbury, made a canon of Christ Church and a prebendary of Gloucester. In view of his aristocratic connections and academic abilities his elevation to the episcopate was only a matter of time, and in August 1791 the crown nominated him to the see of Carlisle, whilst allowing the new bishop to hold both his living and the Christ Church canonry *in commendam*. At Carlisle he proved a very popular diocesan, endearing himself to the diocese as a whole by devoting the episcopal income entirely to the needs of that see. His pleasant and amicable disposition also made him a favourite of royalty; so it was scarcely surprising that, on the death of Markham, he was immediately nominated to the archbishopric of York on 26 November 1807, and at the same time was made a privy counsellor and George III's lord high almoner. Later, as a trusted friend of the crown he served on the queen's council, which took charge of the king during his mental troubles. An eloquent speaker in the House of Lords, Vernon, although usually a stout tory, spoke and voted strictly in accordance with the dictates of his conscience. For example, whilst personally not averse to Roman Catholic Emancipation, he strongly opposed the bill of 1849, which sought to free catholics from their civil disabilities, on the grounds that, 'it failed to provide sufficient safeguards for the Protestant Constitution and the Established Church of England'; and in the division he and 19 other bishops voted against it.

When the Reform Bill was rejected by the Lords on 8 October 1831, the archbishop was absent in Yorkshire; but he voted for its second reading, which was carried on 13 April 1832, being persuaded by the king and Lord Grey to do so. But these two gentlemen were later disgusted to find that Vernon had also voted for an amendment postponing the disfranchisement of the pocket boroughs. Actually he did so under a misunderstanding, not realising it meant the defeat of the bill; and, when Grey resigned, his name was included among those who were opposed to reform. Consequently the citizens of York regarded him as an enemy, paraded his effigy through the streets, and then marched on Bishopthorpe Palace, where they smashed the fence, broke the windows and burnt the effigy in front of the house. Grey returned to office, armed with a royal promise to create new peers if necessary, to force the bill through the Lords. there was no need. None of the bishops, including York, voted against it.

The Church Commission was set up with Vernon as a member; and at first it showed itself to be cautiously conservative. For as Grey informed the archbishop, the cabinet's views on the subject were 'purely of a conservative character and tend to the support of the Church Establishment by the removal of some causes of complaint'. These opinions were certainly shared by the two archbishops: Howley and Vernon (now Harcourt), who 'thought the existing arrangements of the Establishment exceedingly good, that the clergy of the Church of England were doing admirable work, and that if changes were made they ought to be small'.

But such an attitude could not long be maintained. Bishop Blomfield of London, who quickly took over the leadership of the Commission, had very different ideas, which, when put into practice, caused the commissioners to be pelted with abuse and criticism, but revolutionised the Church of England. Harcourt for his part, was only too pleased to shift the odium for reform onto Blomfield's broad shoulders, sat back and let him get on with it. Indeed, he once described the business of the Commission in these words: "till Blomfield comes, we all sit and mend our pens, and talk about the weather'. Sydney Smith, a bitter critic of the Commission, once jested:

> . . . the lay commissioners who are members of the Government cannot and will not attend, the Archbishops of Canterbury and York are quiet and amiable men, going fast down the vale of life . . . the Bishop of London is passionately fond of labour and always in London. He will become the Commission.

When Lord Melbourne offered Dr. Hampden, whose works were regarded in Oxford as tainted with heresy, the regius professorship of divinity at that university, both archbishops petitioned the king against the appointment, and then went to expostulate with the prime minister himself, who gave them the 'brush off'. 'I know very little about Dr. Hampden's works', he told them, 'but I know infinitely more than the right Reverend Prelates'. He then advised the king not to yield 'to unreasonable agitation'; to which his majesty replied tartly that he could hardly regard 'the representations of the two archbishops as clamour'. None the less Hampden got the job.

The tradition at the time that bishops were chosen alternatively from Oxford and Cambridge was abandoned by Melbourne, who favoured Cambridge men. This aroused the wrath of Harcourt, who protested, only to meet with the devastating retort that Cambridge produced ten able men to Oxford's five. Did the archbishop really expect him to nominate inferior clergymen? He further told the archbishop: 'you bishops are dull dogs'. In particular Melbourne disliked elderly prelates, of whom Harcourt was now one. 'Bishops; he informed Queen Victoria, 'should be young else they go off directly and don't learn anything'.

But whatever Melbourne might say Harcourt was not a dull dog. He proved a most popular and hard-working primate, pleasant, amiable, sweet-tempered, given to lavish hospitality, and very generous with his money. He fought like a tiger to protect both the interests and integrity of his diocese. For example, when Lord Russell suggested the possible founding of a bishopric at Southwell, the archbishop bitterly opposed the scheme, and it was abandoned. In 1824 a booklet had appeared by 'a graduate', advocating the setting up of special colleges at the universities for the exclusive training of the clergy. This brought a reply from 'an Oxford Graduate' the following August denying the need for change, in which he quoted with approval the training of deacons at York. 'The examinations for deacons orders', he wrote, 'as held by the archbishop of York are not insignificant and cannot be passed with ease after a few weeks' "reading", as the previous author had alleged'.

However, there were apparently exceptions to this rule. In *Church Revival* Baring-Gould wrote:

> The Revd. John Sharp whose curate I was, used to tell the story of his ordination in 1833. 'Well Mr. Sharp', said the archbishop in the only interview with the candidate, so you are going to be curate to your father, Mr. Sharp of Wakefield. Make my compliments to him when you go home. My Secretary has your testimonials: he will give you full instructions. Be sure to be at the Minster in good time. Good Morning'.

Harold Anson also recalls that:

> When his nephew came to him to be ordained to a family living, he [Harcourt] replied: 'Certainly, my dear John, and I think it will save both you and me some trouble if I shoot through both barrels; so I will ordain you both deacon and priest this afternoon'.

To which, however, Anson added: 'there can be no question that Archbishop Harcourt was, in his day, a man revered and loved'.

Confirmations, too, were not always what they might have been. These were often noisy and disorderly affairs; and we are told that on one occasion when the archbishop appeared to confirm in the Minster, the vergers had to shout above the tumult, 'silence for the archbishop'. Harcourt then mounted the pulpit, and waving his hands over the entire congregation, pronounced the prayer of Confirmation once. However, there is little doubt but that the primate was genuinely interested in securing a better training for the clergy; and when Coleridge proposed to found a college for this purpose to 'serve the British Colonies', Harcourt strongly supported the venture that finally led to the creation of St. Augustine's College, Canterbury.

After the two disastrous fires at the Minster which destroyed its roof and most of the interior ornaments, the archbishop donated a magnificent £2,000 to the restoration fund, and also replaced all the communion plate out of his own pocket. Dean Markham's lavish policy of purchasing and rebinding books had turned the Minster library's credit balance into a deficit; but Harcourt's large installation fee of £50 in 1808 restored its solvency.

An ardent musician, the new primate found on arrival in York that Dean Markham would not agree to his suggestion for a musical festival in the Minster, although a commemorative concert had been staged there for Handel in 1791. But after the installation of the new dean, Cockburn, in May 1823, three such festivals were arranged for 1823, 1825 and 1828, each of which proved more elaborate than the last. Galleries were erected in the Minster, where sacred music was performed by enormous choirs; whilst at the same time secular music was played in the city Assembly Rooms. These rooms had been enlarged to include a concert hall; and here fancy dress balls were also organised, which were attended by many of the clergy with their wives.

But perhaps the most noteworthy, and certainly the most publicised event during Harcourt's long primacy, was his visitation of the Minster in 1841, and its aftermath. Canon William Vernon, the archbishop's nephew, was at loggerheads with Dean Cockburn; and, after the fire of 1829, he pressed with great enthusiasm for the restored choir altar to be moved, so that certain important brasses and the pillars of the lantern tower would be uncovered, but was overruled by the dean. Vernon took this rebuff badly and the archbishop himself had to send for his nephew and sternly rebuke him, ordering him 'to cultivate peace and goodwill, rather than gratify taste'. But far from complying with this injunction the canon found an opportunity of revenging himself on Cockburn after the second fire, by attacking the dean for his maladministration of the restoration fund, and referring to what he dramatically called, 'a mortgaged Minster'. Indeed, so heated became the dispute between them that Harcourt decided to visit the Minster, something that had not previously been done for a century and a quarter. This attracted wide publicity; and the whole matter became further complicated by the furious opposition of the dean and chapter to the Cathedrals' Act of 1840. Cockburn in particular was especially outspoken, threatening, quite illegally, to sell his livings before he was deprived of them.

The visitation itself opened in the Chapter House on 18 January 1841, with the lawyer, Dr. Phillemore, as commissary. Cockburn, of course, was the target, being accused of malpractice in his administration of the Minster's fabric fund. He replied by challenging the legality of the court's jurisdiction, and then, when this was overruled, walked out dramatically, followed by his wife. The public interest was now further titivated by one of the prebendaries bringing up the matter of the dean's livings, alleging that he had accepted money in exchange for a promise to appoint the donor to a parish in his patronage. This was a serious charge, since it amounted to simony, but was denied by Cockburn, who had returned to the court on 23 March. In a towering temper he bade defiance to all 'sneaking and roguery', and very nearly had to be ejected from the courtroom by force.

Phillemore now blundered badly, not only by declaring that the charge was true, without a proper investigation, but actually had the effrontery there and then to deprive Cockburn of the deanery. Equally foolishly Harcourt confirmed the sentence; whereupon the dean promptly appealed to the Queen's Bench, where in an action, the Queen versus the Archbishop of York, Cockburn triumphed. 'The archbishop', it was said, 'had no power whatsoever to deprive the dean of his office, without due process of law'; and the deprivation was quashed. Harcourt could, of course, have prosecuted the dean for simony under the Act of Parliament, but wisely forbore to do so; and Cockburn continued in office until his death some 17 years later. But he never really recovered his old reputation, which was forever tarnished; and bitter feuding in the chapter disrupted the life of the Minster for the rest of his life.

The Cathedrals' Act had changed among other things the method of appointment to the residentiary canonries. Hitherto the dean had nominated them out of the existing prebendaries; but now it was enacted that, after Cockburn's death or resignation, this right would belong to the archbishop. At the same time the 50 benefices, which had previously been attached to various offices in the Minster, with the exception of the 19 attached to the dean and chapter, were also transferred to the patronage of the archbishop. But one clause at least in this Act caused much concern to the archbishop and chapter alike, namely that, after Cockburn's departure, the dean's stipend would be reduced from over £2,000 per annum to a mere £1,000, whilst his heavy expenses, including a great deal of official hospitality and the upkeep of the enormous deanery, remained the same. Harcourt protested, pointing out that in the future no-one, except a very rich man, would be able to accept the deanery, but he was not heeded. None the less his advice was sound as the future would disclose.

When still only a fellow of All Souls, Oxford, Vernon had married Anne Leveson Gower, daughter of the Marquis of Stafford, who bore him 16 children, of whom four at least received preferment at the archbishop's hands either in the York diocese itself or the northern province; two of them at the Minster: Leveson as chancellor of York, and William as one of its canons.

Indirectly Harcourt became involved in the Cato Street Conspiracy. As director of Ancient Concerts the archbishop was entertaining his fellow directors, along with the prince regent and the dukes of Cumberland, Cambridge and Wellington, at his London home on the evening of 23 February 1821, at the very time that the conspirators were planning to murder the cabinet ministers dining together in the next-door house. As Canning remarked afterwards: 'the primate and his friends ran some danger of being assassinated in mistake for the cabinet ministers'.

Early in October 1847 Harcourt, then in his 92nd year, was walking with his chaplain across a wooden bridge over an ornamental pond in Bishopthorpe Palace grounds, when the bridge collapsed precipitating them into the water up to their necks. 'Well, Dixon', said the archbishop, 'I think we've frightened the frogs'. He seemed at first to have taken no ill effects; but passed away peacefully the following 5 November. His stone monument, with its recumbent effigy, designed by Matthew Noble, stands in the Minster. In its obituary notice of him *The Times* remarked, after noting his family connections with powerful politicians, that 'the progress of his professional advancement though not much beyond his deserts, was at least fully equal to them'. It has generally been accepted that he was a sweet-tempered, gentle person; but some nineteenth century memoirs suggest other less desirable characteristics: a quarrelsome temper, and the development of an awe-inspiring, not to say terrifying presence, in his old age.

Thomas Musgrave, who was nominated to York within a week of Harcourt's death, could hardly have differed more from his predecessor. Harcourt had been a high tory, a very wealthy aristocrat, lavish in generosity and hospitality, sweet-tempered, gentle and amicable, at least in most people's opinions, which had earned him immense popularity in the north. Musgrave, on the other hand, the son of a Cambridge tailor and woollen draper, combined in himself a liberal-minded-whiggism with a hard-headed business acumen that was scarcely endearing. In one thing at any rate they were agreed: no change for change's sake in the Church of England.

As senior bursar at Trinity College, Cambridge, from 1825 to 1837, Musgrave rendered the college yeoman service by 'his sound judgment and practical knowledge of business', whilst at the same time demonstrating his liberal political views by collecting signatures for Lord Grey's petition, presented to the Lords on 21 March 1824, asking that all religious tests at the universities should be relaxed, and thus permit the entrance of dissenters. In May the same year he and Sedgwick drew up a protest directed against the Master of Trinity, Dr. Christopher Wordsworth, for compelling Canon Thirlwall, afterwards bishop of St. David's, to resign his tutorship on the grounds of his advanced religious opinions.

The then premier, Lord Melbourne, was looking to Cambridge for able liberal whigs to fill bishoprics and other church dignities; and so in 1837 Musgrave was appointed dean of Bristol, and shortly afterwards nominated to the see of Hereford, vacant by the death of Bishop Edward Grey, a brother of Earl Grey; being consecrated on 1 October 1837 in Lambeth Chapel by Archbishop Howley. At Hereford, Musgrave is remembered as the first bishop to propose holding a harvest festival; but when he approached Melbourne for permission, he met with a flat refusal, 'on the grounds that one would then be obliged to have a thanksgiving for everything'. Here too he is credited with reviving the office of rural dean, and founding a Diocesan Church Building Society. In the House of Lords he was an outspoken champion of the whigs; and, when archbishop-elect of York, flatly declined to sign the bishops' remonstrance, headed by Blomfield of London, protesting against Lord John Russell's determination to appoint Dr. Hampden as his successor at Hereford.

Musgrave himself was enthroned as primate in York Minster on 15 January 1848. Later he supported Gorham against Bishop Henry Phillpotts of Exeter in the famous controversy over infant baptism. 'He issued a charge holding the effects of Infant Baptism to be an open question, and declaring that Gorham's doctrine was legitimate within the Church of England'. Musgrave already knew Yorkshire well, since most of Trinity College's estates lay in that county, for which as their bursar he had long had responsibility. So now his business capabilities did much to improve the diocesan finances, and thereby helped to increase the Church's influence, especially in the larger towns. Generally speaking he was opposed to ecclesiastical reforms, adopting the motto 'Quieta non movere'; and in particular resisted the attempt to revive the deliberative powers of the York Convocation. Archbishop Sumner of Canterbury was equally hostile; but when the Canterbury Convocation met for three days in February 1855, he succumbed to pressure and took part in the proceedings. Musgrave was made of sterner stuff, locking the door of its meeting place and thus preventing the York Convocation from doing business. Despite virulent attacks upon him by high churchmen in parliament he remained completely unrepentant; and when in 1858 they threatened him with a *mandatus* from the court of the Queen's Bench, the archbishop took no notice. Indeed he flatly declined to attend the debate on the subject, where he knew a savage assault would be made upon him, saying he had more important business to attend to in Yorkshire.

This attitude he stubbornly maintained until his death, which actually took place in the very year that the Canterbury Convocation passed its first canon, allowing parents to be godparents. The Convocation of York, he said served no useful purpose, and the majority of the clergy did not want it. So he continued to keep the doors locked, whilst carefully watching the deliberations of its southern counterpart. This was all the easier, because as one cynic declared: 'the Convocation of York was much smaller and therefore more lockable'.

On the whole Musgrave's 12 years as primate were not memorable ones. In 1854 he had a severe illness, and thereafter was rarely seen in public, although he always made himself accessible to his clergy, towards whom he exhibited great kindness and hospitality. A humble man of a naturally retiring disposition, he never gained the popularity that his predecessor had enjoyed in the diocese as a whole, where his liberal principles sometimes came under fire, as indeed they did in London. The windows in his London home were broken by a mob, who were protesting against the Sunday bill of June 1855, which the archbishop favoured and voted for. This would have allowed trading in London on a Sunday.

As we have seen Archbishop Harcourt had prophesied that owing to the reduction of the dean's income to £1,000 by the Cathedrals' Act, it would be virtually impossible to appoint anyone but a very rich man to that office. In addition Cockburn had left the 30 room deanery in such a dilapidated state that the next occupant would have to spend thousands of pounds to make it habitable. The problem was solved by the prime minister nominating the Hon. Augustus Duncombe, 'because he was rich'. Duncombe, son of the Earl of Feversham, and married to Lady Harriet, sister of the Marquis of Queensbury, was very rich indeed; but his clerical experience very meagre. He had ministered for some years in the family living of Kirby Misperton, before virtually abandoning his clerical career and retiring to his estate of Calwich Abbey, Staffordshire, where he had lived for many years to all intents and purposes as a layman. He possessed a piping voice, little eloquence and not much intellectual ability; his sole qualification for the deanery, apart from his wealth, being his common sense, courteous manners, and a reputation for 'caring about people'. These seemed good enough for Musgrave, who strongly recommended him for the office, declaring that 'he was a most amiable and respected man, of sound reasonable opinions, of irreproachable conduct, and an excellent clergyman'. Curiously enough the archbishop's judgment proved a very sound one, for Duncombe was to emerge as one of the great nineteenth century deans of York.

Musgrave died on 4 May 1860 in London, and was buried at Kensal Green cemetery; but, like Markham, he has his memorial in the Minster.

This consists of a base, designed by John Raphael Brandon, with an effigy on top carved by Matthew Noble: 'technical competence and a certain forbidding severity are its most obvious characteristics'. In 1839 Musgrave had married Catherine Cavendish, daughter of Lord Waterpark, who survived him.

The next archbishop, **Charles Thomas Longley**, was to spend barely two years at York, before passing on to Canterbury. The son of the recorder of Rochester and a king's scholar at Westminster, he won high honours at Oxford, where he became a successful don; but then a less successful headmaster of Harrow, before being appointed by Melbourne to the newly founded see of Ripon on 15 October 1836. This last preferment was due to the prime minister's desire to oblige an old friend, Sir Henry Parnell, who also happened to be Longley's father-in-law. Melbourne usually expected to get whole-hearted political support from the men he selected for bishoprics, but in Longley's case he had blundered, since the new bishop voted against the appropriation of money from the Irish Church, the government bill on church rates, the Oxford University Reform bill and the Divorce bill, besides the motion for the revision of the Prayer Book. Indeed, Melbourne told the bishop that his patronage had not secured 'one steady friend, nor one firm supporter of my principles and opinions.'

Longley's note-books, now in the possession of Leeds University Library, which were compiled from the parochial returns of his visitations between 1836 and 1856, portray him as an exceptionally active diocesan bishop at Ripon. The clergy there were generally speaking of very poor quality, since Oxford and Cambridge graduates were reluctant to brave the rough conditions to be found in the West Riding of Yorkshire; and for the first 10 years of his episcopate Longley did not ordain a single graduate curate. Consequently his 20 years at Ripon constituted a time of much up-hill work. Much interested in synodical government, he not only advocated the restoration of Convocation as a deliberating body, but suggested that it might also well contain a house of laymen, Both diocesan synods and ruri-decanal chapters came into being in the Ripon diocese, and later in his Durham diocese; and he proved an enthusiastic promotor of Pan-Anglicanism.

Longley advocated intercommunion with the Episcopal Church of Scotland, Eastern Orothoxy, and the Swedish Lutherans; and was even prepared to enter into relations with Rome. The first American bishop to preach in an English cathedral did so at Ripon. Longley's churchmanship has sometimes been described as Evangelical; but in fact he was a moderate high churchman, who yet had no sympathy with Anglo-Catholicism. Indeed, he firmly suppressed the 'Roman Catholic teaching and practices' he found in existence at St. Saviour's, Leeds, in 1848. He was a firm believer in the Establishment; and in a strong letter to his diocese condemned the Gorham Judgment; just as earlier he had written a letter to the press protesting against the appointment of Hampden to the see of Hereford. Later, as archbishop of Canterbury, he opposed the Colenso Judgment.

Longley's translations first to Durham and then to York were recommended by Lord Shaftesbury, who felt that here was 'a proper man for the job', a moderate middle of the road churchman, who could be relied upon never to come to terms with the Puseyites*. After being confirmed in office as primate on 12 July 1860, the new archbishop immediately set to work to ensure that the York Convocation would be allowed to meet and act, as indeed it continued to do regularly from 1861 onwards. But otherwise Longley left little mark either on the diocese or province. J.C. Thirlwall once spoke of him as 'a weak man'; and one momentous result of such weakness for the Minster was the archbishop's acquiescence in the acquisition of power there by Dean Duncombe. For Duncombe, in his desire to accelerate the rehabilitation of the cathedral and its services, persuaded Longley not only to make him precentor, but also virtually to let him take over the work of the chancellor. Consequently the York chapter as a whole became little more than a cypher, its members not even being provided with an agenda paper before the quarterly meetings; and when the next archbishop, William Thompson, arrived, he found a *fait accompli*. 'This democratic institution', he declared, 'has been turned into an absolute monarchy'. For Duncombe, thanks largely to Longley's weakness, 'had become the Minster'. On 20 October, 1862, Longley himself was promoted to Canterbury, and there we must leave him.

In 1831 he had married Caroline Sophia, eldest daughter of Sir Henry Parnell, who became the mother of three sons and four daughters. The archbishop is best remembered at York as a learned, cultivated, gentleman, courteous to all and very even tempered. These pleasant manners won him many friends among the clergy and laity of the diocese; but as one critic not unfairly commented, he was 'an entirely uninspired ecclesiastic'.

William Thomson, the son of a draper at Whithorn, inherited from his father not only a vigorous mind and a strong will, but also his liberal politics and business acumen. At Oxford he studied logic, producing a thesis, *An Outline of the Necessary Laws of Thought*, which earned him considerable kudos; and, after serving a number of curacies, he returned to his old college of Queen's as tutor, dean, bursar and ultimately provost. The college was then at a low ebb, and Thomson set to work to restore the prosperity of its properties. In the college itself he remedied one abuse after another, agitated for the reform of the examination system, and was the chief architect of the destruction of its closed scholarships and fellowships.

* The Puseyites, followers of Dr. Pusey, represented the extreme wing of the Anglo-Catholic ritualists.

Reformers are rarely popular, but Thomson with his good looks, magnificent physique, and splendid voice was idolised by the undergraduates and exerted a powerful influence on the social life of the college. In 1855 he married Zoë Skene, accepted the important living of All Soul's, Langham Place, and retired for a while from Oxford. But not for long, returning to Queen's as provost within a year. His reign was a memorable one, in the course of which he made the college 'the social centre of Oxford', and radically reformed the entire regulations governing it. It can indeed truly be said that Thomson was the maker of modern Queen's. His Bampton Lectures on *The Atoning Work of Christ*, a thoroughly orthodox production, together with his fine voice and handsome presence secured him the preachership of Lincoln's Inn, a chaplaincy-in-ordinary to the queen, and put him well in the running for a bishopric. So in 1861, after declining Carlisle on the grounds of being himself a native of that diocese, he was appointed to the see of Bristol and Gloucester, where he threw himself whole-heartedly into the business of revolutionising that diocese on an evangelical basis; vigorously suppressing the ritualists.

When Longley went to Canterbury, Palmerston proposed Bishop Waldegrave for the northern archbishopric, but the queen disapproved and suggested instead either Phillpotts or Thomson. Palmerston took no notice and offered York to Tait of London, who declined it; and only then, at Shaftesbury's instigation, turned to Thomson. The latter received the news whilst recovering from an illness at Frewen Hall, Oxford; immediately rose from his sick bed and went to tell his wife. 'My dear', he said '*I* am the Archbishop of York'; to which she replied, 'Oh *do* go and lie down'. A fortnight later Palmerston told Victoria that Thomson had 'thankfully accepted the archbishopric'. But others were not so pleased. Samuel Wilberforce of Oxford, who had hoped for the primacy, was bitterly disappointed, and never forgave the new archbishop. The Puseyites alleged that Shaftesbury had got Thomson appointed because he knew he would suppress ritualistic teaching and worship. Others complained that at 44 he was too young for the office. 'Fancy Archbishop Thomson', wrote the sedate Bishop Stubbs.

Thomson belonged to the evangelical and low church school; and although no zealot, was limited in his theological outlook. Sensible and efficient, he was also on the whole remarkably tolerant, except towards ritualists. These last became especially incensed when the archbishop admitted some 400 Salvationists to communion at St Paul's church, York, in 1882; and again when he rejected their demand that he should prosecute the heretical Charles Voysey, vicar of Healaugh, for his published sermons, *The Sling and the Stone*. Thomson for his part claimed to be of the school of Hooker, but in reality was much more akin to the seventeenth century puritans. He never gave preferment to a ritualist, refused to ordain them, and revoked the licences of extreme curates. The controversy between him and the vicar of St. Matthew's, Sheffield, reached the proportions of a scandal. But Thomson refused to serve on the Royal Commission on Ritual in 1867; although he became a member of the Judicial Committee of the Privy Council that dealt with cases of ritual, and gave the casting vote in the famous trial of Martin versus Mackonochie in 1868. Four years later the two archbishops introduced a bill into the Lords that eventually resulted in the Public Worship Regulation Act of 1874, for which Thomson was violently attacked as 'a traitor', and had to endure a storm of abuse from the ritualists.

During his archiepiscopate Thomson ordained some 810 deacons in the Minster; but strongly resisted pressure to persuade him to lower academic standards for ordination candidates, thus enabling men to get into the ministry through the back door of the Mission Field. For he was only too aware of the decline in the social and intellectual status of many of his clergy, since graduates were reluctant to come north; and there was a steady drain of curates southwards. In order to try and remedy this situation he did his best to improve the endowments of the poorer livings.

In the matter of confirmation he demanded a proper preparation of candidates, put an end to the old rowdy, undisciplined services, and took particular care over his addresses. Furthermore he was quite ready to travel to any village for confirmation, provided its incumbent could muster at least 10 candidates, when the traditional practice of supplying the archbishop with cakes and ale in the vestry after the service was discontinued. Thomson's normal routine was to hold confirmations yearly in the larger towns, every second year in the smaller ones, and every third year in the rural districts. In all he confirmed some 200,000 people.

During his primacy the archbishop consecrated 103 new churches, created 76 new ecclesiastical districts, and raised huge sums of money for these purposes. He was among the first bishops to inaugurate a diocesan conference, and even suggested that each parish should have a parochial church council, but found the majority of clergy opposed to such an innovation.

He greatly valued the Church Congresses, encouraged them to meet in his diocese or province, and, as their chairman, proved himself to be 'the very impersonation of that strength of mind and will that shows its power in controlling a great assembly'. He brought new life into the York Convocation, but his autocratic ways led to a reaction, and in 1884 the Lower House, against his bitter opposition, elected another strong man as their Prolocutor, in the person of Dean Purey-Cust of York. This led to conflict, with Thomson determined to rule Convocation, and the dean refusing to surrender the independence of the Lower House, which was only finally resolved by the dean's resignation.

In 1885 the Canterbury Convocation accepted a House of Laity; but Thomson steadfastly declined to allow it at York, so it was left to his successor, Magee, first to summon the latter, and for Archbishop Maclagan to preside over it.

The disputes with Purey-Cust in Convocation were only one manifestation of the primate's hostility towards the deans of York, with whom, throughout his archiepiscopate he was continually at war. A number of factors contributed to this unhappy situation. Both Duncombe and his successor, Purey-Cust, were wealthy men with aristocratic connections, revealing only too cruelly Thomson's relative poverty and low social status; Duncombe's consolidation of power in the Minster outraged the more democratically-minded archbishop; and the former's publicly expressed opinion that Wilberforce ought really to have become primate, added salt to the wounds. Thomson, too, wished to extend the Minster's usefulness to the Church at large, and therefore sought to interfere with the conduct of its services. Indeed, his ideas on the subject of cathedral reforms were so radical that they seriously alarmed the dean and chapter. Then there was a running battle over the archbishop's claim to be the Ordinary of the Minster, to which Duncombe correctly replied that he was no more than its Visitor. Finally, battle became joined over Thomson's rights, under the Cathedrals' Act, to appoint residentiaries who had not previously been prebendaries. None of these disputes were really resolved during Thomson's life-time; and peace only returned to the Minster with the arrival of his successor.

More than any archbishop before him Thomson won the hearts of working people, being deeply aware of the gulf that was then dividing the working classes from the Church. Sheffield, for example, with its population of 325,341, nearly a third of the entire diocese, idolised him. He frequently visited the city, spoke to thousands of working men in workshops and factories, and took part in three missions there. In 1884 he formed Sheffield into an archdeaconry, but strongly resisted all attempts to turn it into an independent bishopric; for he was determined not to lose it. So when the see of Wakefield was founded in 1888, Sheffield remained outside as a continuing part of the York diocese.

Thomson was a great evangelising prelate. He tirelessly toured the diocese and conducted a whole string of missions. He would not tolerate idleness among his clergy; compelled them to reside on their cures; and as a good business man kept the whole of the see running smoothly and efficiently.

The one legitimate criticism that could be levelled against him was that he worked too hard, tried too much, and would not delegate authority. A suffragan bishop might have helped. In an attempt to galvanise the clergy into more action, he ordered the ruri-decanal chapters to meet frequently and to send records of their deliberations to himself. Religious Education, he maintained, was the cement that held all its other parts together, and must never be treated simply as one subject out of many. The Education Act of 1870 in particular drove him into action; and by the end of his archiepiscopate there were some 589 church day schools in the diocese as compared with only 21 board-schools. He also interested himself in higher education, and laid the foundation stone of Leeds College in 1877.

At Oxford Thomson was attracted by science. As archbishop he helped to bring the laboratories of King's College, London, into existence, and at Church Congress after Congress he pleaded strongly for the Church to accept the new scientific discoveries, which should then be harnessed to Religion. Indeed, when Darwin was buried in Westminster Abbey, Thomson became a member of the memorial fund committee. However, he always firmly set his face against all forms of secularism and unbelief. As the friend of the poor he advocated both better workhouses and the setting up of co-operative businesses; waged an unending war against drunkeness, drug-taking and gambling; and urged his clergy to fight all forms of poverty. The evils of poverty, he said, lay at the root of, and were largely responsible for, the apparent Victorian prosperity. 'The children', Thomson declared, 'were ignorant and therefore godless; women selling their souls and bodies for food; workmen worse housed, worse fed, worse cared for than brute beasts'.

In ecclesiastical matters the archbishop was often quite unpredictable, and frequently ploughed a lone furrow. It was said that he had contributed an essay to the famous controversial book, *Essays and Reviews*, but that it arrived too late for publication. However, after the judgment of the Judicial Committee of the Privy Council had cleared Williams and Wilson of heresy, Thomson circulated a pastoral letter condemning that verdict, for which he received a memorial of thanks signed by some 137,000 laymen.

He was opposed to the suggestion that Colonial Churches should become independent, declaring that their bishops ought to continue to be appointed by the crown, and take the oath of allegiance to the archbishop of Canterbury; but he supported the decision of S.P.G. to withhold funds from Bishop Colenso, on the grounds of his biblical criticisms. None the less he feared that the Colenso issue might be discussed at the Lambeth Conference of 1867, and so declined either to preach at or take any part in it. Then, when Bishop Grey of Capetown, basing himself on the Conference's condemnation of Colenso and its decision that a new bishop should be appointed in his place, selected W. K. Macrorie, vicar of Accrington, Thomson flatly refused to allow him to be consecrated either in his diocese or province. He also faulted the Lambeth Conference on other grounds, namely that it had neither attacked the errors of Rome, nor reaffirmed the principles of the Reformation. Indeed, in his opinion the whole Conference was illegal.

At the Lords his interventions in the debates have been described as 'always on the side of reason and common sense, of tolerance and progress'. He was realist enough, for example to accept that the Disestablishment of the Irish Church was inevitable, but fought hard to preserve that Church's endowments. His attitude towards the Public Worship and Regulation bill of 1874 might be coloured by his dislike of ritualists, but even here he was balanced and statesmanlike in his approach; as indeed in other highly controversial measures such as the notorious Burial Law Amendment bill of 1880, and the Clergy Discipline (Immorality) bill of 1888. He rarely took part in legislation not affecting the Church, but did support the criminal Law Amendment bill of 1883.

Thomson was friendly towards dissent, in an age when most churchmen were not; since he 'recognised the right of other men to their opinions'; which led him on to condemn 'the spiritual tyranny' of Rome.

Despite his hard work in the York diocese, the archbishop was not popular there in ecclesiastical circles. His hostility towards the ritualists and friendship with dissent, his clash with the greatly loved Bishop Wilberforce, the jealousy over his rapid promotion, his quarrels with the dean and chapter, the fact that he never belonged to any particular church party, and the venom he sometimes displayed towards his opponents, all contributed to this lack of the approval which his devoted labours certainly would have merited. Outside Yorkshire some of the best minds in the Church of the day, suspected that Thomson's theology was defective and at times unorthodox; and this may well account for the fact that he, unlike Longley, was never offered Canterbury, rather than the oft-told story of how he once trod on Queen Victoria's train with his large feet and tore it badly. But whatever the reason, the knowledge that he had been passed over, caused him bitter disappointment. In ecclesiastical circles he may have been 'suspect', yet there is little doubt of his immense popularity with the mass of the working people, for whom his doctrines of the Church, the Ministry and the Sacraments were far more acceptable than those offered by more orthodox churchmen. No-one could question his warm heart, great generosity and wise, deep humanity. But against these qualities must be set a love of pomp and splendour, a greed for power and authority, and a cruel streak in his nature that revealed itself both in his letters and actions.

A sensitive man, only too aware of his bourgeois origins, Thomson often reacted to criticism with an over-pugnaciousness that bordered on arrogance. He died after a stroke on 25 September 1890, and was buried like Drummond at Bishopthorpe; but within the Minster his effigy by Sir John Hamo Thornycroft lies on a chest-tomb designed by Bodley, with a dog at his feet. 'The whole thing' commented G. E. Alymer, 'is said to have cost less than £2,000 . . . it is not clear who paid.'

William Connor Magee, an Irishman, a graduate of Dublin University, a robust churchman, and a former bishop of Peterborough, who won great renown as preacher and orator, especially by his eloquence in the House of Lords, was nominated and elected to follow Thomson in the northern archbishopric during February 1891. This appointment met with popular acclaim; yet within a few months he was dead, dying suddenly and most unexpectedly whilst on a visit to London the following

5 May. Buried in Peterborough Cathedral, there is also a small memorial to him in the Minster consisting of a mural tablet of brass set in stone, the work of the ubiquitous Bodley. As archbishop he is probably remembered for two acts: the summoning of the House of Laity to the York Convocation, although he did not live long enough to preside over it; and the restoration of harmonious relationships between the primate and the Minster. The world at large will recall his famous remark: 'he preferred to see England free to England sober'.

The last Victorian primate, **William Dalrymple Maclagan D.D.**, concludes the long list of archbishops covered in this book, that stretches from the sixth to the twentieth century. He was of Scottish Presbyterian origin, who after some military and legal training gained a commission in the 51st regiment Madras Native Infantry and served in India from 1847 to 1849, when he was invalided home. Maclagan then decided to take holy orders, graduated at Peterhouse, Cambridge, with a pass degree, and was ordained to a curacy at St. Saviour's, Paddington. Here and in a second curacy at St. Stephen's, Marylebone, he made his mark to such an extent that Tait, then bishop of London, appointed him organising secretary to the London Diocesan Building Society, where his previous legal training stood him in good stead. Incumbencies followed at St. Andrew's, Enfield, St. Mary's, Newington, and St. Mary Abbot's, Kensington. This last he was reluctant to accept on the grounds 'that his only gift was to say plain things to plain people', to which Bishop Jackson of London replied: 'I want a man to say plain things to that congregation'. He became a notable preacher, whose earnestness and simplicity attracted large congregations, and was particularly successful in his work among the young, in building up Sunday schools, and relieving the sufferings of destitute children.

Like Thomson he was a strong believer in parish missions; and his reputation as a sound churchman became much enhanced when he edited a collection of essays by well-known ecclesiastics entitled: *The Church and the Age*. A moderate high churchman, but no ritualist, his strong personality so impressed itself upon his curates that they, all 17 of them, formed themselves into 'the old Curates Union' and would meet together with their old rector in his subsequent dioceses of Lichfield and York. As an erstwhile presbyterian he always got on well with non-conformists, but set his face sternly against all religious extremists. 'Whenever I hear of fasting communion', he once said, 'I cannot use sufficiently strong language to denounce so great an error.' However, such outbursts were unusual, for he was naturally a sweet-tempered man and hated to hurt peoples' feelings.

In 1878 Disraeli appointed him to the see of Lichfield, and he was enthroned on 11 July in the presence of five American bishops and Bishop Wordsworth of St. Andrews. His first wife, Sarah Clapham, had died of scarlet fever in 1862, and now he married again, the Hon. Augusta Anne

170

Barrington. At Lichfield Maclagan worked hard, training the junior clergy, visiting the deaneries regularly, forming a clerical society, Pastor Order of the Holy Ghost, to help improve the spiritual life of the clergy, and founding a Lay Mission, headed by a Salvation Army officer, H. A. Colvis, for carrying out missionary work in the parishes. Under Mrs. Maclagan's auspices both the Mothers Union and the Girls Friendly Society flourished in the diocese.

In the matter of ordinations and confirmations the bishop insisted on a full and thorough preparation, and ensured that the services themselves were performed with all dignity and reverence. He worked hard to raise the necessary funds to endow the new bishopric of Southwell that was carved out of Lichfield; yet even with a reduced diocese he found the work overwhelming and in 1888 obtained a full-time suffragan bishop, Sir Lovelace Stamer, who was certainly needed as Maclagan himself had been laid low with a severe attack of rheumatism.

Outside his diocese the bishop played an important part at the Church Congresses, where in opposition to Charles Gore and the new school of biblical critics, he stoutly defended the inspiration of the scriptures. A firm believer in christian unity, after attending a conference of Old Catholics at Bonn, he spoke of 'that Anglican dream, the fusion of the Greek and English Churches'; and throughout his ministry sought to promote a united Chistendom.

On 1 May, 1891 Lord Salisbury offered him the archbishopric of York, 'vacant now by the lamentable death of Archbishop Magee'. At first Maclagan hesitated, but finally told Salisbury, 'I ought not to refuse the important office, which the queen has proposed for my acceptance'; and in his sermon at the enthronement promised to concern himself primarily with the spiritual welfare of the diocese and province, whilst ever seeking to strengthen the ties between north and south through their respective convocations. Unfortunately, however, he made a bad beginning by, in one of his early addresses, forthrightly condemning evening communion, then the prerogative of the evangelicals, and so creating the impression that he was an anglo-catholic; especially as he went on to say that he would never promote any clergyman practising it. In so doing he infuriated the evangelicals, and especially the people of Sheffield, a centre of the Low Church, where Thomson had been greatly beloved. But within weeks the archbishop had appointed a prominent evangelical as archdeacon, and the clergy soon grew to appreciate his kind, gentle and courteous character. Indeed, he took particular pains to conciliate Sheffield, and worked hard to make it into a new bishopric, which ultimately came to fruition in 1914 after Maclagan's own death.

Anxious to provide a better training for ordinands, he founded the *Schola Archiepiscopi Eborcensis* at Bishopthorpe Vicarage, which was later transferred to York, but never really got off the ground. He was more successful with 'the Order of Postulants', started in 1898, when men seeking holy orders used to meet annually in August at Bishopthorpe Palace for a quiet day and interviews with the archbishop. A fund was started to help them with their training, and more than 60 of these ordinands were eventually ordained.

In 1893 Maclagan inaugurated the 'Poor Benefices Fund', later affiliated to the Queen Victoria Clergy Fund, which did much to relieve the hardships of impecunious incumbents. Despite the ill-health that continually dogged him the archbishop carried out a strenuous three year visitation of the diocese, covering 650 parishes between 1892 and 1895, when he also confirmed widely in rural as well as urban districts. Ordination services were always made as impressive as possible, and Maclagan insisted that men newly ordained must serve as assistant curates for a reasonable term before being instituted to a living. This latter policy however sometimes brought him into conflict with the gentry, who wished their sons to step straight into the family living. His strenuous work on their behalf earned him the nick-name of 'the Clergy's Bishop'; but he was equally concerned with the welfare of the laity, and was especially interested in building up the Sunday and church day schools.

Maclagan did not confine his activities to the north of England, continuing to work hard for christian unity. Pope Leo XIII's bull invalidating Anglican Orders struck a grievous blow at the hopes that the archbishop and others had entertained of an eventual reunion with Rome; and it was felt that a reply must be made. Mandell Creighton, bishop of Peterborough, was selected for the job, assisted by Maclagan, Stubbs of Oxford and John Wordsworth of Salisbury. The death of the archbishop of Canterbury delayed matters for a time, but eventually Frederick Temple, the new Primate of All England, and Maclagan, after rewriting one of the chapters of the original draft, decided to send this Reply not to the pope as hitherto envisaged, but to the universal episcopate, signed by both archbishops.

Despite this set-back Maclagan persisted in his task, visiting Russia where he received a very warm welcome, in order to investigate the possibility of a union with the orthodox churches of the East as a counter-weight to the papal rebuff. A letter, signed by both archbishops, was despatched to all the members of the Russian Holy Synod, enclosing the Reply to Rome, and containing an 'exposition of the doctrine of the Anglican Church'; and on his return Maclagan expressed his optimism at the York diocesan conference that a United Christendom was within sight, or at least an 'alliance of Christian Brotherhood'. This was a pipe-dream, with little reality behind it, for the Russian Orthodox Church, like Rome seemed only interested in a take-over on their own terms.

In 1902, owing to the physical feebleness of Archbishop Temple, Maclagan had the honour of crowning Queen Alexandra; but he found himself too weak physically to take part in the discussions of the fifth Lambeth Conference, although he attended several of the sessions and gave the blessing at the final service in St. Paul's Cathedral. He was also able to go to Oxford in June 1908 to receive an honorary D.D. and to attend the Manchester Church Congress; but the end was near. Mrs. Maclagan urged him to resign, and he himself felt that 'the time had come to retire to a quiet life for the closing days of his life'. A house, 15 Queen's Gate Place, belonging to Lord Colville in London, was purchased and the archbishop settled down to a peaceful and happy retirement for the next 15 months.

He died on 19 September 1910, and lies buried in the churchyard at Bishopthorpe, next to his old friend, Canon Keble, who had been vicar there. The funeral service was conducted by his successor, **Cosmo Gordon Lang**, who at a subsequent Memorial held in the Minster spoke of Maclagan's rule of sympathy, kindness and gentleness, which was always tempered by firmness. 'But', added Lang, 'the basis of that rule after all was spiritual – he spoke unto you the word of God'.

Finally it might be added as a footnote that although Maclagan was no great musician or poet, he composed some fine hymns with their tunes, which have been incorporated into *Hymns Ancient and Modern*. The best known is 'The Saints of God'.

> THE saints of God! their conflict past
> And life's long battle won at last,
> No more they need the shield or sword,
> They cast them down before their Lord:
> O happy saints! for ever blest,
> At Jesus' feet how safe your rest!
>
> The saints of God! their wanderings done,
> No more their weary course they run,
> No more they faint, no more they fall,
> No foes oppress, no fears appal:
> O happy saints! for ever blest,
> In that dear home how sweet your rest!
>
> The saints of God! life's voyage o'er
> Safe landed on that blissful shore,
> No stormy tempest now they dread,
> No roaring billows lift their head:
> O happy saints! for ever blest,
> In that calm haven of your rest.
>
> The saints of God their vigil keep
> While yet their mortal bodies sleep,
> Till from the dust they too shall rise
> And soar triumphant to the skies:
> O happy saints! rejoice and sing:
> He quickly comes, your Lord and King.
>
> O God of saints, to thee we cry;
> O Saviour, plead for us on high;
> O Holy Ghost, our guide and friend,
> Grant us thy grace till life shall end;
> That with all saints our rest may be
> In that bright Paradise with thee.

173

Postscript

The Victorian and Edwardian age, one of relative peace, stability, and expansion, was now to give place to a vastly different era of war, turmoil and revolution. It would witness two World Wars, the turning of the British Empire into the British Commonwealth and a period of unprecedented social change.

During the first half of this century three men of exceptional stature and ability occupied the archiepiscopal throne of York. Cosmo Gordon Lang was outstanding in the power of his intellect and personality. He could undoubtedly have risen to the top of any profession he had cared to adopt. His successor, William Temple, was a great leader of men, a fine scholar, and a powerful orator, who more than any archbishop before or after him captured the love and imagination of the country as a whole. Indeed he became known as 'The peoples' archbishop'; and his sudden and unexpected death rocked the nation. Cyril Garbett, the least intelligent, a strong, robust and somewhat ruthless character, was probably the most effective diocesan of the three. His abounding energy, drive and hard work galvanised the three sees that he served into new life. Two of the three, Lang and Temple, passed on to Canterbury; and Garbett would undoubtedly have done so had he not been too old at the time of Temple's death. Lang wrote little, and nothing of great substance; but both Temple and Garbett were prolific authors. Some of the former's works will live; those of the latter are already forgotten. Competent modern historians have written their biographies in exhaustive detail, so there is no need to repeat them here.

They were followed by three men, Michael Ramsey, Donald Coggan and Stuart Blanch, all of whom at the time of writing are still alive, as well as the present Archbishop, John Habgood. As no man's place in the tapestry of history can be fairly and firmly established until many years after his death, they will not be included in this book.

The long line of the archbishops of York from the sixth to the twentieth century contains the story of a succession of prelates, who, with a few notable exceptions, cannot be compared with their brother metropolitans of Canterbury although a number of them passed from York to Canterbury; each, in his generation, played an important and constructive role in the history of *Ecclesia Anglicana*. Long may they continue to do so.

Appendix

The Sale and Recovery of the Archiepiscopal Estates during the Seventeenth Century

After the Reformation the wealth of the archbishops of York was greatly reduced; but even so their income compared not unfavourably with that of the chief families in Yorkshire. In 1597 it amounted to £1,889-16-6; whilst 41 years later it had risen to £2,145-13-10. This was about a third less than before the crown, from the 1540s onward, had stripped the archbishopric of many of its estates; but much more than in the dark days of Edward VI, since Queen Mary had restored at least some of what had been taken, notably the Nottinghamshire estates and the lordship of Ripon.

Then, under Elizabeth I the position became stabilised. The remaining manors were largely situated in Nottinghamshire and Yorkshire, together with some smaller estates near London, and at Battersea and Wandsworth in Surrey. However, in exchange for their lost lands the archbishops had received some compensation in the form of confiscated monastic properties. But even under Elizabeth the deprivation was not entirely at an end: York House in the Strand had to be surrendered to the queen, and she demanded and received some long leases on farms at very cheap terms.

Such was the situation on the eve of the Civil War. After the abolition of the episcopate on 9 October 1646, the decision was made to sell church lands in order to compensate the London merchants, who had loaned the money to pay the Scots for withdrawing their army from northern England, and handing over the king to the English parliament. The bishops' lands were first sold and raised some £676,387, seven per cent of which came from the see of York. Most of the purchasers were city merchants, civil servants, army officers and some of the lesser gentry. No peer did so, few knights or baronets, and not many tenants. Nor was there a lively market for resale, possibly from fear of a Restoration, followed by confiscation. But not all the York lands were sold, part of the archiepiscopal estate being retained by the Commissioners for the

Maintenance of a Preaching Ministry, in order to augment poor parochial livings.

One disastrous consequence of this sale of church lands was the destruction of the elaborate administrative system that had been built up over the centuries. Some of the old officials, indeed, continued to work for the new owners; but generally speaking record keeping had got into total disarray by 1660, which added considerably to the problem of restoring the land to their original owners. Another factor, too, that had to be carefully weighed at the Restoration was the paramount need to restore a united nation, and this would hardly be done by ruthlessly taking back the sold properties without any kind of compensation. So throughout the summer of 1660 parliament was much concerned with this problem, and eventually decided to set up a royal commission 'to settle any disputes between owners, purchasers and ancient tenants'. Fortunately, although so many records had been lost, parliament during the Interregnum had caused a detailed survey of the archbishopric to be made. Copies of this were used not only by the commissioners, but later by all diocesan officials down to the end of the seventeenth century.

Hyde*, who was largely responsible for the commission, rightly believed that the purchasers, who had already profited extensively from their acquisitions, were unlikely to offer any determined resistance to their restoration, provided they were offered reasonable terms. So to this end he persuaded Charles II to write a letter to both archbishops stressing the need for compromise. Certainly the new archbishop of York, Accepted Frewen, was only too aware of the problems, namely the lack of documentation about his estates, the very few experienced diocesan officials still remaining who could inform him about them, the important changes in husbandry that had taken place under the Commonwealth and Protectorate, the difficulties he would encounter in getting back his official residences, and above all the many claims on these lands by parliament, purchasers and ancient tenants. As the new spiritual leader of the north he naturally wished to appear conciliatory, and therefore set up a commission of five men, including his nephew, Thomas Frewen, to settle the whole matter; when he himself would be set free to deal with ecclesiastical affairs. This commission started work in the spring of 1661, and, following the advice of the royal letter, treated the purchasers with consideration. The latter in fact were given every opportunity to state their case; with the result that a number of them were able to secure tenancies on the properties concerned.

There was indeed remarkably little legislation arising from these negotiations, for, as Hyde had shrewdly surmised, the purchasers having

---

* On 3 November 1660 Edward Hyde was raised to the peerage by the title of Baron Hyde of Hindon; and at the coronation, 20 April 1661, was further created Viscount Cornbury and Earl of Clarendon.

originally bought the land cheaply and already made a good thing out of it during a lengthy occupation, were not now prepared to make trouble for fear of heavy costs. A good example of the kind of thing that might happen if they pressed their case too far was that of James Danby Esq., who petitioned the commissioners to be allowed to receive the rents until he had recovered the purchasing price of £2,000; but when it was discovered that he had already done this between the years 1649 and 1660, Danby himself had to bear the heavy costs of the enquiry, after his petition had been dismissed.

In many cases it was left to the tenants and the purchasers to come to some agreement among themselves. Frewen wrote to Bishop Sheldon of London: 'Much it has cost me in satisfying purchasers: but the express sum I cannot give, because I left it to the old tenants to compound with them, and deducted it out of fines.' The archbishop's old tenants were anxious to re-establish title to their leases, and on the whole they found Frewen very generous in abating fines by about half; but he found the recovery of the rental income a slow matter. Under the Commonwealth some of the estates had been used to help augment poor parish livings; and in the royal letter Frewen had been urged to continue this policy, which he was very willing to do. 'I made a number of improvements to the incomes of the parochial clergy', he informed the crown. Guisborough obtained £100 per annum, Melton £50, and Whitby £37-13-4; certain assistant-curates also benefited: the curate at Whitby received £40, and others at Fyling, Ugglebarnby and Lythe £42 each. In all £350 were paid out yearly during Frewen's archiepiscopate, and continued under his successors.

Apparently there had been little change under the Commonwealth and Protectorate in the personnel of the tenants, the size of the holdings or the terms of the leases. There were, however, a few exceptions: at Marton, Thomas Hodges, a London merchant, had settled his own family on two of the properties; and at Southwell, the Cludds, Pierpoints and Cartwrights leased a large part of the estate to new tenants. The very fact that the majority of purchasers did not themselves live on these lands, had bought them simply as an investment, and made a substantial profit out of them during the time of possession, all helped to persuade them to relinquish these purchases without a serious struggle. Consequently the recovery of the archiepiscopal estates, although it took time, went relatively smoothly.

There is no comparison to be drawn with the sale of church land after the Dissolution of the Monasteries, which proved irreversible. The archbishopric probably suffered from the voracity of the crown during the late sixteenth century, under the pretence of voluntary surrenders of property, a great deal more than it experienced in the long run from the sale of its lands during the Great Interregnum.

Select Bibliography

Archbishop's Herring's Visitations Returns, 1743, edit. S. L. Ollard and F. C. Walker, 5 vols. 1928.
A House of Kings, edit. Edward Carpenter, 1966.
Allott, Stephen, *Alcuin of York,* 1974.
Bennett, H. L., *Archbishop Rotherham,* 1911.
Brown, C. K. Francis, *A History of the English Clergy, 1800-1900,* 1953.
Bullock, F. W. B., *A History for the Training of the Ministry, 1800-1874,* 1955.
Burnet, Gilbert, *History of My Own Time, 1897-1900,* ed. O. Airy, 2 vols.
Carpenter, Edward, *Cantuar,* 1971.
Chadwick, Owen, *The Victorian Church, 1960-1970,* parts 1 & 2.
Chambers, D. S. *Cardinal Bainbridge in the Court of Rome,* 1965.
Clarke, H. Lowther, *Archbishop Gray* [Grey], 1922.
Collinson, Patrick, *Archbishop Grindal,* 1971.
Collinson, Patrick, *Religion and Protestantism,* 1982.
Deansley, Margaret, *The Pre-Conquest Church in England,* 1961.
Dickens, A. G., *Lollards and Protestants in the Diocese of York,* 1959.
Dictionary of National Biography, 1917–1981 edn.
Dixon, W. H. and Raine, J., *Fasti Eboracenses: Lives of the Archbishops of York,* vol. 1, 1863.
Dolben, Paul, *Archbishop Dolben,* 1884.
Fuller, Thomas, *The Church History of England,* 3 vols., ed. J. Nichols, 1868.
Fuller, Thomas, *The History of the Worthies of England,* 3 vols., ed. P. A. Nuttall, 1840.
Gascoigne, Thomas, *Dictionarium Theologium,* 2 vols. (MS in Lincoln College, Oxford.)
Gibbs, M. and Lang, J., *Bishops and Reform, 1215-1272,* 1934.
Hacket, John, *Scrinia Reserata,* 1692.
Hart, A. Tindal, *The Life and Times of John Sharp, Archbishop of York,* 1949.
Handbook of British Chronology, edit. Powicke and Fryde, 1961.
History of York Minster, edit. C. E. Aylmer and R. Cant, 1972.
How, F. D., *Archbishop Maclagan,* 1911.
Hutton Correspondence, Surtees Society, 1843.
Johnson, Charles, *Lives of Hugh the Chanter, 1060-1161,* 1961.
Kirk-Smith, H., *William Thomson, Archbishop of York,* 1958.
Loyal Martyr, or the Life of Richard Scrope, 1722.

Marchant, Ronald, *The Puritans and the Church Courts, 1560-1640*, 1960.
Markham, C. R., *Archbishop Markham*, 1906.
Nicholl, Donald, *Archbishop Thurstan*, 1964.
Raine, J., *Historians of the Church of York*, 1886.
Ridley, Jasper, *The Statesman and the Fanatic: Thomas Wolsey and Thomas More*, 1982.
Rowden, A. W., *The Primates of the Four Georges*, 1916.
Stephenson, A. M. G., *The First Lambeth Conference*, 1967.
Sykes, Norman, *Church and State in England in the 18th Century*, 1934.
Sykes, Norman, *From Sheldon to Secker, 1660-1768, 1958*.
Vergil, Polydore, History of England, ed. Ellis, 2 vols. (Camden Society.)
Visitation Articles and Injunctions of the Period of the Reformation, edit. W. H. Frere and W. P. M. Kennedy, 1910.
Walpole, Horace, *Works*, ed. Robert Berry, 5 vols., 1798; *Reminiscences*, 1805.
Warkworth, John, *Warkworth's Chronicle*, ed. J. O. Halliwell, 1839.
York Minster Historical Tracts, edit. A. Hamilton Thompson, 1927.

Publications of the Borthwick Institute of Historical Research, University of York

Cooper, Janet E., *Last Four Anglo-Saxon Archbishops of York*, 1970.
Cramp, Rosemary, *Anglican and Viking*, 1967.
Dickens, A. G., *Marian Reaction in the Diocese of York*, parts I & II, 1957.
Dickens, A. G., *Robert Holgate, Archbishop of York and President of the King's Council in the North*, 1955.
Douie, D. L., *Archbishop Geoffrey Plantagenet and the Chapter of York*, 1960.
Gentiles, I. J. and Sheils, W. J., *Confiscation and Restoration: the Archbishopric Estates and the Civil War*, 1981.
Hill, R. M. T., *Labourer in the Vineyard: Visitations of Archbishop Melton in the Archdeaconry of Richmond*, 1968.
Ingamells, John, *Catalogue of Portraits at Bishopthorpe Palace*, 1972.
Royle, Edward, *The Victorian Church in York*, 1983.
Sheils, W. J., *Archbishop Grindal's Visitation, 1575*, 1977.
Sheils, W. J., *Archbishop Richard Scrope, 1398-1405*, Calendar of the Register of, vol. II, 1985.

Articles, Lectures, Theses
and Manuscripts

Arundale, R. A., 'Edmund Grindal and the Northern Province', *Church Quarterly Review*, 1958.

Butler, L. H., 'Archbishop Melton, his Neighbours and Kinsmen', *Journal of Ecclesiastical History*, 1951.

Davies, R. G., 'Alexander Neville, Archbishop of York', *Yorkshire Archaeological Journal*, 1975.

Dickens, A. G., 'The Marriage and Character of Archbishop Holgate', *English Historical Review*, 1937.

Keir, G. L., 'The Ecclesiastical Career of George Neville', *Oxford B. Litt Thesis*, 1970.

Knowles, M. D., 'The Medieval Archbishops of York', *Oliver Sheldon Memorial Lecture, York*, 1961.

'Visitations of the Diocese of York Holden by Archbishop Lee', *Yorkshire Archaeological Journal*, 1902.

Whitelock, D., 'Archbishop Wulfstan, homilist and statesman', *Transactions of the Royal Historical Society*, 1942.

York Minster Library Manuscript, 'the visitations of Archbishop Sandys, 1577; Archbishop Matthew, 1615; and Archbishop Neile, 1637'.

Select Index

Cato Street Conspiracy, 160
Cecil, Robert, 115, 119
Celestine III, Pope, 43-4
Cenwulf, King, 5
Ceolwulf, King, 3
Charles I, King, 120-8
Charles II, King, 128-30
Charlemagne, Emperor, 5
Chatham Annuity Bill, 1778, 153
Chichele, Henry, Archbishop of Canterbury, 25, 80
Church Commission, 156
Church Congress, 166, 173
Churchill, John Duke of Marlborough, 138
Clarence, George, Duke of, 84, 88
Clarke, Dr. Samuel, 144
Clement III, Pope, 43
Clement V, Pope, 23, 53, 57, 58
Clement VI, Pope, 62, 64
Clement VII, Pope, 71
Clement VIII, 98
Clofeshah, Synod of, 4
Cnut, King, 8-10
Cobham, Eleanor, 80
Cockburn, Dean, 158-62
Celenso, John, 164
Comber, Dr. Thomas, 129, 131-2
Commissioners for the Maintenance of a Preaching Ministry, 175
Compton, Henry, 134
Congress of Arras, 80
Constantine the Great, Emperor, 1
Corbridge, Thomas, Archbishop of York, 23, 50, 56-9
Cosin, John, 122
Council of the North, 101-9, 112
Cranmer, Thomas, Archbishop of Canterbury, 99-101
Creighton, Mandell, 172
Cromwell, Oliver, 122, 124, 128
Cromwell, Thomas, 96, 99-101
Cumberland, Duke of, 144, 160
Cynesige, Archbishop of York, 11-2

DARWIN, Charles, 168
David I, King of Scotland, 34-8, 68
Dawes, Sir William, Archbishop of York, 138-40
Deane, Henry, Archbishop of Canterbury, 94
Declarations of Indulgence, 128, 132
Disraeli, Benjamin, 170
Divine Right of Kings, 121
Dolben, John, Archbishop of York, 130-1, 142
Drummond Robert, Archbishop of York, 148-52
Duncombe, Dean, 162, 164, 167

EADBERHT, King, 1
Ealdred, Archbishop of York, 12-4, 16, 28
Eanflaed, Princess, 1
Eanbald I, Archbishop of York, 3-5
Eanbald II, Archbishop of Canterbury, 5
Eardwulf, King, 5
Easdall, William, 121-2
Edgar, King, 7-8
Edgar Atheling, 9, 13
Edwald, Archbishop of Canterbury, 7
Edward, King of the Saxons, 8
Edward the Confessor, King, 8, 12-3, 54
Edward I, King, 23-4, 53-7
Edward II, King, 58-61
Edward III, King, 24, 51-2, 59-69
Edward IV, King, 82-3, 85-8
Edward V, King, 89
Edward VI, King, 98, 102-4, 175
Edward VI's Chantry Act, 102
Edwin, King of Northumbria, 1, 16
Education Act, 1870
Egbert, Archbishop of York, 2-4, 16
Eldulf, Archbishop of Canterbury, 8
Eleanor, Queen, 43
Elfric, Archbishop of York, 10, 11
Elizabeth I, Queen, 98, 107-9, 114-7, 175
Elizabeth Woodville, Queen, 83, 89
Eric, Danish King, 77
Eric Bloodaxe, Danish King, 8
Essays and Reviews, 168
Essex, Earl of, 117
Ethelbald, Archbishop of York, 6
Ethelbert, Archbishop of York, 3-4
Ethelred the Unready, King, 8-11
Eugenius III, Pope, 21, 38, 40
Eugenius IV, Pope, 80
Eustace, Prince, 38-9
Evesham, battle of, 53

FAIR Rosamund, 41
Ferrar, Family of, 125
Finch, Heneage, Earl of Nottingham, 134
Flambard, Ralph, 20
Fleming, Richard, 79
Foliot, Gilbert, 41
Foxe, Richard, 94
Frankland, Richard, 135
Frederick I, King of Prussia, 136
Frederick, Prince, 152
Frederick William, King of Prussia, 136

GARBETT, Cyril, Archbishop of York, 174
Gascoigne, Chief Justice, 75, 80, 98
Geoffrey Plantagenet, Archbishop of York, 22, 28, 41-7
George I, King, 140
George II, King, 141, 145-9
George III, King, 150, 152, 155
Gerard, Archbishop of York, 18, 27, 30-1

185

The particular devices, or family Arms, belonging to several Archbishops of York.

The old Arms of the See.

The present Arms.

S. WILLIAM.	MELTON.	ZOUCH.	THORESBY.	A. NEVIL.	ARUNDEL.
SCROPE.	BOWET.	KEMPE.	W. BOTHE.	G. NEVIL.	L. BOTHE.
ROTHERAM.	SAVAGE.	BAYNBRIDGE.	WOLSEY.	LEE.	HOLGATE.
HEATH.	YOUNG.	GRINDAL.	SANDYS.	PIERS.	HUTTON.
MATTHEWS.	MONTAIGN.	HARSNET.	NEILE.	WILLIAMS.	FREWEN.
STERNE.	DOLBEN.	LAMPLUGH.	SHARP.	DAWES.	BLACKBURN.

Bishops and Archbishops of York

1 Paulinus, 627-633
2 Chad (Ceadda), 664-669
3 Wilfrid I (St. Wilfrid), 669-677
4 Bosa, 678-705
5 John (St. John of Beverley), 705-
6 Wilfrid II, 718-732
7 Egbert, 735-766
8 Ethelbert, 767-780
9 Eanbald I, 780-796
10 Eanbald II, 796-808
11 Wulfsige, 808-837
12 Wigmund, 837-854
13 Wulfhere, 854-900
14 Ethelbald, 900-
15 Hrotheweard (or Lodeward), 904-931
16 Wulfstan I, 931-956
17 Oskytel, 958-971
18 Edwald (or Ethelwold), 971
19 Oswald, 972-992
20 Ealdulf (Abbot of Peterborough), 992-1002
21 Wulfstan II, 1003-1023
22 Aelfric Puttoc, 1023-1051
23 Cynesige, 1051-1060
24 Ealdred, 1061-1069
25 Thomas I, 1070-1100
26 Gerard, 1101-1108
27 Thomas II, 1109-1114
28 Thurstan, 1119-1140
29 William Fitzherbert, 1143-1147 and 1154
30 Henry Murdac, 1147-1153
   William Fitzherbert
31 Roger of Pont-L'Eveque, 1154-1181
32 Geoffrey Plantagenet, 1181-1191
33 Walter de Grey, 1215-1255
34 Sewal de Bovill, 1256-1258
35 Godfrey of Ludham (or Kineton) 1258-1265
36 Walter Giffard, 1265-1279
37 William Wickwane, 1279-1285
38 John le Romeyn (Romanus). 1286-1296
39 Henry of Newark, 1298-1299
40 Thomas of Corbridge, 1300-1304
41 William Greenfield, 1306-1316
42 William of Melton, 1317-1340
43 William le Zouche, 1342-1352
44 John of Thoresby, 1352-1373
45 Alexander Neville, 1374-1388
46 Thomas Arundel 1388-1396
47 Robert Waldby, 1396-1398

48 Richard le Scrope, 1398-1407
49 Henry Bowet, 1407-1423
50 John Kempe, 1425-1452
51 William Booth, 1452-1464
52 George Neville, 1465-1476
53 Lawrence Booth, 1476-1480
54 Thomas Rotherham (or Scott) 1480-1500
55 Thomas Savage, 1501-1507
56 Christopher Bainbridge, 1508-1514
57 Thomas Wolsey, 1514-1530
58 Edward Lee, 1531-1544
59 Robert Holgate, 1545-1554
60 Nicholas Heath, 1555-1560
61 Thomas Young, 1561-1568
62 Edmund Grindal, 1570-1576
63 Edwin Sandys, 1577-1588
64 John Piers, 1589-1594
65 Matthew Hutton, 1595-1606
66 Tobias Matthew, 1606-1628
67 George Monteigne, 1628
68 Samuel Harsnett, 1628-1631
69 Richard Neile, 1632-1640
70 John Williams, 1641-1650
71 Accepted Frewen, 1660-1664
72 Richard Sterne, 1664-1683
73 John Dolben, 1683-1686
74 Thomas Lamplugh, 1688-1691
75 John Sharp, 1691-1714
76 Sir William Dawes, 1714-1724
77 Lancelot Blackburne, 1724-1743
78 Thomas Herring, 1743-1747
79 Matthew Hutton 1747-1757
80 John Gilbert, 1757-1761
81 Robert Hay Drummond, 1761-1776
82 William Markham, 1777-1807
83 Edward Venables Vernon (afterwards Harcourt), 1807-1847
84 Thomas Musgrave, 1847-1860
85 Charles Thomas Longley, 1860-1862
86 William Thomson, 1862-1890
87 William Connor Magee, 1890-1891
88 William Dalrymple Maclagan, 1891-1908
89 Cosmo Gordon Lang, 1908-1928
90 William Temple, 1929-1942
91 Cyril Forster Garbett, 1942-1955
92 Arthur Michael Ramsey, 1956-1961
93 Frederick Donald Coggan, 1961-1974
94 Stuart Yarworth Blanch, 1975-1983
95 John Stapylton Habgood, 1983-

Plate 1. *Tomb of Walter de Grey 1215-1255*

Plate 2. *Coffin lid from tomb of Walter de Grey*

BISHOPTHORPE
The East Front (mainly of the 13th Century) facing the River Ouse

Plate 3. *Bishopthorpe Palace from the river; early 20th century; drawing by D. Hutton*

Plate 4 above.   *Robert Waldby 1396-1398*
Plate 5 top right. *Thomas Rotherham (or Scott)*
                         1480-1500
Plate 6 right.   *Samuel Harsnett 1628-1631*

Plate 7. Richard le Scrope 1398-1407

Plate 8. Thomas Wolsey 1514-1530

late 9. Cawood Castle; 10th century; rebuilt 13th century; enlarged 15th century and damaged during the Civil War

Plate 10. Robert Holgate 1545-1554

Plate 11. George Mountain 1628

Plate 12. York House, Whitehall, in 1616; purchased 1244 and seized by Henry VIII

Plate 13. John Williams 1641-1650

Plate 14. Accepted Frewen 1660-1664

Plate 15. John Sharp 1691-1714

Plate 16. York Minster Library c. 1230

Plate 17. Thomas Herring 1743-1747

Plate 18. Map of Bishopthorpe, Cawood and York

Plate 19. Robert Hay Drummond 1761-1776

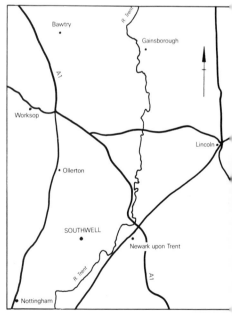

Plate 20. Map of Southwell, Nottinghamshire

Plate 21. Bishopthorpe Palace from the South; detail of a painting by James Roberts, 1777

Plate 22. Southwell Palace; 10th century; rebuilt 13th-16th century

Plate 23. Edward Venables Vernon (afterwards Harcourt)
1807-1847

Plate 24. William Dalrymple Maclagan 1891-1908

Plate 25. York Minster from the North West; Engraving by Woolnoth c. 1900